The Philosophy of Modern Literary Theory

The Philosophy of Modern Literary Theory

PETER V. ZIMA

THE ATHLONE PRESS
London and New Brunswick NJ

First published 1999 by
THE ATHLONE PRESS
1 Park Drive, London NW11 7SG
and New Brunswick, New Jersey

© Peter V. Zima 1999

British Library Cataloguing in Publication Data
*A catalogue record for this book is available
from the British Library*

ISBN 0 485 11540 9   hb
0 485 12150 6   pb

Library of Congress Cataloging in Publication Data
Zima, P. V.
  The philosophy of modern literary theory / Peter V. Zima
    p. cm.
  Includes bibliographical references (p.   ) and index.
  ISBN 0-485-11540-9 (cloth : alk. paper). -- ISBN 0-485-12150-6
(pbk. : alk. paper)
  1. Criticism--History--20th century. I. Title.
PN94.Z56   1999
801'.95'0904--dc21   99-17830
                                                          CIP

Distributed in the United States, Canada and South America by
Transaction Publishers
390 Campus Drive
Somerset, New Jersey 08873

Typeset by
Bibloset

Printed and bound in Great Britain by
Cambridge University Press

Contents

Preface

The main argument underlying this book, which is a short introduction to the problems, theories, and concepts of contemporary
literary criticism, can be summed up in a few words: modern
theories of literature can only be understood adequately if they
are considered within the philosophical and aesthetic context in
which they originated and evolved. As long as they are isolated
from this context and viewed in purely literary terms, as co-existing
and competing approaches to literature, their specific character and
their fundamental aims are obscured.

Riddled with fashions and biased by ideological endeavours
of all kinds, literary theories often appear as products of a
commercialised culture in which the 'idols of the marketplace'
(as Francis Bacon called them) seem to dictate the concatenations
of our thoughts. Sociology and semiotics, two disciplines which
enjoyed the unmitigated admiration of many intellectuals during
the 1960s and 1970s, have long since been compelled by market
forces and political upheavals to yield their privileged positions to
deconstruction, feminism, and postmodernism.

However, nobody should be lured by this shift in popularity or
fashion into believing that deconstruction, for example, is superior
to structuralism, because, for the time being, it occupies the centre
of the marketplace. It would be equally wrong of course to react
with rancour and to assume that deconstruction must be wrong
because it happens to be fashionable. For both sociology and
semiotics survived the fashions of the 1960s and 1970s without
losing their character as complex theoretical systems which no
contemporary social scientist would want to renounce. In very
much the same way, deconstruction will at one point be considered
on its theoretical merits: as a way of thinking which successfully
challenged some of the most deeply engrained prejudices of
structural linguistics and semiotics.

It is one of the fundamental aims of this book, however, to
show that the dialectics of prejudice and challenge can best be

understood against the backdrop of past philosophical and aesthetic debates. The challenge of deconstruction is neither revolutionary nor incomprehensible if it is considered as a Nietzschean reaction to several rationalist or Hegelian premises which semioticians and Marxists have never queried. Thus the idea that a literary text ist a meaningful totality, which is shared by the rationalist semiotician Algirdas J. Greimas and the Hegelian Marxist Lucien Goldmann, loses some of its plausibility as soon as we realise that all of the texts interpreted by them can be interpreted differently and that diverging interpretations proliferate as time passes on. This does not imply, however, that structural semiotics (Greimas) and Marxist sociology of literature (Goldmann) are 'old hat' and that the multiplicity of meaning discovered by reader-response criticism and deconstruction replaces the philosopher's stone. For even poststructuralists and deconstructionists tend to agree among themselves that some interpretations are more plausible than others, i.e. that there are 'limits' to the interpretation process, as Umberto Eco would say. These limits, Greimas would add, cannot be discerned without a clear reference to phonetic, semantic, and syntactic text structures.

In what follows, it will be shown that the debates and controversies hinted at above are not new in all respects, because they have a long philosophical and aesthetic past. Long before the deconstructionists, Nietzsche challenged the Platonic and Hegelian idea that a text expresses truth in a univocal manner and that it is a meaningful totality. On the whole, it will appear that the Kantian, Hegelian or Nietzschean background of literary concepts such as *autonomy, autoreflexivity, world view, work structure* or *signifier* in the sense of Barthes is essential to the understanding of literary criticism in its present form.

In the last chapter a dialogical theory will be mapped out which attempts to mediate between the Kantian idea that art and the Beautiful cannot be defined by conceptual means and the Hegelian (Marxist) idea that works of art are accessible to conceptual analysis. It will be shown on the one hand that literary texts are 'without concept', as Kant and the Kantians would have it, insisting quite rightly on the open-ended character of interpretation and the reception process; on the other hand it will be made clear that interpretation and reception are not arbitrary but permanently guided by phonetic, semantic, syntactic, and narrative structures whose existence is hard to deny.

However, their nature cannot be grasped intuitively or be monologically defined within one type of (Marxist, psychoanalytic or phenomenological) discourse. Starting from critical analyses conducted by Karl Mannheim, Maurice Halbwachs, and Paul Lorenzen, it will be argued that only a dialogue between heterogeneous theories (such as Critical Rationalism and Critical Theory, for example) can break up the doxa which each theory inevitably relies on. The ideological heterogeneity of the theories involved makes it possible to discard the prejudice of scientific groups and to become aware of textual elements or structures beyond collectively sanctioned ideological stereotypes. Naturally, this awareness has nothing to do with a Platonic vision of essences; it is at best a moment of truth which can be superseded in later discussions.

A dialogical approach towards literary theory cannot possibly pretend to be the last word or the *ultima ratio* of literary criticism. For the attempt to expose the philosophical and aesthetic foundations of literary theories inevitably yields a construction which excludes all approaches that cannot be adequately analysed and explained within a philosophical framework. Cultural Studies, the study of post-colonial literatures, the empirical sociology of culture, art, and literature (in the sense of Pierre Bourdieu), Michel Foucault's historical approach, New Historicism, and feminist criticism may differ in many respects, but they all have one element in common: they cannot be understood as *aesthetic theories* and derived from a Kantian, Hegelian or Nietzschean model, because their scope stretches well beyond philosophy into the realm of society, politics, and culture.

One could argue that all of these approaches are *extrinsic* to a philosophical and aesthetic reconstruction of literary theory insofar as they are attempts to explain different aesthetic concepts and models within a particular cultural, historical or political set-up. Cultural Studies, for example, tend to ask why and how aesthetic ideals (e.g. the autonomy of art) are tied up with particular cultural contexts which vary in the course of history. Similarly, Pierre Bourdieu's sociology of culture is a systematic attempt to explain cultural patterns along with aesthetic norms and values as results of economically, socially, and politically sanctioned (institutionalised) power structures. It would therefore be grossly inappropriate to try to present Bourdieu's sociology as an aesthetic in the Kantian, Hegelian or Nietzschean sense – in spite of the fact that his literary interpretations (e.g. of Flaubert's work) are aimed, like those of many Marxists, almost exclusively at the social and historical content.

Although Foucault's philosophy can be considered as Nietzschean insofar as it regards knowledge and truth not as eternal universals (in the sense of Plato) but as results of particular, historically variable power constellations, it cannot be understood as a Nietzschean aesthetic. For it *encompasses* the aesthetic approach on a socio-historical level and hence cannot be reduced to it. A similar argument applies to New Historicism, which evolved under the influence of Foucault's historical approach. It not only investigates the relationship between history and literature, but also views aesthetic norms and values as engendered by social factors and power structures. Therefore its socio-historical context extends well beyond the framework of this book.

Although feminism is so heterogeneous that it is impossible to identify it with one of its positions, it is clear that it cannot be dealt with in the context of the philosophical discussion analysed here. For some feminist approaches can best be understood as attempts to map out a social or literary criticism beyond philosophy. In their article on the relationship between postmodernism and feminism entitled 'Social Criticism without Philosophy: An Encounter between Feminism and Postmodernism' (*Culture and Society*, nos. 2-3, 1988), Nancy Fraser and Linda Nicholson, for example, seem to believe that it is possible and desirable to develop a theory of society which has emancipated itself from male-dominated philosophy. Therefore all attempts to trace feminist discourses back to Kant, Hegel, Nietzsche or Croce are bound to lead to a distortion.

Avoiding this kind of distortion, this book also refrains from a purely additive approach inspired by the encyclopedic pretension of being able to deal with everything. By focusing on the aesthetic point of view, it might shed some light on the origins and aims of literary theories, and on the aesthetic meaning of their basic concepts. At the same time it could help readers to sort out their theoretical problems in a world in which competing fashions and terminologies tend to leave us speechless. The approaches, which have been termed *extrinsic* here, need not be neglected, however. They could be covered in another book that concentrates on the socio-historical contexts in which aesthetics, literary canons, and notions of literature appear and disappear.

Acknowledgements
I should like to thank my wife Veronica Smith for her invaluable advice regarding matters of language and style and for her unflinching support in tackling technical problems. I am very grateful to Mrs Brigitte Pappler for composing and correcting the typescript with patience and endurance.

CHAPTER 1
The Philosophical and Aesthetic Foundations of Literary Theories

The idea that each notion of literary criticism can readily be deduced from philosophical aesthetics and that each literary critic ought to be read in either a Kantian or a Hegelian perspective would be a caricature of the basic purpose of this book. A literary semiotic in the Greimasian sense, for example, is neither Kantian nor Hegelian; yet the sixth chapter will show why it is meaningful to consider it within the present context: like the Hegelian-Marxist theories of art and literature, it is based on a univocal concept of content and tends to disregard the multiple or polysemic character of fiction.

But what exactly is meant by *univocity, content, and polysemy*? Before the various philosophical and aesthetic positions are dealt with, it seems necessary to say a few words about these concepts, all of which are deeply rooted in philosophical traditions, yet at the same time involve contemporary linguistics and semiotics. It has to become clear that they are located at the crossroads of these disciplines and philosophy.

The main question which will be asked throughout this book is to what extent literary texts (works of art in general) univocally express conceptual thought or meaning. It is a question which concerns both the philosophical and the linguistic-semiotic context. Within the latter it has been dealt with extensively since Ferdinand de Saussure (1857-1913) and his disciples who believed that the linguistic sign is composed of two *arbitrarily* connected units: the *signifier (signifiant)* and the *signified (signifié)*. The arbitrary character of their association guarantees their respective *autonomy*: the signifier cannot be reduced to the *concept* (as Saussure also calls the signified), and the latter does not depend for its articulation on a particular signifier, i.e. on a particular phonetic unit. An isolated signifier, a word in a dictionary for example, can have many different meanings – it is *polysemic*. Conversely, a concept can find its expression in different signifiers considered as synonyms.

Later on, the Saussurian linguist André Martinet was quite explicit in pointing out that each language functions on two complementary but autonomous levels: the level of the phonetic units or signifiers and the semantic level of the signified. He calls this dual character of language '*la double articulation du langage*' and tries to show how the linguistic system 'confers upon the phonemes, that is to say upon units without signifieds, the constitution of its signifiers, thereby shielding the latter against the impact of meaning.'[1] In other words, the level of the signifiers is only arbitrarily linked to the semantic level of the signified units, and shifts between the two levels are always possible.

The idea that language has a dual character and that all linguistic processes are to be seen as taking place on at least two levels (phonetic and semantic) is later generalised by John Lyons:

> What Hockett calls duality (. . .) is also referred to in the literature by means of the terms 'double articulation' (cf. Martinet, 1949); and it is generally recognized as one of the universal features of language. Indeed some scholars (notably Hjelmslev, 1953) have proposed that it should be made an essential and defining property of language on a priori grounds.[2]

The Danish linguist and semiotician Louis Hjelmslev (1899–1965) goes one step further than Martinet by coining two new concepts which make it easier to distinguish the phonetic level of the signifier from the semantic level of the signified. He speaks of an *expression plane* and a *content plane*: '(. . .) We have used respectively the designations *expression plane* and *content plane* (designations chosen with reference to Saussure's formulation cited above: "le plan . . . des idées . . . et celui . . . des sons").'[3] Like Saussure and Martinet, Hjelmslev believes that the expression plane (the phonetic level of the sounds) is autonomous *vis-à-vis* the content plane (the semantic level of concepts or ideas).

In what follows it will be argued that Hjelmslev's distinction which systematically develops Saussure's dualism is *comparable* to Immanuel Kant's (1724–1804) dualist theory of knowledge and in particular to his dualist view of the relationship between conceptual and aesthetic cognition. Starting from the assumption that aesthetic knowledge cannot be reduced to conceptual knowledge, Kant points out that an aesthetic judgement ('*Geschmacksurteil*') cannot be deduced from conceptual and logical reasoning and that therefore the Beautiful pleases the human mind '*without a concept*' ('*ohne Begriff*').[4] His view of the Beautiful is analogous to the linguist's view of the expression plane: neither can be viewed as entirely determined by concepts, neither can be reduced to conceptual knowledge. It will appear that Georg Wilhelm Friedrich Hegel (1770-1831) challenged Kant's dualist view of the Beautiful and implicitly denied the autonomy of the expression plane in verbal art.

1 Kant, Hegel, and Literary Theory

Hegel's critique of Kant and the ensuing controversies between Kantians and Hegelians are of considerable importance to modern literary theory insofar as they touch upon the central problem of this theory around which all recent discussions revolve: *the conceptualisation of art and literature*. In the literary context, the possibility or impossibility of conceptualisation is inextricably tied up with the nexus of the expression plane and the content plane in the sense of Hjelmslev. Although Kant, Hegel, and their successors never used linguistic or semiotic terminology, the Kantians and Hegelians among modern literary critics did so quite often. Hence it is perfectly possible to speak of Kantian and Hegelian positions within contemporary literary theory. In fact, it can be argued that it is impossible to understand the latter adequately as long as the Kantian, Hegelian or Nietzschean bias of its competing components is not perceived. But let us return to Kant.

Kant can be considered as the philosopher who founded the notion of artistic autonomy by limiting the realm of conceptual thought. Refusing to conceptualise the notion of the Beautiful, which he mainly associated with nature, he designated a category of objects which were autonomous with respect to conceptual logic. However, this should not be taken to mean that the absence of concepts implies the arbitrary character of aesthetic judgement; for Kant explains: 'Beauty is not a concept of an object, and a judgment of taste is not a cognitive judgment.'[5] He adds elsewhere: 'By an aesthetic Idea I mean a presentation of the imagination which prompts much thought, but to which no determinate thought whatsoever, i.e., no (determinate) *concept*, can be adequate, so that no language can express it completely and allow us to grasp it.'[6] For Kant, beautiful is that which – without a concept – is recognised as the object of necessary pleasure. In defining an object as beautiful, we assume universal agreement on the part of all those who perceive it. This is why Kant speaks of 'necessary' pleasure, as he assumes that the aesthetic judgement is universally valid without a determinate or explicit conceptualisation. (He does concede, however, that an indeterminate, i.e. indefinable concept underlies the universality of aesthetic judgement.)

It should be noted that in discussing the Beautiful, Kant adopts the point of view of the *observer* or *recipient*. He does not ask what ideas beautiful objects express but regards the *Critique of Judgement* (1790) as an inquiry about the correct attitude towards aesthetic phenomena. This attitude not only excludes conceptual definitions but also all attempts to instrumentalise the Beautiful, reducing it to what is economically, politically or didactically useful. Rejecting the utilitarian point of view of Enlightenment philosophers such as Gottsched (1700–1766), who tended to subject works of art to political and didactic ends, Kant expects the competent or ideal observer to regard aesthetic objects with *disinterested pleasure (interesseloses Wohlgefallen)* and to conceive of them as *purposiveness without purpose (Zweckmäßigkeit ohne Zweck)*. In other words, they ought to be considered as *autonomous* with respect to economic, political or affective interests.

This disinterested attitude towards aesthetic autonomy finds a clear and convincing expression in E. M. Forster's commentary on Shakespeare's tragedy *Macbeth*. Forster, who is not a Kantian, puts forward a very Kantian idea when he points out:

> Well, the play has several aspects – it is educational, it teaches us something about legendary Scotland, something about Jacobean England and a good deal about human nature and its perils. We can study its origins, and study and enjoy its dramatic technique and the music of its diction. All that is true. But *Macbeth* is furthermore a world of its own, created by Shakespeare and existing in virtue of its own poetry. It is in this aspect *Macbeth* for *Macbeth*'s sake, and that is what I intend by the phrase 'art for art's sake'. A work of art – whatever else it may be – is a

self-contained entity, with a life of its own imposed on it by its own creator.[7]

Forster's description of the Shakespearian tragedy bears witness to a Kantian belief in the autonomy of art. Although the play can be perceived or read in a *referential* and *didactic* mode in that it *teaches* us something about English and Scottish history and society, its actual *raison d'être*, its value is poetic or aesthetic: it is 'a world of its own', a world 'existing in virtue of its own poetry'. In other words, it should not be reduced to its referential, historical, political, affective or didactic dimensions.

In the second and third chapter of this book, it will be shown that this Kantian conception of artistic autonomy underlies the theories of Anglo-American New Criticism, Russian Formalism, and Czech Structuralism. All of these theories are Kantian aesthetics insofar as they emphasise the autonomy of art and are strongly opposed to all attempts to reduce literature to heteronomous factors such as the author's biography, the social context or the reactions of the reader. I. A. Richards, whose work had a lasting influence on the New Critics, sums up the programme of New Criticism when he points out: 'Every poem, however, is a strictly limited piece of experience, a piece which breaks up more or less easily if alien elements intrude.'[8] Similar statements could be found in Russian Formalism and Czech Structuralism; they will be discussed in some detail in the third chapter.

For the present it may be sufficient to recall the linguistically based literary theory of Roman Jakobson (1896-1982) who made a crucial contribution to Czech Structuralism after leaving the Soviet Union, where he had been one of the most active members of the Formalist movement. Among the six functions of language which he distinguishes in his well-known article on 'Linguistics and Poetics' (1960), he defines the *poetic function* as an auto-referential or self-reflexive message. It is a type of text which is to be read for its own sake, not as an historical, social, biographical or moral document. On the whole, the theories of the New Critics, the Formalists, and the Structuralists can be defined as Kantian because they insist on the autonomy of art, rejecting all attempts to reduce it to a conceptual message pointing towards the real world.

The idea that art is autonomous, self-contained, and impervious to conceptual thought ought not to be considered as 'natural' or universally valid. For within philosophy, it was challenged early on by Georg Wilhelm Friedrich Hegel who rebuked Kant for having separated the *senses (Sinnlichkeit)* from the *concepts (Begriffe)*, thus excluding art from the realm of knowledge and reducing it to mere appearance. Unlike Kant, Hegel does not consider art and the Beautiful in general from the point of view of the spectator or reader but within the perspective of the producer or artist who, according to Hegel, articulates a particular historical consciousness: the consciousness of his time.

Within this perspective, art and the individual work of art no longer appear as objects located beyond or outside the conceptual domain (*'ohne Begriff'*, Kant) but as expressing historical consciousness, a historical content. Starting from the assumption that the development of history is the development of human consciousness, of what Hegel calls the *World Spirit* or the *Weltgeist*, he attempts to show in his *Aesthetics* that the symbolic forms which prevail in the architecture of Egyptian, Indian, and Persian antiquity are incomplete, because their material form and their conceptual content fail to coincide. This fundamental contradiction between matter and concept leads to the decline of the ancient symbolic forms marked by what Gérard Bras calls 'the essential obscurity of symbolism'.[9] According to Hegel, this obscurity is overcome by classical Greek sculpture, in which material appearance and conceptual essence are one.

It seems worthwhile to have a closer look at Hegel's own text, which makes it sufficiently clear that, from his point of view, the congruence of material appearance and conceptual content which characterises ancient Greek art is the ideal of German classical doctrine[10] and of German Idealism in the first half of the nineteenth century:

> In fact the classical ideal is clear because it encompasses the true content of art, i.e. substantial subjectivity, and precisely thereby it finds too the true form, which in itself expresses nothing but that genuine content. That is to say, the significance, the meaning, is no other than that which actually lies in the external shape, since both sides correspond perfectly; whereas in the symbol, simile, etc., the image always still presents some

thing other than the meaning alone for which it furnishes the image.[11]

What Hegel calls 'clarity' is the coincidence of material form and conceptual content, a coincidence which brings about a monosemic or univocal unity of the artistic sign. Translating Hegel's passage into the language of contemporary semiotics, one could say that in spite of his theory of the sign which assumes arbitrariness, he postulates a unity or one-to-one correspondence of the *signifier* and the *signified*, of the *expression plane* and the *content plane*. It goes without saying that these linguistic or semiotic concepts are only applicable to the quoted text if defined in a very broad sense, as meaning 'material expression' and 'conceptual or ideal content'. For in dealing with ancient Greek sculpture Hegel does not inquire into the problems of verbal art, of literature.

However, he does so when discussing the historical period of 'Romantic Art' which not only encompasses European or German Romanticism, but all of medieval art and the art of modern times. As a matter of fact, the notion 'Romantic Art' is co-extensive in Hegel's work with the art of Christianity which succeeds the classical world of ancient Greece and Rome. In Hegel's perspective, Christian or Romantic art appears dominated by its verbal form: by literature, by poetry. The domination of the latter in Christianity is viewed as a result of the disintegration of the classical synthesis, marked by the global correspondence of material appearance and essence, by what Hegel calls *'das sinnliche Scheinen der Idee'*. The break-up of the classical synthesis which Hegel considers as an ideal equilibrium between the material and the conceptual or spiritual (*geistig*) leads to the domination of the word and the concept.

Many of Hegel's remarks about poetry and literature make it sufficiently clear that he tends to disregard what semioticians would call its *expression plane*, focusing entirely on its conceptual aspects: on its *content plane*. It is hardly surprising therefore when he remarks about the poem that 'it is a matter of indifference whether we read it or hear it read; it can even be translated into other languages without essential detriment to its value (. . .).'[12] This emphasis on concept and content and the complementary idea that the verbal art of literature prevails during the era of Christianity leads Hegel to conclude that, at the end of the day, art, as the expression of a lower form of historical consciousness, will be overcome by philosophy: 'Philosophy has the same content and end as art and religion; but it is the highest manner of comprehending the Absolute Idea, because its manner is the highest – the Notion (Begriff).'[13] This is obviously the antithesis to Kant's postulate that art pleases without concept and that the critique of judgement cannot be conceptualised.

Considering the incompatibility of the Kantian and the Hegelian positions, it is hardly surprising to find that the critical debates of the twentieth century were marked by regular clashes between Kantians and Hegelians – not only in the theory of knowledge, in politics and ethics, but also in literary criticism. Modern Marxist critics in particular turned out to be staunch defenders of Hegelian positions and of the idea that works of art are conceptual icons which univocally express political points of view, ideologies or philosophical doctrines.

The two Marxist-Hegelian thinkers who most stubbornly insisted on translating literary works into conceptual systems were György (Georg) Lukács and Lucien Goldmann, whose works will be dealt with in the sixth chaper. Both believed that works of art are to be considered as meaningful totalities genetically linked to *class interests, ideologies* or *world visions* (*Weltanschauungen* or *visions du monde* as Goldmann says). Goldmann's Hegelianism comes to the fore whenever he sets out to demonstrate that each element of a philosophical or literary text acquires a specific, concrete meaning if it is considered as a constituent part of the textual totality which in turn can be linked to the conceptual system of a world vision.

Unlike the Russian Formalists and the Czech structuralists who took the view that literature and avant-garde literature in particular cannot be reduced to a univocal conceptual structure, because they elude conceptual definition by intentional polysemy, Goldmann believed that he could identify the conceptual system underlying Samuel Beckett's work. In a discussion with Theodor W. Adorno, who was fiercely opposed to such 'logocentric' reductions, Goldmann asserts that, if Beckett's work '*is really great*' ('*si elle est grande*'), it overcomes all contradictions and incongruencies in a global world vision '*which can be reduced to a system*' ('*qui peut être réduite en système*').[14] The postulate of 'greatness', put forward by Goldmann almost *en passant*, is of Hegelian origin. For it evokes the Hegelian view of the classical

Greek sculpture as being a meaningful totality, a flawless fusion of spirit and matter.

In the course of the critical debates which took place during the nineteenth and twentieth centuries, the Hegelian stance was not only challenged by the Kantian New Critics, the Russian Formalists, and the Czech Structuralists; it was also treated with open defiance by literary theories which originated in German Romanticism and the Young Hegelian critiques of Hegel's system. Deconstructionists, for example, such as Geoffrey H. Hartman, tend to criticise aesthetic rationalism and Hegelianism from a Romantic and a Nietzschean point of view.

2 From Romanticism and Young Hegelianism to Nietzsche

The first philosopher to systematically challenge Hegel's subordination of art to conceptual thought was his contemporary and rival, Friedrich Wilhelm Schelling (1775–1854), whose romantic aesthetics had a great impact on German philosophy. Although its influence is negligible in European and American literary criticism, its central idea, which also crops up in the poetics of Friedrich Schlegel (1772–1829), should be mentioned here. In Schelling's philosophical system, art occupies a central position in the sense that it is regarded as a mode of thought which makes it possible to conceive and represent whatever 'cannot be represented by way of concepts and conceptual reflexion'[15], as Manfred Frank puts it.

In spite of all the differences which separate him from Kant, Schelling agrees – at least partly – with Kant in considering art as a specific mode of perception which cannot be reduced to conceptual discourse or subordinated to philosophy. Unlike Hegel, who finally turns art into an *ancilla philosophiae*, Schelling regards it – at least in some of his writings – as superior to philosophical thought. In other writings he establishes a correspondence between philosophy and art, defines art as a *particular* mode of perception (in contrast to philosophy which aims at the *general*) and concludes that it is '*the highest potential of the ideal world*' ('*die höchste Potenz der idealen Welt*').[16]

This idea reappears – albeit in a modified form – in the work of the Romantic philosopher Friedrich Schlegel, whose theory of art and of literary criticism had a lasting impact on Geoffrey H. Hartman's notion of literature and on deconstruction in general.

In his famous essay '*Über die Unverständlichkeit*', Schlegel points out that he considers '*art as the core of humanity*' ('*daß ich die Kunst für den Kern der Menschheit halte*')[17], thus defying the rationalists of the Enlightenment period, who emphasised the didactic utility of art, and the Hegelians who believed that art would be superseded by philosophy.

However, the originality of Schlegel's essay does not simply consist in its apotheosis of art which is characteristic of the entire Romantic movement; it is due to the philospher's emphasis on the obscurity or '*incomprehensibility*' ('*Unverständlichkeit*') of language. Turning upside down the rationalist creed according to which language is a means of communication and comprehension, an instrument enabling us to classify and clarify, Schlegel exposes the dark side of language: its irreducible polysemy, its notorious resistance to communication of meaning, and its poetic hermetism. He asks with a grain of Romantic irony: 'But is incomprehensibility something so despicable and bad?'[18] He adds, with one eye on the rationalists: 'Indeed, you would be greatly distressed if the whole world were made quite comprehensible in accordance with your wishes.'[19]

Schlegel, the Romantic philosopher, regards the obscurity of language as an inexhaustible source of poetic inspiration, not as an obstacle to (rationalist) knowledge. Without saying so, he stresses the autonomy of the *signifier* and of the entire *expression plane*, revealing their imperviousness to conceptual meaning: i.e. the impossibility to reduce speech and thought to the signified concept in its pure form. The signifier permanently interferes and causes shifts in the meaning we intend to communicate, shifts due to the fact that the communicated word means something different to the speaker and the listener, to the sender and the receiver.

Such shifts are particularly conspicuous in poetry, which was the model for Friedrich Schlegel and his brother August Wilhelm. It is not by chance that it also became the model for deconstruction, a theory which is not simply irrational or obscure, but – quite rationally – reveals the imponderabilities of an autonomous expression plane which incessantly causes shifts in meaning. These shifts are the gist of language, according to the deconstructionists, not its shortcomings. This is what Geoffrey H. Hartman has in mind when, inspired by Schlegel, he insists on the vital role of obscurity in the process of imagination: 'To withhold from imagination its dark nourishment means desiring its death.'[20] We are not too far away here from F. Schlegel's praise of the incomprehensible. In the seventh chapter, the Romantic and Nietzschean roots of deconstructionist theories will be laid bare.

In a rather different political context, marked by the critique of society, religion, and ideology, the Young Hegelians queried the validity of Hegel's systematic thought. Among them were not only Karl Marx and Friedrich Engels (whose theory of art is Hegelian and will be commented on in the sixth chapter) but also less known authors such as the anarchist Max Stirner (1806-1856), Arnold Ruge (1803-1880), Ludwig Feuerbach (1804-1872), and Friedrich Theodor Vischer (1807-1887), whose aesthetic theory departs considerably from Hegel's. The common denominator of all these thinkers is their rather rebellious social criticism which is partly due to the fact – as Martin Eßbach aptly points out[21] – that many of them could not embark on a university career or find a socially acceptable alternative.

Unlike Hegel, who in his *Philosophy of Law* and in his *Philosophy of History* wrote an apology of the modern (Prussian) state, the Young Hegelians set out to unmask the state and its mechanisms of domination. 'He knew', writes Sidney Hook about Ruge, 'that it was a clerical, romantic, feudal class state.'[22] He realised, in other words, that the Prussian state did not represent the universal idea, as Hegel would have it, but particular class interests. Hook's point of view is confirmed by Löwith and (more recently) Eßbach who draw our attention to the widening rift between the Young Hegelians and the state institutions.[23]

This political rift explains why the radicals among Hegel's disciples began to question the foundations of their master's philosophical system, which was an apology of the existing order in the sense that it pretended that the individual's and the group's interests could be reconciled with those of society at large and that the state was instrumental in this process of reconciliation. Along with Hegel's system, the Young Hegelians, especially Friedrich Theodor Vischer, criticised Hegelian aesthetics which attempt to reconcile all aesthetic phenomena (including nature) with conceptual, philosophical thought.

Although Vischer's critique is not as radical and global as that of Stirner, Feuerbach or Marx, it radically queries Hegel's faith in conceptual domination: the idea that there is a fundamental identity between the thinking Subject (philosophical thought) and its objects. In his *later* writings, especially in *Kritik meiner Ästhetik* (1887), he clearly departs from Hegel's postulate that the aesthetic object, although it primarily addresses the senses, can be grasped with the help of concepts, for in the Beautiful 'general truth is contained as an object of contemplation (Anschauung), without having previously existed in a conceptual form'.[24] Later on, he explains: 'We also exclude the *theoretical* interest, the drive of our mind to know truth. When we contemplate the Beautiful we do not feel obliged to understand it first.'[25] At this point, Vischer not only breaks with Hegel but also with his own voluminous *Ästhetik* (1847-1858) which is Hegelian in most respects.

His partial return to the Kantian position (which does not make him a Kantian) is particularly important for modern literary debates. For Walter Benjamin's and especially Theodor W. Adorno's aesthetic and literary theories have to be understood in this context: as discourses which oscillate between the Hegelian and the Kantian position, between Hegel's quest for conceptual truth in an artistic form ('*sinnliches Scheinen der Idee*') and Kant's '*ohne Begriff*'. The sixth chapter will show to what extent Adorno considers both the Hegelian and the Kantian position as reductionist: Hegel may be right in stressing the importance of philosophical truth in art ('*Wahrheitsgehalt*', Adorno), however, he completely neglects the ambiguous or polysemic character of the artistic form (the *expression plane* in literature), which defies conceptual definition. Kant quite rightly insists on the non-conceptual nature of the Beautiful, but entirely disregards the truth it expresses, albeit negatively, critically. Adorno's emphasis on the critical potential of artistic form explains his virtuoso oscillation between Kant and Hegel and his – often neglected – affinity with Vischer. It is not by chance that Adorno refers to Vischer in his posthumous *Aesthetic Theory* (1970).

Not only Adorno's aesthetic and literary theory was influenced by Vischer but also that of the Russian theoretician, Mikhail M. Bakhtin. Writing under ideology-obsessed Stalinism, Bakhtin not only rejected the idea that literary texts could be pinned down to political positions, but along with it the Hegelian notion of classical harmony and of the work of art as harmonious totality.

In Vischer's aesthetics he found a theory of the *grotesque* which is a straight negation of the classical ideal. Unlike Hegel and the Hegelian Marxists Lukács and Goldmann who believed that in 'great' works of art no contradiction is left unresolved, Vischer revealed the disparities of the grotesque in art and literature.

Bakhtin took up some of his arguments in his two remarkable books on Rabelais (*Rabelais and his World*, 1928) and Dostoevskij (*Problems of Dostoevsky's Poetics*, 1928). He continues the Young Hegelian critique of Hegel's classicist apology of political and aesthetic totality, confirming the link established by Vischer between the grotesque and the *culture of popular laughter* (*kultura smĕcha*): 'Hegel completely ignores the role of the comic in the structure of the grotesque, and indeed examines the grotesque quite idependently of the comic. F. Th. Vischer differs from Hegel. He sees the burlesque, the comic as the essence and the driving force of this genre.'[26] And Bakhtin quotes from Vischer's *Aesthetic* when he adds: 'The grotesque (. . .) is the comic in the form of the miraculous, it is the mythological comic.'[27] He concludes: 'Vischer's definition has a certain profundity.'[28]

'Profundity' could be read as an indication that in some respects Bakhtin continues the Young Hegelian Critique of Hegel. Like the Young Hegelians, Vischer, Feuerbach, and Ruge, he objects to the aristocratic tone, the monologue, and the repressive aspects of the Hegelian system, proposing alternatives in the realm of ambiguity and laughter (Vischer), materialism (Feuerbach), and partisan politics (Ruge). Bakhtin can be read as a 'Young Hegelian' in the sense that he opposes ambivalence, polyphony, and aesthetic disparity to Hegel's ideal of classical harmony, to his notion of an integrated and meaningful totality. In the fifth chapter it will become clear to what extent Bakhtin's literary theory can be viewed as a critical and polemical reaction to Marxist-Leninist aesthetics, which are of Hegelian origin.

However, Young Hegelian philosophies are not only important because they inaugurated a critique of Hegel's system which in turn influenced Walter Benjamin's, Theodor W. Adorno's, and Bakhtin's approaches to art and literature; they are also important because they made Friedrich Nietzsche's radical critique of European metaphysics possible. It goes without saying that Nietzsche's thought cannot be considered as just another brand of Young

Hegelianism. It is a well-known fact, however, that Nietzsche was familiar with Max Stirner's anarchist treatise *Der Einzige und sein Eigentum* (1845) and that his radical repudiation of Christianity and the Christian moral code would hardly have been possible without Ludwig Feuerbach's and Bruno Bauer's critiques of religion.[29]

Unlike Hegel's philosophy which is a secularised quest for truth inspired by Platonic and Christian metaphysics, Nietzsche's philosophical critique can be read as a sustained effort to demolish the whole metaphysical edifice, in particular its central concept of truth. In contrast to Hegel who relentlessly seeks to overcome ambiguities and contradictions by integrating them into ever higher syntheses which make up his system, Nietzsche reveals the ambivalent and contradictory character of key values and concepts of European metaphysics. 'The fundamental faith of the metaphysicians', we read in *Beyond Good and Evil*, '*is the faith in antithetical values.*'[30] In other words, metaphysics are based on oppositions such as *essence/appearance*, *truth/lie*, *good/evil*, *virtuous/vile* etc. Long before the deconstructionists who, as will be shown in chapter seven, doubt the very possibility of such neat distinctions, Nietzsche seeks to subvert 'the fundamental faith of the metaphysician' by revealing the affinity of all opposites and by exposing in a sacrilegious way the vile character of virtue, the evil roots of the morally Good, and the lies underlying truth.

In his well-known text '*Über Wahrheit und Lüge im außermoralischen Sinn*', Nietzsche lays bare the trivial or even vile origins of metaphysical truth: '*mankind's metaphoric drive*' ('*Trieb zur Metaphern-bildung*')[31] which makes metaphysical truths appear as fortuitous constellations of metaphors, metonymies, and other rhetorical figures. 'What, then, is truth?' – he asks and answers: 'a mobile army of metaphors, metonymies, anthropomorphisms'.[32] This dissolution of metaphysical truth in the volatile figures of rhetoric inevitably leads to a radical upgrading of the *expression plane* of language and to a concomitant downgrading of the *content plane*, of its conceptual components.

Time and again Nietzsche defends the ambiguities and polysemies of reality and language against attempts to domesticate them by univocal conceptual definitions, by 'truth'. It is not surprising to find that he considers music as the highest form of art; for the polysemic sound of music, music as pure *phoné*, defies conceptual definition. In

Nietzsche's work it becomes the unattainable model towards which not only the other arts but even philosophy should aspire.[33] It is quite inevitable of course that a philosophy geared towards music should place art above conceptual thought, thus inverting the hierarchy established by Hegel. Polemicising against Hegel, Nietzsche defines art as 'the *good* will to hold on to appearance' ('der *gute* Wille zum Scheine').[34] With the help of art he sets out to fight metaphysical truth and Christian morals.

Globally, his philosophy could be interpreted as a gathering of all the radical tendencies in Young Hegelianism, tendencies which later reappear in Bakhtin's literary theory, in Roland Barthes' semiotics and especially in Derrida's, Paul de Man's, J. Hillis Miller's, and Geoffrey Hartman's deconstruction. In all of these theories, Hegel's (Lukács', Goldmann's) attempts at a conceptual definition of art and literature are condemned as 'metaphysical' or 'logocentric' (cf. chapter 7). Following Nietzsche, Roland Barthes stresses the impossibility of translating the polysemic signifiers of literary *and* philosophical texts into conceptual systems, into 'structures of signifieds'.[35] Jacques Derrida and the American deconstructionists go one step further in trying to show that purely conceptual thought does not exist and that theories which pretend to domesticate rhetorical figures (metaphors, metonymies) by conceptual means finally deconstruct themselves. Paul de Man adopts a Nietzschean point of view when he upgrades the 'rhetorical dimension of discourse' (its metaphors, metonymies, synecdoches), projecting it onto an epistemological level: 'Difficulties occur only when it is no longer possible to ignore the epistemological thrust of the rhetorical dimension of discourse, that is, when it is no longer possible to keep it in its place as a mere adjunct, a mere ornament within the semantic function.'[36] Far from being mere ornament, the rhetorical figure is the epistemological gist of discourse and cannot be reduced to concepts.

The global situation of deconstruction between Hegel and Nietzsche is sketched by the Yale deconstructionist, Geoffrey H. Hartman, who discerns two main directions in Derrida's thought: 'One is the past, starting with Hegel who is still with us; the other is the future, starting with Nietzsche who is once again with us, having been rediscovered by recent French thought.'[37]

Although contemporary French thought cannot be globally

characterised as Nietzschean (there are still enough Kantians, Hegelians, and Marxists around), it is certainly true that Barthes, Derrida, Foucault, and the American deconstructionists cannot be understood adequately as long as the Nietzschean elements in their works are not acknowledged. It is equally important, however, to detect the Hegelian components of Marxism and the Kantian bias of Anglo-American New Criticism and of Russian Formalism. In what follows, the main arguments of this introductory chapter will be developed in more detail within the context of literary theory.

CHAPTER 2
Anglo-American New Criticism and Russian Formalism

In spite of all the differences between Russian Formalism, which was inspired by the verbal experiments of the Futurists, and Anglo-American New Criticism, which was influenced by T. S. Eliot's conservative poetics, the common aim of the New Critics and the Formalists seems to be of paramount importance: it is the assertion that art is autonomous and should not be reduced to a historical or social document or to a testimony of the psyche. Both groups, Formalists and New Critics alike, were therefore strongly opposed to Positivism (which is an attempt to base literary theory on the study of causal relations between empirical data such as the author's biography, historical facts, etc.) and to Marxism. Their unflinching allegiance to the idea of aesthetic autonomy explains why dealing with them in a single chapter or in a systematic account such as Ewa Thompson's book *Russian Formalism and Anglo-American New Criticism*[1] makes sense.

However, the idea of aesthetic autonomy is not, as the previous chapter has shown, an invention of the Russian Formalists or the New Critics. It dates back to Kant's *Critique of Judgement* which insists on the impossibility of conceptualising the Beautiful and on the necessity of considering it with a disinterested attitude (*interesseloses Wohlgefallen*), i.e. without subjecting it to heteronomous criteria of utility. It is hardly surprising therefore that the aesthetics of the Formalists and especially the New Critics are better understood if considered in a Kantian context. In the case of the Formalists it will become clear that their fatal clashes with the Russian Marxists were not simply 'political' but originated in a fundamental incompatibility between Kantian and Hegelian notions of literature.

This incompatibility is mitigated in Benedetto Croce's (1866-1952) philosophy, which appears as a Hegelian project if considered in a historical or social perspective (in many respects Croce considered himself as a disciple of Hegel), but which is clearly Kantian from an aesthetic point of view. Hegel, argues Croce, adopts an 'intuitive' attitude towards the *concept*, 'when intuition signifies (. . .) that philosophy must spring from the bosom of divine Poetry, *matre pulchra filia pulchrior*'.[2] This is clearly an extremely unorthodox interpretation of Hegel, for it ignores the Hegelian intention to subordinate art and poetry to philosophy as a superior form of historical consciousness, thus inverting the hierarchical order of the German philosopher.

The consequences of this inversion come to the fore when Croce argues in his influential *Estetica* (1902) that in all works of art the *expression* (*espressione*) is crucial and that one of the fundamental philosophical errors begins 'when we try to deduce the expression from the concept (. . .).'[3] He denounces this error as an 'intellectualist error'[4], thereby confirming Kant's thesis that the Beautiful pleases without concept. Although Croce's notion of 'expression' bears a certain resemblance to Hjelmslev's *expression plane*, it should be pointed out that the two ought not to be treated as synonyms: not only because the Italian philosopher has a much wider concept of linguistics than Hjelmslev and a rather vague one, but also – and above all – because he applies the word 'expression' to all arts, not only to literature. Nevertheless, Croce's orientation towards expression coincides with an aversion towards all kinds of 'content analyses' which focus on the ideas articulated in literary works.

This Kantian attitude has three consequences, all of which are of considerable importance for Anglo-American New Criticism: 1. Croce views each work of art as a particular, unique, and incommensurable construct or *expression* which – in the case of literature – cannot be translated into another language without losing its original character, without being transformed into a 'new expression'.[5] It is not surprising that Croce speaks of the 'impossibility of translations'[6] thus anticipating some of the deconstructionist theories, and insists on the 'original value'[7] of good translations. The good translation becomes a new and autonomous work of art. 2. The focus on the expression and the Kantian rejection of conceptualisation lead Croce to believe that all generic theories (of the novel, the drama or the poem) encroach on the essentially unique and incomparable character of individual novels, dramas or poems. There is no such thing as 'the novel'; there are but individual novels such as Emily Brontë's *Wuthering Heights* or Joseph Conrad's *Lord Jim*. The concept of *genre* is dismissed by Croce as an 'empty phantasy' which has to yield to the analysis of the individual work: to what the New Critics later called *close reading*. 3. The rejection of generic concepts such as Classicism, Romanticism, and Realism entails a dismissal of *literary history*. Unlike Hegel who subjected the individual work of art to the general idea inherent in the process of history, Croce in 1902 (not in his later works, however)[8] subordinates historical development to artistic intuition.

Anglo-American New Criticism and Russian Formalism, which developed in the first half of the twentieth century, are Kantian and Crocean in character insofar as they both insist on the *autonomy of literary works* and on the impossibility to conceptualise them: i.e. to reduce them to heteronomous factors such as philosophy, religion, politics or morals. In what follows, it will be shown that New Criticism can be read as an aesthetic synthesis of Kantian and Crocean principles and that Formalism is marked by the somewhat contradictory collusion of Kantian and avant-garde orientations.

1 Kant and Croce in the New Criticism

'When we are considering poetry we must consider it primarily as poetry and not another thing.'[9] This quotation from T. S. Eliot's *The Sacred Wood* could be read as expressing the basic rule which all New Critics – Brooks, Ransom, Wimsatt, Blackmur, Empson – adhered to without reserve. It is not by chance that Eliot's influence within New Criticism was strong and lasting; for the New Critics were preaching what Eliot practised in the realm of poetry: the autonomy of art and its disengagement from social action and politics. In this respect, an analogy or elective affinity can be assumed between Eliot's, Brooks', Ransom's or Wimsatt's poetics and Kantian aesthetics which draw a clear line between the Beautiful and the Useful.

However, the Kantian components of New Criticism are not due to a mere analogy or historical coincidence, for the New Critics knew Kant's *Critique of Judgement* and were lastingly influenced by it. W. K. Wimsatt's *The Verbal Icon*, one of the major contributions to New Criticism, reveals just how much the latter owes to the philosophies of Kant and Croce:

> The highly respected individuality of the poem owes its obvious debt to the Kantian aesthetic judgement 'without concept' and the corresponding intuition-expression of Croce. In such instances as these – and they are cardinal instances – the literary theorist must be grateful to the metaphysician and the aesthetician.[10]

Wimsatt's reference to the *poem* has a symptomatic value here: for most New Critics regarded poetry as the highest form of autonomous literature and of literary autonomy. On aesthetic and political grounds the *roman engagé* of Realism, Naturalism or Existentialism was not their favourite model. For this type of novel can be read as a permanent challenge to the very idea of artistic autonomy.

But what does Wimsatt, what do the New Critics mean by 'the individuality of the poem'? Individuality in this particular context has three aspects, all of which can be related to Kantian and Crocean aesthetics: 1. emphasis on the expression plane of poetry and on the fact that a conceptual paraphrase of paradoxical and ambiguous lyrical texts is inconceivable; 2. the idea that a poem can only be analysed as an entity *sui generis* and that as such it is inaccessible to conceptual thought; 3. finally, the notion that works of literature and art are unique and incomparable and that every attempt to explain them within an historical, political or philosophical context amounts to a heteronomous reduction.

The last two points presuppose the first: whenever the level of the signifiers or the expression plane is deemed to be the central element, all attempts to understand literature within non-literary contexts are considered with suspicion as potential heresies of heteronomy. The third point is explicitly related by Wimsatt to Kant's and Croce's aesthetic positions, as the above quotation from *The Verbal Icon* shows. Although Wimsatt at one point criticises Croce's notion of literary autonomy as being 'extreme'[11], he stresses elsewhere 'that the critic who wishes to retain his humanism and his identity as a literary critic will have to persevere in his allegiance to the party of Coleridge and Croce'.[12] The party of Coleridge and Croce is the party of radical autonomy which it defends against all non-poetic intrusions. Ransom, Wimsatt, and

Brooks tend to agree with I. A. Richards's view of Coleridge's *The Ancient Mariner*: 'As the poem stands, it is of a kind into which ulterior ends do not enter.'[13]

However, Richards, whose central idea that the nature of poetry is mainly affective is rejected by the New Critics, is well aware of the fact that there is a kind of poetry which, far from being self-contained and an end in itself in the Kantian sense, was written for heteronomous (moral, affective, political or religious) purposes and hence cannot be adequately understood within an aesthetic of autonomy. Unfortunately, the New Critics have seldom heeded his insight 'that poetry is of more than one kind, and that the different kinds are to be judged by different principles'.[14] Their very Crocean assumption was that all poetry which deserves to be considered as such is autonomous and incommensurate.

The method of *close reading* which they adopted and which resembles in many respects the traditional French *explication de texte* and the German *werkimmanente Interpretation* introduced by Wolfgang Kayser[15], is based on the postulate that a literary text should primarily be understood in itself − primarily, because the New Critics never explicitly denied that literature contains metaphysical, moral, religious or political components. These, however, were considered to be secondary, inessential for the 'reading of the poem itself'[16], as Cleanth Brooks puts it in *The Well Wrought Urn*. This focus on the text as such explains why the New Critics were neither interested in *what* literature communicates, nor in the question *why* it is written (for what emotional, moral or political purposes), but almost exclusively in the question *how* it is made. It will appear that this specific interest in the *how* makes their thought akin to that of the Russian Formalists.

This emphasis on the *how* and the *expression plane* is common to all New Critics. Cleanth Brooks and Robert Penn Warren regard poetry primarily 'as a way of saying'[17] and draw a clear line between literature, which according to William Empson derives its vitality from ambiguity and indeterminacy, and science which relies on 'statements of absolute precision'.[18] Their opinions are substantiated by John Crowe Ransom who claims that poetry conveys a particular kind of (intuitive) knowledge which is incommensurable with the conceptual thought of science. In *The New Criticism* (1941), which could almost be read as a manifesto, he asserts that poetry breaks with conventional logic. Unlike the logician who aims at universal truth, the poet seeks the particular which has no conceptual equivalent, no scientific paraphrase. Using the terminology of the American semiotician Charles Morris, with whom he disagrees in many other respects, he defines the work of art globally as an 'iconic sign'[19] the particularity of which eludes conceptual (scientific) definition. Ransom's train of thought is Kantian in the sense that it insists on the impossibility of conceptualising the aesthetic phenomenon and the necessity to recognise a special kind of poetic cognition located beyond the realm of concepts.

This is by and large the perspective adopted by Cleanth Brooks in *The Well Wrought Urn*. Unlike Hegel, who takes the view that poetry can be translated into other languages without damage and explained by conceptual means, Brooks concludes that 'the poem itself is the *only* medium that communicates the particular "what" that is communicated'.[20] In full agreement with Croce he points out that 'the finer aspects of poetry elude translation'[21] and dismisses all philosophical, religious, psychological or sociological attempts to deduce poetry from heteronomous principles.

Within this context the three fallacies which the New Critics relentlessly denounced are to be understood: the *genetic*, the *intentional*, and the *affective* fallacy. In reality it seems sufficient to distinguish only *two* fallacies, because the *intentional fallacy* can be subsumed under the encompassing concept of the *genetic fallacy*. The basic idea underlying the critique of the fallacies is that the literary text ought not to be confused with the *context of its production or genesis* ('genetic') or with the *intentions* (i.e. the biography) of the author ('intentional'): 'The Intentional Fallacy is a confusion between the poem and its origins, a special case of what is known to philosophers as the Genetic Fallacy.'[22] The *affective fallacy* consists in an erroneous identification of the text with the reactions of the readers: 'The Affective Fallacy is a confusion between the poem and its results (. . .).'[23]

It is not difficult to understand this critique of the *fallacies* against the backdrop of Kantian and especially Crocean aesthetics, as Wimsatt and Brooks' *Literary Criticism. A Short History* (1957) shows. The authors deal extensively with Croce and, having rejected all brands of Hegelian and Hegelian–Marxist criticism (chap. 21: 'The Real and the Social: Art as Propaganda'), they reveal in the 23rd chapter ('Expressionism: Benedetto Croce') just how strong Croce's influence within New Criticism was.

In spite of a few critical remarks concerning Croce's attempt to identify the *aesthetic* with the *linguistic*, they fully approve of the Italian philosopher's 'dismissal of the affective art theories which he groups under the headings "hedonistic" (. . .) and "sympathetic" (. . .)'.[24] Here it becomes clear to what extent Croce's *Aesthetic* anticipates the critique of the fallacies. Adopting a more general point of view, one could argue that the basic tenet of New Criticism, namely that a literary text is a unique, particular, and individual phenomenon which cannot be dissolved in universal principles, is also Croce's fundamental creed: 'But to the inviolable general rule Croce opposes the inviolable individual – the individual which must not be touched by conceptual abstraction if it is to retain its aesthetic validity. (The beginning of his whole philosophy, as he himself has confessed, was his criticism of the genres.)'[25] It now becomes clear why the New Critics were not primarily interested in literary history or in genre theory, but in the analysis of the individual text: in its unique 'way of saying', as Cleanth Brooks and Robert Penn Warren put it.

Finally, it should be asked how Croce's lasting influence within New Criticism came about and how it can be explained in a social and historical context. His direct influence is partly due to the fact that his major work *Estetica* (1902) was translated into English by Douglas Ainslie as early as 1907 and published under the title *Aesthetic As Science of Expression and General Linguistic*. Croce's influence was reinforced by the publication of his article 'Aesthetic' in the *Encyclopaedia Britannica*. This article introduced the word 'aesthetic' into the English-speaking world, identifying it with the Italian philosopher's name and doctrine.

However, Croce's importance for the New Critics is not simply due to the influence of his works; it should also be viewed in terms of an elective affinity between the liberal individualism of the Anglo-American group and Croce's political liberalism and radical individualism which he staunchly defended as founder of the new (post-1945) Liberal Party, as senator, and minister of education (1920/21). The liberal individualism, which he shares with most of the New Critics and which also has a strong conservative and idealist bias, is the social basis upon which his aesthetic individualism rests: the idea that art is autonomous and that each work of art is a particular, unique entity that can only be understood on its own merits.

It is not surprising that this idealist conception of art as a self-contained world located beyond history and society is not only incompatible with literary history as a *history of genres* but also excludes all *sociological* approaches to literature. One of these is Pierre Bourdieu's theory of art as a social institution and of literary criticism as a strategy to promote certain forms of art for economic, political, and ideological reasons. From this point of view, Croce's and the New Critics' attempts to institutionalise one *particular form of art* – namely art as an autonomous entity – are to be seen as part and parcel of an institutional strategy which aims at sanctioning individualism and autonomy on an aesthetic level. The strategic trick, according to Bourdieu, consists in declaring a particular definition of art to be universally valid: by a *'universalisation of the particular case'* (*'universalisation du cas particulier'*).[26] The fatal defect of this strategy consists in ignoring the socio-historical conditions which make this universalisation possible.[27]

The other sociological approach which reveals some of the shortcomings of Kantian and Crocean aesthetics of autonomy is Marxist (i.e. Hegelian in many respects). The Marxist argument, which will be considered in the last section of this chapter in conjunction with Czech Structuralism and in chapter five, is quite complex, but can – for the time being – be summed up in one sentence: New Critics and Russian Formalists only have an eye for the *how*, for the question how literature is written or composed; they completely neglect the questions *why* it is written in a particular social set-up and *what* political aims or interests it articulates. At the end of this chapter the controversies between Russian Formalists and Marxists will be considered in more detail. Let us now return to another brand of aesthetic autonomy in the Kantian sense: to the Russian Formalists' view of literature as technique.

2 Russian Formalism between Kantianism and the Avant-Garde

Although it is not possible to identify all of Russian Formalism with Kant's philosophy and in particular with the *Critique of Judgement*, because, as Ewa Thompson points out[28], Bergson, the Vienna Circle, and other philosophers also influenced the Formalists, it makes sense to consider the Formalist theories as oscillating between two extremes: Kantianism and the Futurist avant-garde. The tension between these two poles which is absent from New Criticism explains some of the contradictions and vicissitudes which haunt the Formalists.

Like the New Critics, they tend to identify literature with the *expression plane*. Starting from the assumption that literary works and works of art in general convey (intuitive) forms of knowledge which are beyond the grasp of conceptual thought, they adhere to the Kantian postulate that art addresses the mind and the senses without conceptualisation. Ewa Thompson quite correctly defines the common denominator of the two literary theories when she explains: 'Thus the evolution of concepts in both critical movements had a Kantian basis.'[29] She reminds us of the fact that the Formalists were not really conscious of the philosophical foundations of their premises, some of which they inherited from the Symbolist poet Andrej Belyj (1880-1934). This lack of consciousness which was transmitted to contemporary literary theory makes a reconstruction of the aesthetic premises of New Criticism, Formalism, Structuralism or Deconstruction seem all the more urgent. Confirming Ewa Thompson's postulate that Formalism is − at least partly − of Kantian origin, Aage Hansen-Löve points out: 'This concept of form used exclusively as an "aesthetic category" in the sense of Kant, is very akin to early Formalism because it is opposed to content (. . .).'[30] This means that the aesthetic position of Formalism is partly determined by the opposition between Kantianism and the Futurist avant-garde, partly by that between *expression plane* and *content plane*.

The main argument can be summed up in a few words. Although Formalists like Viktor Šklovskij (1893-1984) and Boris Ejchenbaum (1886-1959) pleaded in favour of aesthetic autonomy in the Kantian sense, their definitions of the work of art and its functions are closely related to the revolutionary *engagement* of the European avant-garde movements, especially to that of the Russian Futurists. Considering the basic tenets of Kantian aesthetics (as discussed in the first chapter), i.e. the idea that the appropriate attitude towards art and beauty is one of 'disinterested pleasure' and that the Beautiful pleases without conceptualisation (without conceptual definition), the contradiction between Kantianism and the *engagement* of avant-garde movements becomes obvious. For we cannot adopt a disinterested attitude towards a work of art and at the same time expect artistic production to violate established norms and values in order to bring about a new, avant-garde vision of reality. However, this is precisely what the Formalists and their Futurist allies demanded. In spite of their notion of artistic autonomy which they tirelessly defended against the Marxists and Marxists-Leninists, they openly sympathised with the Futurists who advocated an aesthetic transformation of the real: a kind of cultural revolution. This revolutionary vision cannot be reconciled with any brand of Kantianism.

But what exactly was Russian Formalism in a historical and social context? It was a literary and theoretical movement which originated partly in the Moscow Linguistic Circle (founded in 1915), partly in the OPOJAZ-Group (founded in 1916 in St. Petersburg). The name OPOJAZ (*Opščestvo Izučennija Poetičeskogo Jazyka / Association for the Study of Poetic Language*) is symptomatic insofar as it reveals the fundamental aim of early Formalism which is akin to that of New Criticism: the analysis of the poetic or lyrical text. Like the New Critics, the early Formalists tended to identify literature with poetry. In this respect they followed the Futurist poets Velimir Chlebnikov (1885-1922) and Aleksej Kručënych (1886-1968) whose experimental texts belong to a lyrical genre considered by many Formalists as a model of future literature.

However, this orientation towards experimental poetry is not characteristic of Formalism as a whole: it is a dominant trend within the early OPOJAZ which Peter Steiner defines as 'mechanistic Formalism'.[31] The main representative of this current of thought was Viktor Šklovskij. Steiner quite rightly reminds us of the fact that the other two brands of Formalism, the 'morphological' and the 'systemic', are not less important. While the theory of the literary system, the theory of literary evolution, which will be commented on later on, was mainly developed by Jurij Tynjanov (1894-1943), Vladimir Propp (1895-1970) was responsible for the research into literary morphology which yielded revolutionary results in his well-known book *Morphology of the Folktale* (1928). This book is not only important because it had a lasting impact on

Algirdas Julien Greimas' *structural semiotics* (cf. chapter 6), but also because its search for textual functions and *deep structures* (*structures profondes*, Greimas) clearly contradicts the Kantian premise 'without concept'.

It becomes clear at this stage that Formalism – like New Criticism – was not a homogeneous theory, but a loose set of complementary ideas oscillating between Kantianism, the avant-garde, and other philosophical positions. However, the complementary character of Formalist ideas yielded a relatively coherent terminology oriented simultaneously and in a somewhat contradictory manner towards Kant's *aesthetic autonomy* and the avant-garde concept of *innovation*. On the one hand the Formalists defended the idea (which they share with the New Critics) that art is a phenomenon *sui generis*, on the other hand they expected works of art to fulfil an innovative function by introducing new and revolutionary techniques in order to change our vision of objects and individuals. This is why, especially in the first and second phase of the Formalist movement, they emphasised the *literariness* (*literaturnost'*) of literature and its innovative techniques. It will become clear that other key concepts of Formalism such as *de-familiarisation* (*ostranienie*) and *de-automatisation* are *aspects of innovation*.

The global development of Formalism is put into perspective by Aage Hansen-Löve who shows to what extent literariness or the question what makes literature 'literary' (a specific 'way of saying', as the New Critics would put it) was the dominant problem of the first phase. The second phase was marked by the study of *composition techniques*: by what Šklovskij calls *priëm* (translated into French as *procédé*, into German as *Verfahren*). The research of the third phase was geared towards a systematic inquiry into problems of literary history and the sociology of literature.

Hansen Löve's view of the three phases confirms Peter Steiner's account insofar as it also detects a trend towards systematisation and an orientation towards historical and social factors. This orientation indicates that no absolute opposition should be postulated between Formalism and Marxism and that, as will be shown in the last section of this chapter, a fruitful dialogue might have evolved had it not been for the repressive policies of the Leninist party initiated by Stalin after Lenin's death in 1924.

An antagonism between the two positions exists nevertheless, and it can best be understood as a twofold contradiction between Kantian autonomy and Hegelian (Marxist) heteronomy, reinforced by an antagonism between the expression plane and the content plane. The Formalist intention to subordinate content to expression clearly appears when Šklovskij proclaims: '*A new form does not appear in order to express a new content but in order to replace an old form which has lost its characteristic of an artistic form.*'[32]

In other words, the driving force of *literary evolution* (Šklovskij, Tynjanov) is neither social change nor Hegel's idea, but *formal innovation*. The new techniques of parody, for example, as developed in Laurence Sterne's *Tristram Shandy* or the revolutionary techniques of Brecht's Epic Theatre break with traditional narrative and Aristotelian drama and make both look obsolete in the eyes of the reader or the spectator. In this context Jurij Tynjanov explains *literary evolution* as a dialectic between *automatisation* and *de-automatisation*: the old, established literary forms, he argues, are being automatically perceived by readers, i.e. without critical reflection and without new insights, until innovation or *de-automatisation* puts an end to literary routine by introducing new techniques, new forms or an entirely new language.

Innovation as de-automatisation, as a radical break with narrative routine, is vividly exemplified by the first lines of John Barth's postmodern story *Lost in the Funhouse*:

> For whom is the funhouse fun? Perhaps for lovers. For Ambrose it is *a place of fear and confusion.* He has come to the seashore with his family for the holiday, *the occasion of their visit is Independence Day, the most important secular holiday of the United States of America.* A single straight underline is the manuscript mark for italic type, *which in turn* is the printed equivalent to oral emphasis of words and phrases as well as the customary type for titles of complete works, not to mention.[33]

In very much the same way as Brecht's theatre which every now and then interrupts the action and makes actors comment on it, the postmodern narrator interrupts the flow of narration in order to comment on the typography or the composition in general. This new technique of narrative interruption and essayism makes conventional narration appear insipid and uninspiring; it solicits imitation by other authors, is widely applied and in turn transformed into a literary *cliché* or *routinised*.

A more radical break with literary convention is the attempt of the Russian Futurists Velimir Chlebnikov and Aleksej Kručënych to introduce an entirely new language by detaching the *signifiers* from the *signifieds*, thus radicalising the *autonomy of the expression plane*. It is not surprising that the Formalists were fascinated by their experiments in *transmental language* which disconnected the phonetic from the semantic level: 'By calling a lily *euy*', writes the Futurist Nikolaj Gorlov, 'Kručënych causes the organic unity of language to disintegrate; he destroys language as a factor of social order.'[34] Elsewhere he asks: 'What is a phonic image?' and explains: 'It is the combination of the sound elements of a word which address the psyche independently of the semantic content.'[35] It becomes quite clear at this stage that the Futurists did actually intend to radicalise the autonomy of the expression plane and that their revolution of the word was a revolution of the expression, the phonetic level. In this respect their programme was akin to that of Dadaism, Italian Futurism (*parole in libertà*), and, to a certain extent, Surrealism. The phonetic transmental language was meant to transform words into things, into *slova-vešči* (*word-things*) freed from their semantic ties with the social world and from conceptual constraints.

As far as the *transmental language* was concerned, Formalists like Šklovskij, Tynjanov, Ejchenbaum and Jakubinskij agreed that it is a valuable avant-garde instrument for liberating the word from metaphysical, religious, and ideological connotations: from conventional meanings. In spite of this avant-garde rhetoric which one would seek in vain in New Criticism, the Formalists tend to agree with the New Critics that literature (poetry) is autonomous because it is a specific 'way of saying' and not a meaning being conveyed 'anyway'. The sounds of the expression plane, Jakubinskij points out, are almost irrelevant in practical (communicative) language; not so in verse language: 'Thus, various considerations compel us to recognize that in *practical language sounds do not attract our attention*. It is the other way round in verse language. There, one can claim that sounds enter the bright field of consciousness and do attract our attention'.[36] As in New Criticism, it is the orientation towards the expression plane which guarantees the autonomy of literature *vis-à-vis* the semantic world of socialised meanings.

In Formalism, this orientation is not limited to poetry but extended into the world of prose. When Boris Ejchenbaum for example analyses the narrative use of *spoken language* or *skaz* (*skazat'* = to tell) in Nikolaj Gogol's short novel *The Coat*, he is again predominantly interested in the 'way of saying', i.e. in the expression and the phonetic particularities of the text. Instead of presenting the reader with a psychological analysis of the hero's character, he gives the latter a characteristic name which evokes awkwardness: Akakij Akakijevič. Like all the other protagonists, Akakij is best characterised by his *skaz*, by his way of speaking: by his disconnected and clumsy way of narrating, by his incoherent discourse, his interrupted sentences, his stammer. By imitating language mimetically, by reproducing its phonetic particularities and oddities, the narrator conveys a vivid impression of people's psyche, their social status, their problems. For Ejchenbaum – as for Šklovskij and Tynjanov – what counts is the *how*: the way of saying and the narrative technique.

The theoretical approach of the Formalists was summed up in the Sixties by Roman Jakobson in his well-known thesis that the poetic message is marked by auto-referentiality, or, as Jakubinskij would put it, that in poetic language the sounds themselves (and not the meaning they convey) attract our attention (see above). However, Jakobson's autonomous conception of art and his Kantianism seem to contradict the enthusiasm he showed for Futurist aesthetics and their revolutionary connotations in his early years. For in his article on Futurism ('Futurizm'), which was published by the review *Iskusstvo* in 1919, the central idea is not artistic autonomy or auto-referentiality, but aesthetic *engagement*, the violation of the ruling norm. 'The new art', Jakobson writes about Futurism, 'has broken with the static forms, it has broken with the last fetish of the static – with the notion of beauty. (. . .) Whatever was true for yesterday's artists, is today a lie, says the Futurist manifesto.'[37] This repudiation of the notion of beauty is inconceivable within conventional Kantian aesthetics and it can only be understood as an avant-garde element incompatible with Kantianism.

Naturally, the contradiction between Kantian and avant-garde aesthetics disappears if one assumes, as some people do, that the Jakobson of the Sixties, the author of 'Linguistics and Poetics' (1960), had simply forgotten his early allegiance to Futurist ideals. Unfortunately, it is not as simple as that, and Thomas G. Winner is probably right when he points out that 'the fundamental ideas which so interested Jakobson, the eighteen-year-old *zaum* poet and friend and associate of Majakovskij, Chlebnikov, Kručonych, and Malevič, never lost their fascination for him.'[38] However, this fascination seems incompatible with the Kantian principle of 'disinterested admiration' and with Jakobson's own definition of artistic autonomy as auto-referentiality. For the Futurist vision of a cultural revolution which many Futurists (e.g. N. Gorlov) associated with the Marxist-Leninist project, is eminently political and excludes autonomy and auto-referentiality.

Nevertheless, the contradiction between Kantian autonomy and Futurist heteronomy is not absolute in Formalism, for there is an element which Kantian and avant-garde aesthetics have in common: the idea that art appeals to us *without concepts*. In a particularly interesting comment, Ewa Thompson reveals the Kantian implications of another key concept of Formalist theory which can also be considered as an aspect of innovation: *de-familiarisation (ostranienie)*. Things familiar to us can be estranged from our routine perception by virtue of a new point of view, a new perspective. When in *Huron le naïf*, for example, Voltaire makes us look at Europe from the point of view of an Indian, our perception changes: it is de-familiarised in the Formalist sense. In a similar way, Tolstoj, in his short novel *Xolstomer*, describes reality from the point of view of an old horse and thus succeeds in making phenomena such as ownership and greed appear in a new light.

> He manages, writes Ewa Thompson, by means of 'strange' arrangements of elements, to express something that would not be otherwise expressed and perceived. His presentation 'occasions much thought, without, however, any definite thought', one would like to repeat after Kant. *Xolstomer* is a presentation of a Kantian 'aesthetic idea' of greed and ownership, of the uselessness of selfish life, of life's sadness – in general: Kant's concept might not have been familiar to Šklovskij in its original version; the latter argues, however, along Kantian lines.[39]

In other words: an avant-garde (Futurist, Surrealist, Brechtian) concept such as de-familiarisation has a Kantian aspect to it, insofar as it occasions much thought without being definable by specific concepts. In spite of all the fissures and contradictions which a close scrutiny of Formalism reveals, the relative unity of Formalist theory is based on the idea that works of art cannot be translated into conceptual systems. This idea is simultaneously of Kantian and avant-garde origin.

3 The Aborted Dialogue between Marxists and Formalists

Unlike the Formalists, most Russian Marxists of the revolutionary period were Hegelians whenever art and literature were concerned. In the fifth chapter it will become clear that Marx and Engels were materialist Hegelians in aesthetic matters and that their Hegelianism consisted in the assumption that works of art express, albeit indirectly, specific, univocal meanings which can be conceptually defined. According to Marxists such as Lunačarskij, literature, like philosophy, fulfils primarily a cognitive function by conveying ideas, by shedding light upon a particular socio-historical constellation. According to Lunačarskij, the fundamental difference between literature and philosophy consists in the fact that the latter primarily addresses the intellect, whereas the former speaks to the senses.[40] As in Hegel's case, this difference does not imply a resistance to conceptual translation on the part of literature. On the contrary, Lunačarskij, Trockij, and Lenin firmly believed that art and literature have conceptual, philosophical equivalents which are made accessible to the senses in music, painting or poetry. This is why they were mainly interested in the *ideological content* of literary texts, not in the formalist question *how* these are composed.

In *Literature and Revolution* (1924), Trockij criticises the Formalists for having developed an idealist and abstract method geared exclusively towards the analysis of sounds, techniques, and rhetorical figures, and quite incapable of answering the essential question *why* in a particular social and historical situation certain artistic forms appear and not others. He goes on to say that 'only Marxism can *explain* why and in what circumstances a certain artistic movement developed in a given historical period'.[41]

In other words: the Marxist is not so much interested in Kant's question *how* a work of art (the Beautiful) should be viewed or contemplated and to what extent it defies conceptual definition, but repeats Hegel's question in a materialist context: *why* a work of art is produced at a particular moment of history and what class interests and ideas it expresses. The Formalist questions *how* art is made and *how* it should be looked at are superseded by the *genetic* questions *why* it emerges in a certain period of time and what ideological, philosophical or religious interests it articulates. In the fifth chapter, this *genetic question*, which is of considerable importance in Lucien Goldmann's *Genetic Structuralism*, will be discussed in more detail, and it will be shown that it is deeply rooted in Hegelian aesthetics.

For the time being it seems more urgent to ask if and how the Formalist and the Marxist questions are methodologically related. For it would be somewhat superficial to assume that the conflict between the two groups of critics was simply political and that the Formalists were idealists who defended the autonomy of art (i.e. its dissociation from politics), whereas the Marxists insisted on its political function. Although this assumption is not wrong, as the various histories of the Formalist School show (Erlich, Hansen-Löve, Steiner)[42], it misses one important point: the fact that the political conflict was simultaneously a conflict between aesthetics and methods, between Kant and Hegel. As the following chapters will show – especially chapter 5 – it would be a mistake to solve the conflict unilaterally by opting for one of the two positions.

Quite early on, some of the most lucid critics of Formalism who were by no means orthodox Marxists or Marxists-Leninists insisted on the necessity of combining the two competing methods and of relating the Formalist *how* to the Marxist *why* and *what*. In his remarkable book on *The Formal Method in Literary Scholarship. A Critical Introduction to Sociological Poetics* (Leningrad, 1928), Pavel N. Medvedev (1891-1938), a close fried of Mikhail M. Bakhtin (cf. chap. 5), lays the foundations of what could nowadays be considered a sociology of the fictional text. Unlike the other Marxists (including Trockij and Lunačarskij), he does not oppose content and form, content plane and expression plane, but maintains that the form itself is a social phenomenon. Placing literature in the sphere of social interaction and communication, Medvedev asserts that the poetic qualities of genres such as the novel, the drama or the epic poem ('*Poema*': e.g. Achmatova's *Poema bez geroya*) should be viewed as cultural facts which acquire different semantic and ideological functions in different communication systems. Thus the Victorian novel which in some cases may have fulfilled a critical function, raising, albeit timidly, the question of female emancipation, may in present-day society acquire the function of a nostalgic genre with rural, imperial or aristocratic connotations.

From Medvedev's point of view the methodological deadlock which partly accounts for the sterility of the Marxist-Formalist polemic, can be avoided or overcome as soon as the dichotomy form/content (expression plane/content plane) is abandoned and the textual structure itself (its semantic, syntactic, and phonetic elements) is considered as socially significant; that is, as soon as social values and interests are related to the semantic elements of the text and the latter linked up with the syntactic and possibly phonetic particularities of literary production. In other words, only an approach which succeeds in representing social facts as textual structures (and vice versa) is likely to overcome, on a methodological level, the opposition between the Formalist questions concerning the *how* of literary texts and the Marxist concern with the *why* and the *what*.

To a certain extent such an approach was envisaged by Formalists such as Tynjanov and Ejchenbaum who introduced the complementary concepts *literary fact* (*literaturnij fakt*, Tynjanov) and *literary life* (*literaturnij byt*, Ejchenbaum). Texts, argues Tynjanov, which in the past were not considered as having a literary function, can become 'literary': the diary and the letter, for example, which are important forms of social communication, become *literary facts* when they are used for the composition of novels by Jane Austen (*Lady Susan*), Rousseau, Goethe or Karamzin. Ejchenbaum's concept of *literary life* is complementary to *literary fact* because if refers to institutionalised non-literary publications such as newspapers and magazines which may have a considerable influence in the literary world. Thus a sociological explanation of Charles Dickens's prose cannot possibly ignore the fact that Dickens was also a journalist, reporter of the *Morning Chronicle*, and author of the *Sketches by Boz* which were originally published in newspapers (as were his novels). Especially Dickens's early work cannot be considered independently of his work as a journalist and of a journalistic style that is omnipresent in his prose.[43] If it had been systematically developed in relation to the concepts of *literary fact* and *literary life*, the concept of *literary evolution* might have become a lot more concrete: for the development of literature is somewhat more complex than Tynjanov's dialectic of *automatisation* and *de-automatisation*. Social facts such as the *letter*, the *diary*, and, in contemporary society, radio, film, and television have a considerable impact upon it, as the symbiotic relationship between novel and film shows.

Unfortunately, the Formalists were prevented from pursuing their research by the Marxists-Leninists who, for political reasons, were not interested in a genuine dialogue. However, the aborted dialogue of the 1920s and 1930s was resumed in the 1970s and 1980s in Britain, France, Germany, and the USA, where Tony Benett, Gérard Conio, Hans Günther, and William G. Walton intervened in order to reveal the importance of the methodological problems involved.[44] Thus Tony Benett emphasises the importance of Formalism for Bakhtin and the ulterior development of literary theory: 'If Bakhtin's work defines and occupies a theoretical space that is situated "beyond Formalism", that space was produced only by "working through" Formalism.'[45]

The investigations of contemporary authors such as Benett show, among other things, that in spite of their errors, their simplifications, and their repressive policies, the Marxists were not entirely wrong, because the Formalists never really succeeded in answering the question *why* certain forms, genres or ways of writing appear under certain social conditions and disappear with the latter. This means, as will also be shown in the fifth chapter, that the Marxist question is meaningful as long as it does not distract from the crucial question which the Formalists and the New Critics have in common: *how* is a literary text constructed and what makes it a literary text?

CHAPTER 3

Czech Structuralism between Kant, Hegel, and the Avant-Garde

It has been customary to consider Czech and Slovak Structuralism as a continuation of Russian Formalism in a new context marked by the influence of Saussure's structural linguistics. Although this continuity certainly exists, because Roman Jakobson (1896-1982), one of the most prominent Russian Formalists and linguists, was at the same time one of the most important members of the *Prague Linguistic Circle* (*Cercle Linguistique de Prague, CLP*, founded in 1926), it should not be overemphasised. For Prague Structuralism is not only a linguistic and semiotic, but also an aesthetic theory, deeply rooted in Czech and German philosophical traditions, and a result of philosophical debates and controversies which took place in the first decades of the twentieth century.

Most of these controversies were dominated by the fundamental opposition between Kantian and Hegelian-Marxist perspectives. Kant's influence was reinforced by the fact that Johann Friedrich Herbart's (1776-1844) Kantianism was predominant in Czech aesthetics, especially in the theories of Otakar Hostinský (1847-1910) and Otakar Zich (1879-1934), who were Jan Mukařovský's (1891-1975) predecessors and mentors. While Hostinský attempted an empirical foundation of Kant's and Herbart's theories of aesthetic judgement[1], Zich insisted on the autonomous character of the work of art and on the Kantian postulate that the latter cannot be deduced from heteronomous systems such as philosophy, religion or political ideology. Starting from Kant's assumption that the Beautiful cannot be conceptually defined, he located *meaning*, in the sense of Johannes Volkelt's (1848-1930) *Bedeutungsvorstellung*, not in the individual work itself but in the heterogeneous, contradictory, and controversial process of its reception. Like Kant and Herbart, he believed that art stimulates thought without being identifiable with particular, clearly definable concepts. Mukařovský inherited this Kantian attitude towards art, and his theory is marked by the tension between the attribution of meaning and the idea of a polysemic work, the meaning of which cannot be fixed because it permanently changes in a never ending process of interpretation and reinterpretation which also involves its functional (institutional) transformation.

In this respect there is a fundamental affinity between Mukařovský's and Jakobson's notions of art and hence between Czech Structuralism and Russian Formalism. For the Czech semiotician and philosopher tends to agree with the Russian linguist and literary critic that art and literature are auto-reflexive in the sense that they draw our attention to the way they are made or written: to the 'way of saying', as the New Critics would put it. In what follows it will be shown to what extent the Prague Structuralists revived the Formalist interest in the question *how* literary texts are made and how they distinguish themselves from communicative language which is frequently marked by *automatisation* (automatised perception).

They shared this interest with the Czech avant-garde – Poetism and Surrealism – which resembled the Russian Futurists in focusing on literary *expression* and on the process of *de-automatisation*. Like the Formalists, the Structuralists were simultaneously Kantians and followers of the avant-garde in the sense that literature appeared to them as an experiment oriented towards the expression plane and defying conceptual definition (*monosemy*). At the same time they preferred the point of view of the spectator, listener or reader to that of the producing artist expressing forms of consciousness in the process of history. In this respect they were also Kantians rather than Hegelians or Marxists.

In spite of this Kantianism which was transmitted by the Herbartian tradition in Czechoslovakia after the First World War, the Structuralism of the Prague Linguistic Circle cannot be entirely dissociated from Hegelian philosophy. In his important article on 'Structuralism in Aesthetics and Literary Science', Mukařovský mentions Hegel's influence (along with that of Kant, Herbart, Husserl, and others)[2], and Oleg Sus explains 'that G.W.F. Hegel is not the historical patron of contemporary Czech structural semiology and semantics; nevertheless, he played a special, indirect role in the genesis of those theories'.[3] How is this role to be defined?

Globally speaking, there are two Hegelian elements underlying Mukařovský's structuralism, elements which are incompatible with a Kantian stance: the historical conception of art and the concomitant sociological idea that art and individual works of art can have an impact on a society's system of values and norms. The historical perspective implies a functional understanding of art that is incompatible with Kant's timeless definition of the Beautiful: whatever seemed beautiful, valuable or admirable in one historical period (Classicism or Romanticism) may seem despicable or ridiculous in another (Realism or Modernism). This way of looking at things is also a challenge to Kant's postulate of *disinterested pleasure* (*interesseloses Wohlgefallen*). If the value of a work of art (of art in general) is controversial because art is involved in collisions and controversies between *aesthetic norms* and *aesthetic ideologies*[4], then a disinterested attitude becomes inconceivable. It is interesting to observe how Czech Structuralism – from Mukařovský and Vodička to Červenka, Jankovič, and Chvatík – oscillates between Kantian, Hegelian, and avant-garde positions and how it copes with the aesthetic tensions resulting from this oscillation.

1 Roman Jakobson's and Jan Mukařovský's Kantianism
One of the major events which had a considerable impact on the development of Structuralism was the publication of the *Theses* of the Prague Linguistic Circle in 1929, when the First International Slavistic Congress was held in Prague. While most of the theses deal with structural and functional problems of language and frequently attempt to historicise Saussure's 'synchronic' or systematic approach, the third thesis is an attempt to distinguish communicative from poetic language. It gives the Structuralist manifesto a clearly Kantian orientation by postulating that in every day language the word is a *means* of communication whereas in poetic language it becomes an *end* in itself, thereby acquiring an '*autonomous value*' ('*des valeurs autonomes plus ou moins considérables*').[5] This argument is completed by the Kantian idea that, whenever we contemplate a work of art, our attention is not focused on the *signified* (the *content plane*, Hjelmslev would say), but '*on the sign itself*' ('*sur le signe lui-même*'), as the authors put it.[6] In other words, we are not – or rather should not be – primarily interested in *what* is said but *how* it is expressed.

This is exactly what the young Roman Jakobson meant when, in an article on the Russian avant-garde poet Velimir Chlebnikov he defined Russian poetry of that period as a discourse '*oriented towards the expression*' ('*vyskazyvanie s ustanovkoj na vyraženie*').[7] This emphasis on the expression (on the *how*) is not only Kantian insofar as it excludes conceptual univocity, but also closely related to the practice of the avant-garde which (as was shown in the second chapter) was anxious to keep aloof from metaphysical, ideological or religious meanings. In an interview with Krystina Pomorska which took place in the early 1980s, Jakobson locates his own early lyrical experiments in an avant-garde context: 'I obstinately insisted on the avoidance of meaningful words in order to concentrate on the elementary components of the word, on the sounds of language in themselves (. . .).'[8]

In the 1930s, when he was already a member of the Prague Linguistic Circle and professor at the Masaryk-University in Brno, Jakobson pursued this train of thought by insisting on the need to dissociate poetry from biography, from the poet's life. In his important article 'What is Poetry?' ('*Co je poezie?*', published in *Volné směry* 30, 1933/34), he denounces all attempts to treat poetry as a document of the author's psyche or as a text about reality in general. His arguments are reminiscent of the 1926 Theses and of the notion of poetic autonomy expounded by the New Critics: 'Poeticity is present when the word is felt as a word and not a mere representation of the object being named or an outburst of emotion, when words and their composition, their meaning, their external and inner form acquire a weight and value of their own instead of referring indifferently to reality.'[9] In other words: poetic language should not be read in a referential context but for its own sake.

This idea is worked out on a linguistic level in Jakobson's well-known article 'Linguistics and Poetics' (1960) where he distinguishes six functions of language: 1. the *emotive function* which is linked to the *sender* or *author* of a message; 2. symmetrically, the *conative function* which is related to the *receiver* or *listener*; 3. the *metalingual function* which is geared towards the *code* in question; 4. the *phatic function* which is oriented towards the *contact medium*; 5. the *referential function* which designates the *context* of communication, and finally 6. the *poetic function* which becomes an *end in itself*.[10]

In spite of the fact that the New Critics hardly ever ventured into the realm of linguistics there are some striking affinities between what they call the *genetic* or *intentional fallacy* and Jakobson's *emotive function* and between what they call *affective fallacy* and Jakobson's *conative function*. Translating the discourse of the New Critics into the linguistic discourse of the Structuralists, one could say that the genetic or intentional fallacy consists in confusing the poetic with the emotive function, while the affective fallacy consists in confusing it with the reactions of the listener or the reader. In both cases, the autonomy of poetic language is overlooked, negated.

However, it should be borne in mind that this kind of misreading is only possible because almost every poem, every literary text can also be read on an emotive, conative, metalingual, or referential level. This is due to the fact that most works of literature contain the other functions and hence cannot be reduced to their poetic component. Marx and Engels were not entirely wrong when they insisted on reading Balzac's work as a treatise on French society and economy. Nor were Freud and his disciples wrong when they attempted to explain literary works as documents of the author's psyche. As Peter Steiner points out, Jakobson was well aware of all these facts:

> When in 1935 Jakobson lectured on Russian Formalism at Masaryk University in Brno, he called the equation of the poetic work to the esthetic or poetic function 'unquestionably erroneous: a poetic work is not confined to the esthetic function alone, but has in addition many other functions . . .' He continued: 'Just as the esthetic work is not exhausted by its esthetic function, so the esthetic function is not limited to the poetic work'.[11]

Later on, the problem which arises whenever one attempts to relate the poetic function of a literary text to its other functions was solved by Jakobson, Mukařovský, and the other Prague Structuralists by the concept of the *dominant*: in art, it was said, many different (political, moral, cognitive) functions may coexist, but the aesthetic function, i.e. auto-reflexivity or auto-referentiality, dominates all of them and guarantees the autonomy of the artistic object, its specific character. Jakobson defines the *dominant* as follows: 'The dominant may be defined as the focusing component of a work of art: it rules, determines, and transforms the remaining components. It is the dominant which guarantees the integrity of the structure. – The dominant specifies the work.'[12] A dominant may be the prosodic pattern or the verse form of a text – and this form or pattern makes the competent reader consider the text for its own sake and its political or emotional components as part and parcel of the aesthetic structure and function. However, there are border-line cases, e.g. political poems by Auden or Brecht, where the aesthetic dimension seems to exist for the sake of the political intention. It will be shown that the Prague Structuralists deal with this problem by introducing the complementary concepts of function, norm, and value.

In spite of all their theoretical efforts, the border-line cases mentioned here threaten to 'deconstruct' their definition of the dominant. For it is a definition based on hierarchy, as Josip Užarević aptly points out in his contribution to the Roman Jakobson-Congress held in Moscow in 1996: 'The differences between messages (soobščenie) imply a hierarchical relationship between functions (one function being dominant, the others secondary).'[13] But who is to decide? Which function dominates in the Bible, the *Chanson de Roland* or Chaucer's *Canterbury Tales*: the aesthetic, the political or the religious?

Like Jakobson, Mukařovský was well aware of the problems which the coexistence of heterogeneous functions in art and literature can entail. However, he did agree with Jakobson that art could be defined by the domination of the aesthetic function over all the other functions. 'The aesthetics of language', he explains, 'differs therefore from communicative language by virtue of the aesthetic relevance of the utterance as a whole.'[14] This is another way of saying that in literary texts the aesthetic function, i.e. the function which transforms the text into an auto-referential message, dominates.

This notion of aesthetic autonomy is not only Kantian, but at the same time anti-Hegelian, because it excludes Hegel's postulate that art and literature can without loss of substance be translated into other media or languages and into the conceptual discourse of philosophy. This aspect of Hegel's thought is explicitly challenged by Mukařovský who, in an important article on 'Art and World Vision' ('*Umění a světový názor*'), denies the possibility of translating works of art into conceptual language. Distinguishing three aspects of *world visions* – i.e. world vision as *noetic foundation of a society*, as *ideology of a class* and as *philosophical system* – Mukařovský insists on the impossibility of bridging the gap between these conceptual systems and works of art or literature. In an analysis which is reminiscent of Kantian discourse, he admits on the one hand that great works of art – such as Shakespeare's *King Lear* or Goethe's *Faust* – cannot be understood independently of the noetic foundations of a society, of ideologies or philosophies, but on the other hand rejects all attempts to make literary texts express such noetic systems univocally. He tends to treat such attempts with irony and scepticism, pointing out that 'considerations concerning the so called philosophy of certain literary works tend to be comments on the literary critic's own philosophy, illustrated by quotations from the analysed text'.[15]

This argument is Kantian and anti-Hegelian insofar as it traces the limits of conceptual thought: literature and philosophy are two autonomous and distinct worlds which cannot be telescoped, whatever systematic efforts Hegelians and Marxists may undertake in order to achieve this. Their efforts will be assessed in some detail in the fifth chapter; for the time being it may be sufficient to draw attention to their Hegelianism which consists in postulating analogies or homologies between conceptual systems and works of literature. In his major work *The Hidden God* (1955), Lucien Goldmann for example tries to convince us that Jean Racine's tragedies express the ideas and crises of the seventeenth century Jansenist theology, which he associates with the social position and the interests of the *noblesse de robe*. Unlike the Kantian semiotician he does believe in a univocal relationship between philosophy and literature, thus exposing himself to a Kantian scepticism which suspects that the Hegelian Marxist Goldmann projects his own *world vision* (*vision du monde*) into Racine's polysemic text.

However, Mukařovský and his heirs – Květoslav Chvatík, Milan Jankovič, and Miroslav Červenka – do not deny that literature, philosophy, and political ideology are closely related and that literature generates meanings. Their concept of *semantic gesture* (*sémantické gesto*) is a case in point. It is a Kantian concept par excellence, and its Kantianism is primarily contained in the word 'gesture': it hints at meaning without fixing it. In other words, art and literature are meaningful and trigger off semantic processes (especially on the level of reader-response; cf. sections 3-4) without articulating meanings univocally.

The importance of meaning in the reading process is brought out by Mukařovský[16] and Miroslav Červenka: 'Semantic gesture is not something separable from the total semantic process of the work of art or from the perceiver's activity in the process of constituting the aesthetic object.'[17] But what exactly is meant by the 'semantic process of the work of art'? Should a semantic content be attributed to the literary text itself or only to its interpretations by readers? Chvatík is quite clear on this point when he argues that the concept of *semantic gesture* also refers to the constitution of meaning in the 'process of the work structure'.[18] This interpretation is confirmed by Jankovič who reminds us that in Mukařovský's analyses of Mácha's poem *Máj*[19] the semantic content of the text is implicitly defined as the interaction of all formal and thematic layers (at this early stage Mukařovský does not yet use the term semantic gesture which he introduces later).

The Kantian character of this term comes to the fore in Milan Jankovič's more recent work *Nesamozřejmost smyslu* (*The Nonobvious Character of Meaning*) where the *semantic gesture* is defined by 'the necessary indeterminacy of its content or rather its irreducibility to current meanings'.[20] This redefinition of one of the key Structuralist concepts is reminiscent of Kant's famous dictum that the Beautiful stimulates thought without being reducible to definable concepts. This is undoubtedly the reason why the term *semantic gesture* was so difficult to define and why, as Jankovič aptly points out, it still admits 'different interpretations and applications'.[21] For it is an attempt to define that which by definition defies conceptualisation. This is a Kantian dilemma *par excellence*, a dilemma eliminated by Hegel at the expense of art.

2 Hegel and the Avant-Garde in Mukařovský's Theory: Structure, Function, Norm, and Value
Unlike New Criticism which based its concept of literary auto-nomy on the complementary aesthetics of Kant and Croce, Czech Structuralism – like Russian Formalism – underwent contradictory influences: its aesthetics are not simply Kantian but bear the imprint of heterogeneous philosophies such as Hegel's

dialectics, Husserl's phenomenology, Durkheim's sociology, and of contemporary avant-garde practice. In the present context, Hegel and the avant-garde deserve particular attention, because their influence on Czech Structuralism is a global challenge to Kantian autonomy.

Hegel's presence in Czech Structuralism is mainly felt in conjunction with the historical perspective adopted by Mukařovský and his successor Felix Vodička: a perspective which clearly excludes Kant's view of the Beautiful as something static that does not undergo alterations in the course of time. – But what exactly is the function of this historicism in Mukařovský's work? In the first place, it is meant to account for the fact that meaning and value of a work of art are subject to permanent change: the semantic potential or *semantic gesture* of a literary text for example is developed in the course of time and its value may change as new readers apply new aesthetic and non-aesthetic *norms* to it (see below).

However, the literary text is not merely an object in the historical process, an object of interpretation or critical evaluation, it is also an agent of history, for it may contribute decisively to the transformation of *social norms* and *values*. Mukařovský writes about this aspect of literary evolution: 'Art appears to us as a mighty catalyst in the transformation of the world of values.'[22] Here the Kantian notion of art and beauty as more or less static phenomena which are to be contemplated with disinterested pleasure is superseded by a historical conception of art which participates in aesthetic, moral, and political conflicts, thus transforming the social system of values.

This historical and conflictual model of art not only contradicts Kant's non-historical notion of the Beautiful; it is also incompatible with his postulate of *disinterested pleasure*, of disinterested contemplation. For works of art which become involved in social change and the transformation of a value system cannot possibly elicit a disinterested response on the part of the reader, listener or spectator. On the contrary, they will define themselves dialogically and polemically in relation and in opposition to other works of art, in opposition to established norms, values, and hierarchies. Like the works of Shelley and Flaubert, like the plays of Harold Pinter or Thomas Bernhard, they will partake in aesthetic, moral, and political controversies, contesting and possibly subverting the established cultural order.

In Mukařovský's theory this dialogical and polemical conception of art is affiliated to the aesthetics of the European avant-garde of the Twenties and Thirties. In this context Mukařovský mentions the 'dialectical contradictions between art and society'.[23] His descriptions of these contradictions are reminiscent not only of the Surrealist and Futurist revolts against the bourgeois order but correspond in many respects to the central arguments advanced by the most important theoretician of the Czech avant-garde, Karel Teige.

Teige, who advocates a cultural revolution, proclaims: 'The new poetry, *whose theory is Poetism*, is dedicated *to this cultural revolution.*'[24] (Here the functional analogies between Russian Futurism and Czech Poetism as avant-garde movements and between Formalism and Structuralism as avant-garde theories are striking.) Although Mukařovský never endorsed Teige's revolutionary programme, nor that of Russian Futurism or French Surrealism, his conception of art and in particular his idea that art survives by incessantly violating established norms, bears the marks of avant-garde theory and practice. And this conception is incompatible with Kantian aesthetics which locate art and beauty in a static perspective above the interests and conflicts of society.

In approaching Mukařovský's terminology – concepts such as *structure, function, norm,* and *value* – it is important to realise to what extent the tensions between his Kantianism, his Hegelianism, and his sympathy for avant-garde ideas yield a highly original theoretical synthesis which may not form a harmonious totality, but which can be considered as a stimulating encounter of Kantian, dialectical, and avant-garde thinking. It is probably true that the Kantian element is predominant in Jakobson's and Mukařovský's works. However, in the case of Mukařovský it is a highly original brand of Kantianism: historicised by dialectical thought and literally modernised by a permanent dialogue with the avant-garde movement, in particular with Czech Poetism.

On the whole, Mukařovský was primarily a Kantian, but a Kantian anxious to take into account the arguments of materialist dialectics and the aesthetic practice of Poetism, Futurism, and Surrealism. In this respect his thought appears complementary to that of Theodor W. Adorno, who started from dialectical, Hegelian premises, but incorporated so many avant-garde elements into his aesthetic theory that calling him a Hegelian or a Marxist would reduce his aesthetics to a caricature. Mukařovský's and Adorno's originality seems to consist in their heresy, in the fact that they were heretics with respect to their origins: with respect to Kant and Hegel. In this context it seems appropriate to read one of Mukařovský's statements about Kant: 'Kant's "interesseloses Wohlgefallen" ought to be considered cum grano salis.'[25] Its validity and applicability are limited by Mukařovský's concepts of *structure, norm, function,* and *value* which open up a Hegelian, historical, and sociological perspective.

The concept of structure in particular could be regarded as an attempt to synthesise Hegel's view of totality as a semantic whole, which endows each of its elements with a particular meaning, and Saussure's view of the linguistic system as a functional totality in which each element acquires a meaning by interacting with other elements. Thus in English the semantically related words *lake, pond, tarn, loch, firth, bay* or *water* (Wast Water, Derwent Water) form a subsystem which would change considerably if one of the elements were lost and had to be replaced by one of its neighbours: e.g. *lake* by *pond* or *firth* by *bay.* In this case, *pond* or *water* would have to be used for *lake.*

In an important article on 'The Concept of Totality in the Theory of Art', Mukařovský distinguishes the concept of *structure* from the related concepts of *composition* and *context.* A composition is only recognised as such if it is complete: a sonnet, for example, has to be complete, i.e. composed of 14 lines, if it is to be identified by the reader as a sonnet. In other words, a sonnet is a composition, the main criterion of which is completeness. The same argument applies to the idea of context, exemplified in Mukařovský's article by the sentence and the detective novel: as long as a sentence is incomplete (e.g. I didn't read the book, because . . .) it does not make sense; as long as the outcome or *dénouement* of a detective novel is not known, the meaning of the novel as a *whole* remains unclear.

According to Mukařovský, the concept of *structure* differs substantially from the other two concepts by virtue of its openness: a structure can be incomplete or fragmentary and still be recognised as such. In spite of its fragmentary, i.e. incomplete character a novel such as Kafka's *The Trial* can be conceived as a structure on a semantic and narrative level. We need not know how it ends or whether it ends (according to Uyttersprot the last scene of *The Trial* may not have been intended as the last scene)[26] in order to consider it a meaningful, structured whole. There are parallels in architecture and other arts: in order to be able to reconstruct a Greek or Roman temple the archaeologist need not be familiar with all of its elements, as long as the remaining fragments contain some essential clues. All this does not mean of course that compositions (sonnets) or contexts (detective novels) are not structures; it does mean, however, that structures need not be compositions or contexts in the sense of Prague Structuralism.

The avant-garde character of Mukařovský's concept of structure is not only due to its openness, but also and above all to its contradictory nature. Unlike Hegelian totality, which is tinted by Classicism, Structuralist totality does not imply harmony: 'The fewer contradictions an artistic structure contains, the weaker its individuality, the more it approaches the general, impersonal convention.'[27] Artistic originality and innovation thus appear to be inextricably tied up with the contradictions of artistic structures. According to Mukařovský, such contradictions are essential for the individuality of a work of art insofar as they oppose traditions, conventions, and stereotypes or what the Formalists called *automatisation*. Like the Futurists and the Formalists, Mukařovský considers art a dynamic, contradictory, innovative, and *normbreaking* element of culture.

Unlike moral, legal, linguistic or scientific norms which demand conformity and obedience, the aesthetic norm presupposes rebellion and disobedience. The modern artist – the Poetist, the Futurist, the Surrealist – is not rewarded for conforming to the established norm, but for breaking it, for inventing new norms and criteria. Naturally, Mukařovský is aware of the fact that this was not always the case and that in the days of French Classicism, for example, only artists who strictly adhered to the normative canon (e.g. to the Aristotelian unity of space, time, and action in drama) could hope to be rewarded by the King and his critics.[28] However, Mukařovský, like the young Jakobson, is not a classicist, but a modernist and a thinker of the European avant-garde: to him artistic activity appears almost identical with normbreaking innovation: 'Summing up, we may say that the specific character of the aesthetic norm consists in the fact that it is broken rather than obeyed.'[29]

Mukařovský's conception of the aesthetic norm has far-reaching consequences for his historical and sociological theory of art and literature. For if we assume that works of art, literary and non-literary texts negate the established normative order, thereby decisively contributing to its transformation, we also have to assume that they will fulfil different *functions* whenever a normative system undergoes global change. The Bible, for example, which in a society dominated by religion (e.g. European society of the eleventh century) was read exclusively as a holy book, may undergo functional change in a secularised society of the twentieth century, where some groups (e.g. literary critics) read it as a literary text that inspired many works of art. Similarly, the novels of D.H. Lawrence, which caused several scandals because they violated aesthetic, moral, and political norms, have undergone a functional change: they are now read – mainly by students of English literature – as 'classics of modernism'. The same could be said of Goethe's *Werther*, a text no longer condemned for moral reasons as an apology of suicide, but analysed and commented on by philologists who compare it with other epistolary novels such as Rousseau's *La Nouvelle Héloïse*.

Thus the relationship between *norm* and *function* appears to be essential. Changes within the normative system of culture entail functional changes of literary and other artistic works. At the same time these works – Lawrence's *Sons and Lovers*, Flaubert's *Madame Bovary* or Pinter's *The Caretaker* – are instrumental in transforming the system by breaking the norm; they are in turn transformed by the system which makes them undergo functional changes. Now it becomes clear what Květoslav Chvatík means when he argues that 'the functional point of view is fundamental for the Prague School'.[30]

The interaction between *structure, norm,* and *function* makes it possible to raise the delicate question concerning the *aesthetic value* of literary works in an historical and sociological context. This question is answered by Mukařovský in conjunction with the concepts of structure, norm, and function: the more contradictions a literary text or a work of art contains, the more contradictory interpretations it admits, the more likely it is to survive different norm systems and to assume new functions within these systems. Mukařovský explains 'that the aesthetic value of a work of art is greater and more durable the more strongly this work resists a literal interpretation within the perspective of a generally accepted system of values of a certain period and a certain milieu'. He goes on to say that 'the multiplicity, differentiation, and polysemy of the material work (can be considered) as a potential aesthetic advantage'.[31]

This is obviously an avant-garde conception of art: the contradictory, differentiated and polysemic text which resists a univocal interpretation and an integration into an existing norm system is constantly being reinterpreted and constitutes a permanent challenge to established ideologies, aesthetics, and stereotypes. Negativity or permanent negation of the norm could be considered the salient feature of this conception.

A contradictory or polysemic text like Emily Brontë's *Wuthering Heights*, Stéphane Mallarmé's poems or Franz Kafka's *The Trial* continues to elicit competing interpretations, criticisms, and evaluations because it cannot be identified with a particular epoch and its aesthetic norms. Its function varies from epoch to epoch and from culture to culture as religious, existentialist, psychoanalytic or deconstructionist discourses re-interpret it, thus making it undergo semantic and social changes. And this capacity to change and to survive normative systems, that is to maintain the momentum of its semantic or hermeneutic potential or its topicality, is considered by Mukařovský as the core of *aesthetic value*. One could also say that the aesthetic value of a work of art resides in its structural capacity for semantic and functional change within different normative and cultural systems. However, this capacity for survival also has a Kantian aspect to it: the ability of a sign to resist conceptual reduction.

3 Symbol and aesthetic object: From Mukařovský to Vodička
In order to understand Felix Vodička's theory of literary evolution, of reader response, and literary criticism it seems necessary to deal in some detail with Mukařovský's definition of the work of art as a *semiological fact*: as a *material symbol* and as an *aesthetic object*. His attempt to distinguish a material from an aesthetic object is

particularly important for theories of interpretation and literary reception. In the past it was assumed by the New Critics, proponents of the French *explication de texte*, and critics such as Wellek and Warren[32] that it made sense to look for the actual meaning of a poem or a novel and to capture it in a correct interpretation. Mukařovský's challenge to this hermeneutic confidence is the fundamental insight that a polysemic literary text (work of art) admits many contradictory interpretations and that the process of interpretation is open-ended, i.e. can go on forever.

While the work of art as a *material symbol* (e.g. Pablo Picasso's *Guernica* or Franz Kafka's *Before the Law*) does not change as far as its thing-like quality is concerned (Mukařovský speaks of *díla-věci*, of *works as things*), the work of art as an *aesthetic object* changes almost incessantly. Picasso's paintings are constantly being reinterpreted and the semantic potential of Kafka's work will probably never be exhausted, considering the bewildering proliferation of its exegeses. In this context Mukařovský distinguishes three aspects of the work of art:

> Every work of art is an *autonomous* sign which is composed of 1. the 'work as thing' which functions as a symbol of meaning; 2. the 'aesthetic object' which is anchored in the collective consciousness and has the function of 'meaning'; 3. the relationship with the things referred to which does not imply denotation of a particular existence – for we are dealing with an autonomous sign – but of the global context of social phenomena (science, philosophy, religion, politics, economy, etc.) of a given environment.[33]

Although Mukařovský clearly defines art as an autonomous sign, he is well aware of its communicative (biographical, historical, philosophical) functions. However, he considers these functions to be secondary, because they are dominated by the aesthetic function which weakens the referential dimensions of art, reinforcing and reasserting its autoreferential dimension so strongly emphasised by Jakobson. This dimension is responsible for the fact that a literary text for example cannot be read as an 'authentic document' (Mukařovský), for it combines fact and fiction, thus forming a heterogeneous aesthetic structure.

But what exactly is the *aesthetic object* which according to

Mukařovský is anchored in collective thought? It is the collective interpretation of a work of art in a particular socio-historical context. This interpretation is historically variable, and the reception of Hermann Hesse's work illustrates what this means: while German readers and critics of the 1920s and 1930s tended to read Hesse's short stories and novels within the Neo-Romantic and Wandervogel traditions, his work was radically reinterpreted by young American readers and critics of the 1960s as a psychedelic manifesto of the Beatnik and Hippie Generation. Hesse's work considered as a *material symbol*, as a typographic artefact, may not have changed substantially (Hesse died in 1962, *Der Steppenwolf* came out as early as 1924), but the aesthetic objects constructed in the USA were quite different from the German, the European ones. In spite of this difference, they were extremely influential in Europe, and the rebellious students of 1968 tended to read Hesse within an American perspective: as a leading writer of the peace-movement, as a discoverer of the aesthetic unconscious and of the relevance of oriental wisdom for Europe. Within literary criticism, Hesse's work as an aesthetic object undergoes a third metamorphosis when it is considered as an example of modernism and compared with the works of D. H. Lawrence or Thomas Mann.

It may have become clear at this stage that aesthetic objects do not only vary in history, as Mukařovský would have it, but that different aesthetic objects or conceptions of a particular work may *coexist* within a certain period of time, within a society. Mukařovský has not sufficiently emphasised this fact, but it goes without saying that during the 1960s Hesse could be read *simultaneously* as a modernist, an author of the rebellious student movement, a psychoanalytic writer, and a Neo-Romantic. Each reading of his work depends on the aesthetic norms prevailing within a certain group of readers or critics at the moment of reception.

The greatest merit of Felix Vodička's approach is probably his attempt to base the whole of *literary history* on Mukařovský's distinction between *material symbol* and *aesthetic object*. Criticising the Russian Formalists for having proposed a far too mechanical notion of *literary evolution* (which they reduced to a dialectic between *automatisation* and *de-automatisation*; cf. chap. 2), Vodička opens a historical perspective within which the transformation of literature as an aesthetic object is viewed as part and parcel of the general transformation of aesthetic and non-aesthetic norms and values. Commenting on the difference between Russian Formalism and Czech Structuralism, Peter Steiner aptly points out: 'We are not, however, back at the Formalist split between art and non-art, since the work of art is not monofunctional. Extra-aesthetic functions do not disappear from the aesthetic sign but participate in its meaning.'[34]

In this context Vodička explains the innovative thrust of literature in conjunction with changing social norms and values. Like Mukařovský he starts from the assumption that the work as material symbol is polysemic and hence should not be identified with one of its possible historical interpretations: 'Since, consequently, there is no correct and single aesthetic norm, there also is no single evaluation, and a work can become subject to multiple evaluation, in the process of which the shape of a literary work (its actualization) constantly changes in the mind of the perceiver.'[35] The term *actualisation* or *concretisation* was first used by the Polish literary critic Roman Ingarden and will be discussed in the next chapter: it means the realisation of the semantic potential of a work, its systematic interpretation on all levels. One might say that the *concretisation* is the individual and collective activity that brings about the *aesthetic object*.

According to Vodička the latter is a result of the complex interaction 'between the structure of the work and the evolving literary norm'.[36] Considering the fact that the structure is a constant which corresponds to the material symbol, the task of literary history consists in analysing the transformation of aesthetic objects within different normative, social, and historical contexts. In this perspective *literary evolution* (*literární vývoj*, Vodička) no longer appears as a purely formal dialectic between automatisation and de-automatisation, but as a social process of normative change within which literary aesthetic objects and the concept of literature as such are constantly being re-defined. The different religious, aesthetic, political or moral layers of the Bible, for example, can be *foregrounded* differently in different social groups: it can become a religious, literary, feminist or historical object.

Vodička believes that the construction of aesthetic objects – as foregrounding of the different layers or dimensions of a work of art – is the main task of the *literary critic*. 'It is his duty', he explains, 'to comment on a literary work as an aesthetic object (. . .).'[37] Literary critics are not merely expected to articulate subjective emotions or value judgements, but to evaluate the literature of their time within the contemporary system of norms and values. In pursuing this goal, the critic also defines the *function* of a literary text within a particular socio-historical situation. This is of course a somewhat conservative notion of literary criticism as evaluation of contemporary works. For critics who merely apply the dominant norms and values will hardly be able to appreciate the norm-breaking activities of original, avant-garde artists. They will tend to condemn the latter in the name of the ruling taste.

In spite of this conservative slant in Vodička's literary history it may be said without exaggeration that Prague Structuralism constitutes a major contribution to aesthetics, the sociology of literature, and reader-response criticism. Its contribution to aesthetics consists in an original (albeit unstable) synthesis of Kantian, Hegelian, and avant-garde ideas. This synthesis finds a clear expression in Vodička's comments on the capacity of great works of art to survive whole systems of norms:

> *The vitality of a work* depends on properties a work potentially embodies in itself with regard to the evolution of the literary norm. If a literary work is evaluated positively even upon a change of norm, it has consequently a great life span in comparison with a work whose aesthetic appeal is exhausted with the extinction of the norm of the time.[38]

One important aspect of this passage is the avant-garde idea of non-conformity: the work of art which counts cannot be reduced to a particular social system of norms and values; it goes constantly *beyond* this system. The other important aspect is Kantian: only the work which cannot be reduced to the *concepts* of a particular aesthetic or ideological system, which pleases perpetually without a definite conceptualisation, is fit for survival, is valuable. In this respect Mukařovský's and Vodička's theory of aesthetic value can be said to be Kantian. The Hegelian aspect, finally, is the *historical* approach to normativity, evaluation, and function: the function and value of art changes in the course of history.

In the next chapter it will be shown to what extent Prague Structuralism influenced the theories of reader–response criticism and especially the *aesthetics of reception* (*Rezeptionsästhetik*) of the so-called Constance School. It will become clear that the whole of reader–response criticism is based on the Structuralist idea of the work as a dual structure: as a polysemic artefact or material symbol on the one hand and as an interpreted aesthetic object on the other. All attempts to involve the readership in the history of literature implies a rejection of the traditional idea that a literary work has a particular meaning and that this meaning can be fixed once and for all by systematic exegesis yielding the 'correct interpretation'.

In retrospect, it is becoming clear that Czech Structuralism constitutes a vital link between Russian Formalism and German reader–response criticism. With its differentitation of *material symbol* and *aesthetic object* it made literary theory focus on the role of the reader, thus enabling the critics of the Constance School (Jauss and Iser) to reconsider the whole of literary history from the point of view of *reception*. At the same time it revealed the illusory character of the traditional search for a correct interpretation.

CHAPTER 4

Problems of Reader-Response Criticism: From Hermeneutics to Phenomenology

What had been declared a fallacy and a heresy by the New Critics (cf. chap. 1) was, several decades later, to become one of the fundamental tenets of reader-response criticism: namely the idea that the meaning of a literary text is not contained in the object itself, but in the reactions of the reader. 'The Affective Fallacy', the New Critics held, 'is a confusion between the poem and its results.'[1] Reacting to this thesis, the American critic Stanley Fish turns it on its head, arguing that the meaning of the poem *is* in its results, i.e. in the *reading process*. As will be shown in the last section of this chapter, he believes that New Critics, semioticians, psychoanalysts, and Marxists committed the fundamental error of considering the literary text as a static whole, thereby losing sight of the crucial fact that readers do not perceive it as a semantic totality, but experience it as an ambiguous and often contradictory process at the end of which a meaning comes about that is subject to change: to re-reading and new modes of reader-response or reception.

Almost simultaneously with Stanley Fish, the two German critics Hans Robert Jauss and Wolfgang Iser, founders of the so-called Constance School and German reader-response criticism (*Rezeptionsästhetik*), challenged Wolfgang Kayser's influential doctrine according to which literary theory ought to look for 'the correct interpretation' or the 'actual meaning' of a text.[2] In postwar Germany, this doctrine was particularly well implanted in schools and universities, where it had acquired an authoritarian bias. Who else but the teacher or professor of literature was qualified to expound the 'correct meaning' of the interpreted text? In a radical critique of this somewhat authoritarian practice which is not typical of Germany, but also to be found in Anglo-American New Criticism and in the so called *explication de texte* which still prevails in numerous French schools, they invoked the useful distinction made by Mukařovský and Vodička between the text as *material symbol* and the text as *aesthetic object* (cf. chap. 3). The material symbol, according to the Czech structuralists, is polysemic and can generate many contradictory meanings which, in the course of time, take on the shape of competing collective interpretations or aesthetic objects. As in the case of Stanley Fish, meaning is thus removed from the text as a material construct and transferred into the realm of aesthetic objects: into the reading or reception process. Considering the fact that this process, which is a process of constant re-interpretation and re-adaptation to the prevailing social and aesthetic norms, generates a large number of contradictory meanings, the concept of meaning as a homogeneous totality intended and created by an omniscient, God-like author is radically questioned.

At this point it becomes clear why American reader-response criticism and German *Rezeptionsästhetik* are predominantly (albeit not exclusively) Kantian: like Kant in his *Critique of Judgement* and unlike Hegel in his *Aesthetics*, they both adopt the point of view of the spectator, the reader. They do not ask with Hegel what kind of authorial or historical consciousness a work of art expresses, but how it is perceived or understood by ever-changing reading publics in different historical set-ups. This is why in his 'Literaturgeschichte als Provokation', which was initially (1967) published at Constance University as a lecture and a kind of manifesto, Jauss pleads in favour of a literary history which would no longer be based on the consciousness of the artist as producer, but on the heterogeneous reading public which is responsible for the continuing *change* of literary meaning.

Recognising the importance of this change also implies a slackening confidence in the Hegelian idea that each work of art expresses a *conceptually definable meaning*. Meaning, as Jauss, Iser, and Fish argue, is not a metaphysical entity that can be defined once and for all, but an open-ended evolution within which the text as material symbol functions as a catalyst. This conception of art and literature can be considered Kantian, because it follows Kant's tenet '*ohne Begriff*', 'without concept'. All rationalist and Hegelian attempts to identify works of art with conceptual systems are doomed to failure, the reader-response critics say, because artistic meaning is irrevocably fragmented in the course of a contradictory reading process, in the course of history.

This emphasis on an open-ended process at the expense of the concept or the *content plane* in the sense of Hjelmslev entails an orientation of reader-response criticism towards the *expression plane*, towards the text as signifier. Although Jauss, Iser, and Fish do not believe that the polysemy of the literary signifier is unlimited, they tend to consider the text as a polysemic signifier rather than as a system of signifieds, as Barthes would say. In many respects their notion of the polysemic text corresponds to Mukařovský's notion of *material symbol*.

In what follows it will become clear that reader-response criticism and even the *Rezeptionsästhetik* of the Constance School are not homogeneous theoretical systems. While Hans Robert Jauss' theory is firmly anchored in modern German hermeneutics dominated by the work of Hans Georg Gadamer, Wolfgang Iser's approach is phenomenological in the sense of Husserl and Ingarden. While Jauss – at least in theory – is primarily interested in the reactions of historical reading publics, Iser analyses the *semantic potential* of literary texts from a phenomenological point of view: their inexhaustible capacity to generate new meanings by virtue of *indeterminacy*. In other words, Iser is more interested in the text and the unfolding of its potential in the reading process, while Jauss would like to focus on the expectations and reactions of reading publics in the course of history.

1 From Gadamer to Jauss: The Hermeneutics of Reader-Response
Hans Georg Gadamer, whose major work *Wahrheit und Methode* (1960) lays the foundations of contemporary German hermeneutics, has decisively contributed to the rise of reader-response criticism in Germany by emphasising the cognitive functions of art and literature: literature as a source of truth. It is important to note, however, that Gadamer's conception of aesthetic truth is not identical with Hegel's. While Hegel holds that in spite of its sensuous (*sinnlich*) character art can be translated into conceptual thought (i.e. philosophy), Gadamer explicitly denies this possibility. Although he praises Hegel for having associated art with the historical search for truth, he criticises his attempt to subordinate art to the concept: 'Certainly, inasmuch as it makes

the truth of the concept all powerful, which resolves all experience within itself, Hegel's philosophy at the same time disavows the way of truth that it has recognised in the experience of art.'[3]

This critique of conceptual domination in Hegel's aesthetics justifies a partial return to Kant which Gadamer makes plausible by insisting on the tendency of art to exceed the narrow limits of conceptual definition. He refers to its inexhaustible character 'by which it resists conceptual translation'.[4] However, Gadamer's 'return to Kant' is only partial, because he continues to share Hegel's belief in aesthetic truth. He turns against Kant when he pointedly asks: 'But is it right to reserve the concept of truth for conceptual knowledge? Must we not also admit that the work of art possesses truth?'[5]

Gadamer's answer to these crucial questions is clear and it is a synthesis of Kant and Hegel: art can only be understood adequately as a permanent quest for truth. This truth, however, cannot be conceptually defined; it is polysemic and an inexhaustible source of interpretation. Unlike in Hegel's and Kant's thought, where truth was primarily a matter of conceptual reflexion, in Gadamer's philosophy it becomes both an aesthetic and an historical concept. It is no longer seen as a system of monosemic definitions, but as an open historical process, a permanent dialectic of question and answer in which the work of art fulfils the function of a catalyst. A literary text, Gadamer argues, can only be understood as a set of answers to certain historical questions or problems. Thus Shakespeare's *King Lear* may be read as an answer to the question concerning the relationship between reason and folly. However, it is a rather ambiguous, polysemic answer which can be re-read and re-interpreted at any time in history. It is a truth that cannot possibly be reduced to a conceptual definition. According to Gadamer, it goes well beyond 'the original historical horizon within which the recipient and the producer of the work of art were contemporaries'.[6] It continues to signify in our time and to influence our answers to contemporary questions concerning reason, folly, love, jealousy, and death. In other words, aesthetic truth is an endless process in which questions and answers of the past are inserted into our contexts and thereby actualised, renewed: they become questions and answers 'for us'. One could also say that they signify within our *horizon of expectations* or *Erwartungshorizont*. Gadamer – like Jauss – uses this conceptual metaphor which was originally introduced into philosophy and sociology by the early Karl Mannheim (1853-1947)[7] in order to describe the global historical context within which texts and works of art are understood, interpreted, and applied to contemporary problems, needs, and practices.

However, the adaptation of literary texts to new historical horizons of expectations does not imply a simple, unilateral integration of the old into the new; it rather presupposes a permanent dialogue between old and recent phenomena: between the first horizon of expectations which a literary work like *King Lear* evoked and later horizons (questions, problems, values, norms) which it encounters in the course of history. This dialogue or *understanding* (*Verstehen*), as Gadamer calls it, is represented by him as a *fusion of horizons* or *Horizontverschmelzung*: 'Understanding, rather, is always the fusion of these horizons which we imagine to exist by themselves.'[8] In what follows it will be shown how Jauss adapts this hermeneutic terminology to his own aims and purposes.

Like Gadamer he is convinced that a Hegelian conceptualisation of literature has to be avoided if the historical vitality, the historical dynamism of literary texts is to be understood. It is not by chance that, in an interview with Rien T. Segers, he tries to revive the Kantian aesthetic tradition which is based entirely on the notion of perception and on the question how the Beautiful is to be *perceived*. 'The last great aesthetic of perception (*Wirkungsästhetik*)', he points out, 'was Kant's critique of aesthetic judgement.'[9] Jauss tends to believe that Aristotle's and Kant's aesthetics of perception ought to be considered as historical exceptions because the historically dominant aesthetic theories – from Plato to Hegel – were oriented towards the artist and the production process. 'The great exceptions within the philosophical tradition', he explains in his article '*Paradigmawechsel in der Literaturwissenschaft*' (1969), 'are the Aristotelian Poetics in Antiquity and Kant's *Critique of Judgement* in modern times.'[10]

His attempt to renew and reinforce the Aristotelian and especially Kantian tradition should be considered within the social, political, and institutional context of postwar Germany. While official East German criticism was dominated by the Hegelianism of Marxist-Leninist aesthetics, the rebellious students of the late

Sixties had the names of Marxist critics such as Benjamin, Lukács, Goldmann, and Gramsci written on their banners. Jauss' attempt to bring about a change in the critical 'paradigm' should be seen against the backdrop of this political situation in which the Hegelian tradition was being continued by the Marxist-Leninists and the Neo-Marxists, whereas the Kantian renewal advocated by Jauss and his disciples was meant to reassert the autonomy of art (*vis-à-vis* philosophy and ideology) and the importance of the reader.

Although it was primarily an ideological response to the Hegelian-Marxist aesthetics of artistic *production*, *Rezeptionsästhetik* was also a reaction to the so-called *werkimmanente Interpretation* founded by Wolfgang Kayser in his influential book *Das sprachliche Kunstwerk* (1948). As was already pointed out in the introduction to this chapter, this type of literary criticism completely neglected the reader and the historical context of literature; like *New Criticism* and the French *explication de texte* it was geared towards the text itself and its correct interpretation. In the 1950s and 1960s it was popular with teachers of literature who, having experienced the National-Socialist annexation of art, were anxious to avoid political debates.

Apart from being a political and polemical reaction to Marxism and *werkimmanente Interpretation*, Jauss' reader-response criticism also has a postmodern dimension. Almost simultaneously with Foucault, who diagnoses the 'death of the author'[11], Jauss proclaims the end of authorial meaning and – like Foucault – rejects all attempts to discover the real meaning of a text intended by the author. Although he differs sharply from deconstruction and Roland Barthes' semiotics, he tends to agree with Barthes and Derrida that there is no such thing as 'the meaning' of a text. Like Stanley Fish he projects meaning into the polymorphous process of reader-response history. This attempt to substitute a *plurality of meanings* for *the authentic meaning* pursued by Proust, Kafka, the Existentialists, and the Marxists, could be considered as postmodern.

According to Jauss, the history of literature as such ought to be envisaged from the point of view of the reader (the reading public) and not in the perspective of the writer or producer: '*A renewal of literary history demands the removal of the prejudices of historical objectivism and the grounding of the traditional aesthetics of production and representation in an aesthetics of reception and influence.'*[12] The idea is not simply to propose reader-response criticism as a new component of literary research, but to operate a paradigmatic reorientation within literary criticism and literary history in particular: both should focus on the historical reading public and its changing horizons of expectations.

How are these horizons to be defined? What do they consist of? The early Karl Mannheim, who was the first theoretician to use the German word *Erwartungshorizont* in a treatise on the sociology of culture[13], associated it closely with the concept of *world view* or *Weltanschauung* which he defined as the sum total of values, norms, and interests underlying the point of view of a social group. Complementarily, the *Erwartungshorizont* or *horizon of expectations* refers to the collective expectations, hopes, and apprehensions of a group at a particular moment of history. In other publications he analyses in detail the *world view* and the complementary expectations of the conservative bourgeoisie in the eighteenth and the nineteenth century.

In the reader-response theory developed by Jauss, the notion of *Erwartungshorizont* is detached from the concept of *world view* and exclusively applied to the historical reader who is not presented as a collective or a group, but as a kind of generalised individual. Readers, as imagined by Jauss, have at least three options in reacting to a new, innovative work of literature: 1. They can reject it as incomprehensible, worthless, immoral or ugly if they are shocked by its avant-garde or non-conformist character. 2. In certain cases they may overlook its innovative, revolutionary elements and assimilate it to their routinised aesthetic, moral, and emotional expectations. 3. The third case is the only interesting one for Jauss – as it was for Gadamer: particularly active and alert readers may go beyond rejection and assimilation by recognising the innovative nature of the literary text and by reacting to it in a creative mode through changes in their horizon of expectations.

Whereas the first case (outright rejection) is amply illustrated by literary scandals, such as the condemnation of D. H. Lawrence's *Lady Chatterley's Lover* or Gustave Flaubert's *Madame Bovary*, the second case (tacit assimilation) is less spectacular but equally detrimental to the reception of the new. When André Gide, one of the first readers of Marcel Proust's *Du côté de chez Swann*, criticised the text as dull and banal, he certainly overlooked its innovative potential, as his revised judgements on the subject made clear later on. The creative reaction to literary innovation seems particularly interesting to Jauss and Gadamer, because it brings about what they call a *Horizontverschmelzung*: a *coalescence* or *fusion of horizons*. Creative readers adapt their aesthetic, cognitive, and social expectations to the new horizons revealed by the innovative text.

The horizon of expectations as defined by Jauss may be considered as consisting of at least three components: 1. the literary or aesthetic, 2. the psychological, and 3. the social. Towards the end of this section it will become clear that Jauss is primarily interested in the first component: in the literary expectations of the reader whom he tends to identify with the reader-as-author. He tends to neglect both the psyche and the social background of the reading public, thus incurring massive criticism from Marxists and other sociologically-minded theoreticians.

The changes which certain texts bring about in the consciousness of their readers are due, among other things, to what Jauss calls the *aesthetic distance* (*ästhetische Distanz*) between reader and text. This distance is greatest when a work of art radically negates the established values and norms of the public. Beckett's *Endgame* or *Waiting for Godot* are cases in point: both dramas infringed the normative horizons of the cultivated audience whose expectations were geared towards dramatic action, meaningful dialogue, and a more or less conventional *dénouement*.

The early Jauss whose work had not only been influenced by Mukařovský's theory of artistic production as a norm-breaking process, but also by Adorno's negative aesthetics (cf. chap. 5), tended to defend the phenomenon of *aesthetic distance* as the critical dimension of art which prevented it from falling pray to the commercialisation of culture. In his important article 'Racines und Goethes Iphigenie' (1973), he attempts a systematic reconstruction of the aesthetic distance which separated the very first public from Racine's *Iphigénie* (1674) and Goethe's *Iphigenie* (1779-1787) and which was later on obliterated by interpretations with a strong humanist bias rooted in the humanist ideology of 19th century France and Germany. The original aesthetic distance brought about by the untamed and socially dangerous emotions represented by Racine and by the Enlightenment ideas put forward by Goethe was eliminated and the two dramas were reduced to ideologically acceptable and hence consumable clichés: '*the tender Racine*' ('*tendre Racine*') and '*the myth of feminine purity*' ('*der Mythus des rein Weiblichen*').[14] Both ideological myths are neoclassical or classicist in the sense of the nineteenth century: they suppress the critical dimension of art, thus speeding up its integration into bourgeois culture. In his article, Jauss proclaims his ambition to deliver both dramas from '*the beautiful appearance of the timeless truths of Classicism*' ('*schönen Schein eines zeitlos wahren Klassizismus*') and to rediscover the critical, humanitarian, and Enlightenment character of Goethe's drama ('*Goethes im Ansatz aufklärerisch-humanitäres Drama*').[15] But isn't this a rather Hegelian quest for the 'correct' historical interpretation? – We shall return to this question towards the end of this section.

Considering later developments of Jauss' theory, it is interesting to note that its attachment to avant-garde and critical concepts such as norm-breaking and aesthetic distance did not last. In a later phase of his intellectual development which might be called postmodern, Jauss abandons his avant-garde stance and seeks a compromise 'between the two extremes of the *norm-breaking* and the *norm-fulfilling* function'[16], as he puts it in *Ästhetische Erfahrung und literarische Hermeneutik*. The postmodern idea behind this compromise is that modernism and the avant-garde were too negative about aesthetic pleasure and that *aisthesis* as norm-breaking negativity had to be completed and compensated by *catharsis*: by the reader's or onlooker's affective identification with heroes, actions, and emotions. Jauss refers to the 'communicative function of literature' and allows for 'admiring identification'.[17] The question is of course whether this kind of identification does not considerably further the integration of the spectator or reader into the patterns of commercialised culture.

One of Jauss' favourite postmodern texts which combines Horace's *delectare* and *prodesse* with aesthetic distance (*aisthesis*) is Italo Calvino's *If on a Winter's Night a Traveller*. Jauss believes that in this novel Calvino achieves a 'symbiosis of mass and high-brow culture which also characterises other works of postmodernism'.[18] But can Calvino's experimental novel be univocally defined as postmodern? Jauss seems to think so, in very much the same way as he assumes that Goethe's *Iphigenie* is a 'humanitarian drama' with an Enlightenment message. This assumption, however, seems to contradict Kant's aesthetic principle *'ohne Begriff*, 'without concept', which Jauss pretends to defend against the Hegelians among the Marxists. Here it becomes clear that his attempt to read 'horizons of expectations' into individual works of literature tends to lead to a conceptual and historical definition of these works in the Hegelian sense.

Hence there seems to be a global contradiction in Jauss' theory between the Kantian postulate that polysemic works cannot be conceptualised because they are being constantly re-interpreted in the course of the reading process, and the (latently Hegelian) assumption that the 'horizons of expectations' (*Weltanschauungen*, Mannheim would say) can be conceptually defined. Is 'postmodernism' not just another historical label which Jauss chooses to stick on Calvino's text, but which will be superseded by other concepts in the course of time?

Or are there fundamental structures underlying each text, structures that no group of readers – whatever their historical position – can afford to ignore? Jauss has always denied this. However, he seems to agree with Eco (cf. chap. 6) that it is possible to distinguish arbitrary from plausible interpretations, 'that the historically progressing concretisation of meaning of literary works follows a certain logic (. . .) and that in spite of the changing horizons of interpretation it is possible to distinguish arbitrary from consensus-based (. . .) interpretations'.[19]

If this is the case, then inevitably the question crops up what this consensus as a criterion for lasting plausibility is based on. The only convincing answer to this question is: the phonetic, syntactic, and semantic structures of the text. Although it may be easier to describe the phonetic and the syntactic structures than the semantic ones (because semantic theories diverge more strongly than theories of syntax and sound), descriptions of semantic features are not arbitrary, as will be shown in the sixth chapter in conjunction with Greimas. It is therefore surprising that Jauss has not attempted to answer the question to what extent the varying modes of reception depend on invariable text structures and how the nexus between *literary production* (*sender*), *text* (*message*), and *reader* (*recipient*) is to be described. (Cf. R. Jakobson's six functions in chap. 3.1.)

Jauss' neglect of the process of literary production was pointed out early on by East German Marxists who, faithful to the Marxian scheme of *base* and *superstructure*, argued that any theory of reception or reader-response ought to be based on a materialist theory of literary production. In their collective volume *Gesellschaft, Literatur, Lesen* (1973), which was meant to be a global critique of West German *Rezeptionsästhetik*, they blame Jauss for his idealism which, they believe, is responsible for his neglect of the material conditions of literary production: of the class allegiance of writers, their economic situation, and their position within the literary institution. Discussing the literary work and its status in Jauss' theory, Manfred Naumann and Karl-Heinz Barck point out: 'It is projected exclusively into the process of reading – and not into the system of communication, that is to say into the relationship between the production and the reception of literary works.'[20]

Extending their critique into the realm of the reading public, they add that Jauss' key concept of *Erwartungshorizont* is also idealist because it has a purely literary character, thus excluding the social and economic components of the reading process. Insofar as Jauss deals almost exclusively with the reading experience of writers (Goethe, the author of *Werther*, reading Rousseau's *La Nouvelle Héloïse*, Valéry, the author of *Mon Faust*, reading Goethe, etc.), the horizon of expectations that was meant to describe the reactions of historical or contemporary readers, turns into an instrument of text analysis. This criticism is confirmed by Jörn Stückrath who reminds us of the fact 'that Jauss' interest in the reader is above all an interest in the reader as author'.[21]

Considering this metamorphosis of reader into author, it is not surprising that the East German Marxists criticise Jauss for using a concept of *reading public* that is far too abstract as it fails to take into account the division of society into groups and classes with different interests and often colliding horizons of expectations. This critique was later on confirmed by theoreticians such as Joseph Jurt who developed a sociology of the reading public and the reading process.[22]

In spite of the fact that some of the critical arguments put forward by the Marxists were valid – their idea that a theory of reception has to be linked to a theory of production, that the horizon of expectations has important social and ideological components, and that the reading public is socially heterogeneous – these arguments were embedded in a Hegelian aesthetic which, for political reasons, aimed at a univocal definition of the literary text that was meant to elicit a univocal response by the reader.

According to the Marxists, the revolutionary writer does not merely intend to free the reader from prejudice and provoke a new perception of things (as Jauss would have it): 'he intends to provoke a *correct* perception of things'.[23] And it goes without saying that this correct perception coincides with that of the Party. Therefore Wolfgang Iser is perfectly right when he points out: 'Hence the Socialist way of reading texts is considered a norm in order to safeguard the monosemic character of reception.'[24] In the fifth chapter the Marxist habit of reading literary texts as univocal conceptual messages will be discussed in more detail in a philosophical and aesthetic context.

2 From Ingarden to Iser: The Phenomenological Perspective
Unlike Jauss, who tends to disregard the structure of literary texts, the Polish theoretician Roman Ingarden (1893-1970) sets out from a clear distinction between the *ontology* and the *phenomenology* of literature. Following Edmund Husserl (1859-1938), the founder of modern phenomenology, he defines ontology as an inquiry into the *essence* of things and phenomenology as an inquiry into the *perception* of things. While his first major work, *Das literarische Kunstwerk* (1931), is a systematic attempt to develop an ontology of literature and to describe the essential structures of literary works, his second book, *Vom Erkennen des literarischen Kunstwerks* (1936), deals systematically with the perception of works by readers.

The two books have two salient features in common: their focus on the essence or general structure of works of art and on the potential or ideal reader and their complementary refusal to analyse individual texts in detail or to take the reactions of empirical readers into account. In this respect, Ingarden's ontologically and phenomenologically based reader-response criticism diverges from Jauss' theory which – at least in principle – is oriented towards the historical reader. As a disciple of Husserl he believes that empirical sciences such as psychology, sociology, and empirical literary research should be founded upon the *essential cognition* (*Wesenserkenntnis*, Husserl) of ontology and phenomenology.

This is undoubtedly an idealist value judgement which could be criticised from a materialist point of view[25], but which in Ingarden's case allows for a clear-cut distinction between what he (following Husserl) defines as *real* or *autonomous* (*seinsautonom*) and *intentional* or *heteronomous* (*seinsheteronom*) *objects*. While *real* objects can – at least in principle – be analysed and known on all levels and in all respects, intentional objects contain many empty spaces or *indeterminacies* (*Unbestimmtheitsstellen*). An existing table is a real object insofar as it can be divided into its constituent parts, measured, weighed, and subjected to chemical analysis. At least in principle, none of its elements is inaccessible to our knowledge. In this regard it is qualitatively, ontologically different from a table in a novel or in a drama. In the fictional context, a table imagined by an author is no longer a *real* (*autonomous*), but an *intentional* or *heteronomous* object (heteronomous, because depending on a creator's consciousness). Its intentional or heteronomous character makes it impossible for us to analyse it empirically, and our knowledge of it as an object is entirely dependent on the information which an author-narrator is willing to convey. If we are told that somebody 'sits at a table' or 'lounges on a sofa', we are entitled to imagine any kind of table or sofa that fits the context of the novel or drama. As *intentional objects* the fictional 'table' or 'sofa' are full of *indeterminacies* (*Unbestimmtheitsstellen*, Ingarden).

When we read, for example, in Charlotte Brontë's *Jane Eyre* 'she lay reclined on a sofa by the fire-side'[26], we may imagine all kinds of sofas and fire-sides which fit the middle of the English nineteenth century: a green, red or brown sofa and a small, large, ornate or simple fire-place with a large fire burning or logs glowing away slowly amid grey columns of smoke. All of these images may crop up in the reader's mind and are made possible by the indeterminacies of the text which nevertheless imposes limits on our imagination: we are not free to imagine an avant-garde sofa made of plastic or other synthetic materials or an electrically heated fire-place with illuminated plastic logs.

According to Ingarden, the intentional object *par excellence* is the *centaur* (also mentioned by Jean-Paul Sartre in *L'Imagination*)[27]: 'In this case the pure intentionality of the object comes to the fore'.[28] As long as we accept that a centaur is a creature in Greek mythology with the head, arms, and torso of a man and the body and legs of a horse, we are free to imagine any colour, dimension or character we like. A centaur is not a *real* or *autonomous* object and is unlikely to become one, whatever other results genetic experiments may yield in the future. Considering that objects in literary texts are not real, but merely 'would-be objects', it is not surprising that according to Ingarden the author's, narrator's or hero's judgements which refer to these objects are *quasi-judgements* (*Quasi-Urteile*) that can only be related to a fictive context. These judgements cannot be expected to fill out all the gaps or *indeterminacies*. On the contrary, many statements or allusions create new uncertainties or imponderables, thus provoking the creative drive of the readers.

They are called upon to bring about what Ingarden calls the *concretisation* of a literary work. Within the *ontological* (structural) limits of a text many different, divergent, and even contradictory concretisations are conceivable. It is a well-known fact that Kafka's *The Trial*, for example, has been read and interpreted in a theological, modernist, psychoanalytic, Marxist, existentialist, and deconstructionist context. With every new *concretisation* in the sense of Ingarden a new *aesthetic object* in the sense of Mukařovský and Vodička appears. It is now possible to understand why Vodička (cf. chap. 3) decided to use the phenomenological concept of concretisation. Every new concretisation leads to the constitution of a new aesthetic (existentialist, Marxist, modernist or deconstructionist) object. It could be argued that it is the task of the critic as a reader to suggest new concretisations to the general reading public, concretisations yielding new aesthetic objects.

As in the case of Czech Structuralism, the idea that the literary text as a *material symbol* (Mukařovský) or as an *ontological* fact (Ingarden) is marked by *indeterminacies* which may elicit diverging *concretisations*, leads to the rejection of all Hegelian and Marxist attempts to read literature as a univocal message. Reacting to the Marxist search for a univocal definition of literature, Ingarden emphasises that 'the idea of the work in the sense of a *true sentence*'[29] is inconceivable. He nevertheless believes that a kind of ideal content is expressed by the *essential structure* of a work: by what he calls the *Wesenszusammenhang*.[30] However, this essential structure, he argues, 'cannot be defined conceptually'.[31] The Kantian agnosticism which comes to the fore in this remark is of phenomenological origin. As an *intentional object*, the phenomenological argument runs, a literary text contains many indeterminacies that cannot be eliminated. The irreducible rest is the non-conceptual, polysemic residue. It is interesting to observe how the phenomenologist arrives at conclusions that are quite similar to those of the Kantian New Critics and the Prague Structuralists. It is not surprising therefore that Vodička in particular was very interested in the phenomenological concept of *concretisation*.

In spite of its crucial insights into the constitution and perception of literary texts, Ingarden's theory has several shortcomings, especially if considered from a semiotic and sociological point of view. For some of its key concepts, such as *indeterminacy* (*Unbestimmtheit*), could have been defined more concretely in a linguistic, semantic or semiotic context: as *polysemy*, for example. (The concept of *polysemy* will be discussed in more detail in chap. 6.1., where it will be related to Greimas' concept of *isotopy*.)

In a sociological perspective, the theory appears flawed because it presupposes an unchanging, non-historical notion of art and literature. Ingarden does not seem to take into account the socio-historical emergence of artistic autonomy and the complementary fact that his own definition of literature is part and parcel of this historical process. Some postmodern theories, for example, would not consider literature as ontologically different from non-literature.[32]

The neglect of the socio-historical dimension leads to a contradiction in Ingarden's approach. From an ontological point of view, the literary work appears autonomous and unchanging, from a phenomenological point of view, however, it appears as an object of varying perceptions, concretisations and evaluations, i.e. as an *aesthetic object* in the structuralist sense involved in permanent change. K. Rosner describes what he calls Ingarden's 'compromise with history':

Practically, it means that a literary work as an object of an aesthetic experience is historically determined and changing. However, a fairly high price has been paid for this compromise with history: for it leads to a separation and opposition of the results of ontological and aesthetic analyses, while in *Das literarische Kunstwerk* Ingarden attempted to consider both aspects in the same terms.[33]

Finally, Ingarden's analysis of the reading process as concretisation could be criticised for not taking into account the dynamics of reading described by Stanley Fish. The reader, Fish would argue, does not simply eliminate indeterminacies, considering the text as a coherent totality or system, but reads and re-reads ambiguities, contradictions, and allusions, constantly revising previous impressions, interpretations, and definitions. Although Wolfgang Iser has never adopted Fish's slightly deconstructionist conception of reader-response, he proposes a re-orientation of Ingarden's approach by taking into account the active part of the reader and the historical dimension of indeterminacy.

In the field of philosophy and aesthetics he stands relatively close to Ingarden, insofar as he tends to adopt a Kantian point of view when it comes to defending literary autonomy and repudiates the Hegelian idea that art can be conceptually defined. He criticises the interpretation theories of the nineteenth century which 'sought to interpret the work in the Hegelian sense as the "sensual appearance of the idea"'[34], and emphasises that literary meaning 'cannot be reduced to a "thing"'.[35] He insists on the qualitative 'difference between image and discourse'.[36]

In view of such arguments, it is not surprising that he feels far more akin to Kant than to Hegel and his Marxist disciples. In an attempt to grasp the non-conceptual mode of literary meaning he suggests that 'the aesthetic nature of meaning constantly threatens to transmute itself into discursive determinacy – to use a Kantian term, it is amphibolic: at one moment aesthetic and at the next discursive'.[37] Bearing in mind that in ancient Greek *amphibolia* means *ambiguity*, this amounts to saying that the ambiguity of art precludes its conceptual, univocal definition, or that it 'pleases without concept', as Kant would have it.

As a Kantian phenomenologist who (unlike Ingarden) is familiar with contemporary semiotics, Iser prefers to read literature on the expression plane rather than on the content plane: 'The iconic signs of literature constitute an organization of signifiers which do not serve to designate a signified object, but instead designate *instructions* for the *production* of the signified.'[38] In other words: texts do not convey conceptually definable messages, but instructions for the production of meaning in the reading process.

And this is what Iser calls *Wirkung* or the *global effect* of a polysemic text upon its readers: the often ambiguous semantic, narrative or syntactic stimuli emitted by the text and transformed into manifold meanings by the ever changing readership. Starting from the phenomenological (Ingardian) assumption that the literary text offers its readers a semantic potential which they may realise (or make concrete) in different ways, Iser envisages a more active reader than Ingarden: a reader who communicates with the text, recomposing and rewriting it as it were, thus becoming a second author. Although Iser accepts Ingarden's idea that a text is an integrated schematic whole, the components and structures of which cannot be arbitrarily re-grouped, he emphasises the *reciprocity* between text and reader. Far from being a passive observer who fills in gaps, thus completing or fulfilling a preconstructed scheme or programme, the reader takes part in the construction of meaning. Iser criticises the 'passive' character of Ingarden's concept of *concretisation* which does not allow for the creativity of successive readers whose divergent perspectives invariably lead to the emergence of competing concretisations.

In an attempt to describe the textual framework that structures the orientations of the reader, Iser distinguishes three levels: 1. the *repertoire*, 2. the *strategies*, and 3. the *realisation* of the text in the course of the reading process. What exactly does he mean by this terminology?

He defines the *repertoire* as a system of literary and non-literary conventions, norms, and values which forms the nexus between the literary text and non-literary systems such as politics, religion, and philosophy in a given society: 'The repertoire of the text is made up of material selected for social systems and literary traditions.'[39] Insofar as the repertoire absorbs social and aesthetic norms along with the techniques of older texts, it constitutes the referential component of fiction. According to Iser, the *repertoire* of *Joseph Andrews* not only consists of allusions to literary scenes and stereotypes of Fielding's time, but also of the corresponding social norms and values. In other words, through its *repertoire* the literary text reacts to the aesthetic, social, political, religious, and emotional problems of its time. However, its reactions, evaluations, and commentaries are by no means univocal and leave ample space for the imagination of the reader.

While the *repertoire* bridges the gap between fiction and reality, the *strategies* are the semantic and narrative techniques implemented by authors and narrators in order to guide readers through the intricacies of the text, arranging the course of events and preparing the expected or unexpected dénouement. Adopting a Saussurian point of view, one could argue that the *repertoire* has a paradigmatic structure (because it does not fix the order or succession of facts and events), whereas the *strategies* which have a predominantly narrative character, are comparable to the syntagm: they establish a certain temporal order, thus fixing a chronological perspective. 'After all', Iser explains, 'the ultimate function of the strategies is to *defamiliarize* the familiar.'[40]

Among the most important strategies are the narrative techniques which make the acting figures, their situations, and actions appear in a certain – positive or negative, comic or tragic – context. They are responsible for the foregrounding of certain characters, actions, and events and for the omission of others. Thus at the beginning of the 14th chapter of Thomas Hardy's *A Pair of Blue Eyes*, certain events are omitted, whereas others are focused on by the narrator: 'It has now to be realized that nearly three-quarters of a year have passed away. In place of the autumnal scenery which formed a setting to the previous enactments, we have the culminating blooms of summer in the year following. – Stephen is in India, slaving away at an office in Bombay (. . .).'[41] One of the narrator's strategies consists in making a leap from autumn to next year's summer; the other consists in foregrounding the visual impressions ('culminating blooms') which eclipse all other sensations. However, the strategies and omissions of the narrator may incite the reader's imagination to extend or even rewrite the text, taking advantage of its *indeterminacies*. The active reader thus turns into a second writer.

In a more recent work entitled *Das Fiktive und das Imaginäre* (*The Fictive and the Imaginary*), Iser returns to the Kantian idea 'without concept', when he points out that the literary text has a dimension 'which is accessible to experience without being open to global, let alone exhaustive definition'.[42] Hardy's text illustrates what is meant: although most readers will *experience* the quoted passage in similar ways (summer succeeds autumn), the metaphoric expression 'culminating blooms' is likely to elicit very different kinds of imagery with different readers and cannot be conceptually defined.

This argument also applies to the sequence 'three-quarters of a year have passed away' which is an *indeterminacy* (*Unbestimmtheits-stelle*) in the sense of Ingarden and Iser. It can be filled out in many different ways (as an episode full of events or emotions, for example) or simply taken into account as an abstract statement. Similarly, the information that 'Stephen is in India, slaving away at an office', can be filled with emotional content (concerning especially Stephen's thoughts about Elfride back home) or simply perceived as factual information. Thus each reading turns into a more or less creative, more or less original *realisation* (Iser) of Hardy's novel.

Iser's 'realisation' is not simply a new word meant to function as a substitute for Ingarden's *concretisation*: it accentuates Iser's attempt to envisage the reader's response as a creative process, not as a mere filling in of semantic gaps. The *realisation*, Iser explains, is 'the reader's production of the meaning of the text'.[43] This is substantially more than what Ingarden was prepared to concede to the competence of the reader. As with the Czech Structuralists, the bulk of literary meaning shifts from the sphere of production to that of reception.

Meaning comes about in a process during which potential readers are incited by the author and the narrator to revise their expectations and to reconsider characters, actions, and situations in a new perspective. The motor of this permanent revision is a dialectic of *expectation* and *remembrance* (*protention* and *retention* in the sense of Husserl) which in all its aspects constitutes the process of reading.

Within this process, Iser's key concept, the *implied reader* (*der implizite Leser*), is defined as 'the role of the reader as incorporated in the novel'.[44] It is a dynamic role whose productive force is permanently being stimulated by the *indeterminacies* (*Leerstellen*, Iser) of the text. However, its dynamic character should not be confused with arbitrariness: 'It is here that the strategies play their part in laying down the lines along which the imagination is to run.'[45] In this context the *implied reader* is redefined as a textual element, that is as the ideal reader whom a given textual structure *requires*. One could also say that the ideal reader is the well-informed recipient who is able to realise optimally the semantic, narrative, and pragmatic potential of a text. Unlike the real historical or contemporary reader, unlike the fictive reader whom the author addresses in a novel[46], the *implied reader* is a theoretical construct without empirical existence, for he represents the entire potential of a text that may unfold in the course of the reading process. Hence the implied reader cannot be equated with empirical readers most of whom 'realise' merely those parts of the text structure which appeal to their particular aesthetic, psychic or social predispositions.

With the notion of *implied reader* which Iser introduced following W. Booth's theory of the *implied author*[47], he goes beyond Ingarden insofar as he considers the creativity of the reader on a par with that of the author. In conjunction with Thackeray's *Vanity Fair* he shows to what extent the criteria of social criticism which are not made explicit in the novel have to be reconstructed by the readership in accordance with the *repertoire* and the *textual strategies*. Their presence thus depends on the creativity of the perceiving imagination. However, there are limits to this imagination, and Iser, arguing along the lines of his *implied reader* theory, says about Sterne's *Tristram Shandy*: 'Obviously, his work allows for different approaches, all of which ought to be realised if possible – and not merely those which agree with one's own propensities.'[48]

Iser also differs from Ingarden as a historian of literature. It was pointed out earlier on that Ingarden pays little attention to the historicity of literature, considering it in a purely ontological and phenomenogical context. Unlike the Polish scholar, Iser adopts an innovative historical point of view when, in *The Implied Reader*, he describes the increase of indeterminacy from Bunyan to Beckett. Especially in the literature of modernism, he argues, indeterminacies such as narrative 'gaps', voluntary omissions, enigmatic allusions, and polysemies proliferate to such a degree that *concretisation* or *realisation* becomes a challenge to the reader. In Beckett's novels, in Joyce's *Ulysses* or *Finnegans Wake*, allusions and polysemies abound, and the narrator hardly ever explains anything: the readers are left to their own devices.

Iser's programmatic remark concerning the historical increase of indeterminacies is quite clear: 'We have to explain the increase of indeterminacy which can be observed since the eighteenth century in literary texts.'[49] Unfortunately, his attempts to explain this phenomenon in a historical context are hardly convincing. He argues, among other things, that an essential function of literature consists in providing answers to those metaphysical and ethical questions which are left open by philosophical, political, religious, and scientific systems. In this context one might ask in what respect the increase of indeterminacy could be read as an answer 'to those questions which are raised by these systems'[50]. Iser's own answer is somewhat disappointing: he takes indeterminacy in literature to mean that the certainties we are looking for in order to satisfy 'our elementary needs'[51] are negated by modern literature. But to what extent is this negation a literary reaction to contemporary political, scientific or religious systems? Iser does not really answer this question.

He could have pointed out that these systems are full of rather unconvincing answers and that the function of modern literature therefore consists in rediscovering the blanks or open questions which are being glossed over by ideologues. But he does not argue along these lines. Like Ingarden's phenomenology his approach suffers from a sociological deficit which is partly due to the fact that problems of ideology, domination, and communication in a postmodern market society are not dealt with. Hence it is hardly surprising that the socio-historical function or dysfunction of literature cannot be adequately explained.

3 Stanley Fish's Alternative

Fish's alternative can best be understood as a reaction to the kind of phenomenological criticism developed by Iser. While Iser, as was pointed out earlier on, sets out to trace the textual structures (*repertoires, strategies*) which guide and limit the creativity of readers, Fish (1989) is strongly opposed to the idea that there are structures inherent in texts and discerned by all competent individuals. There can be no dialectic, he argues, between structures and readers, between the object and the perceiving subject, because textual structures are in no way objective. He simply denies the possibility to distinguish 'between what is already given and what must be brought into being by interpretive activity'.[52]

According to Fish, there can be no dialogue between text and reader, because the reader 'supplies *everything*'.[53] The textual meaning is not due to constants within the object but entirely dependent on the reading process: 'The stars in a literary text are not fixed; they are just as variable as the lines that join them.'[54] In other words, readers are entirely responsible for the constitution of meaning, and their activities cannot be checked or controlled by a recourse to objective features. Inevitably the question crops up *what* readers react to and *what* they actually read if nothing can be said about the object.

Fish tries to make his point by criticising Iser's interpretation of Allworthy in Fielding's *Tom Jones*, an interpretation adopted by Iser in order to explain the possible reactions of the reader. Here is Iser's text:

> Allworthy is introduced to us as a perfect man, but he is at once brought face to face with a hypocrite, Captain Blifil, and is completely taken in by the latter's feigned piety. Clearly, then, the signifiers are not meant solely to designate perfection. On the contrary, they denote instructions to the reader to build up the signified which presents not a quality of perfection, but in fact a vital defect. Allworthy's lack of judgment.[55]

Iser's idea is quite plausible: he believes that competent readers will revise their judgement concerning Allworthy, as soon as they realise that he is incapable of recognising hypocrisy.

However, Fish, who has a very different notion of plausibility and of perfection, argues as follows: 'But one can easily imagine a reader for whom perfection is inseparable from the vulnerability displayed by Allworthy, and for such a reader there would be no disparity between the original description of Allworthy and his subsequent behavior.'[56] This also implies that such a reader would only perceive continuity where Iser revealed a contradiction or 'gap' between Allworthy's 'perfection' and his 'lack of judgement'. Fish obviously tries to prove that Iser's reading does not impose itself universally for structural reasons and that – consequently – meaning is to be found exclusively in the reading process and not in the text.

Unfortunately, Fish's train of thought is neither very convincing in this particular case, nor, as will appear later on, in general. To define 'perfection' as being 'inseparable from vulnerability', i.e. lack of judgement, is quite unusual, to say the least. For *perfect* (Lat. *perficere, perfectus* = *complete, made complete*) indicates a faultless totality without lacks or deficiencies (the Dutch translation *volmaaktheid* = *completion* further confirms this notion of perfection). Transposed into the realm of international politics, Fish's argument would mean that Chamberlain's 'perfection' could be seen as 'inseparable from his vulnerability': from his inability to see through Hitler's hypocrisy. However, Churchill, who had a lot more common sense than the theoretician Fish, defined and denounced it quite correctly as incompetence (i.e. the opposite of perfection). Iser's argument would most certainly be confirmed within structural semiotics (cf. chap. 6), where Allworthy's 'lack of judgement' would also appear as 'incompetence' or as a lack of *savoir faire*: a lack which turns his perfection into mere appearance.

It is interesting to observe that Fish's theory was not always as radically reader-oriented as in his critique of Iser's approach and in his later works. In one of his most important theoretical articles entitled 'Literature in the Reader' (1970), Fish still believes that the reader's reactions can somehow be related to textual features (although he does not say how): 'The argument in "Literature in the Reader"', he explains later on, 'is mounted (or so it is announced) on behalf of the reader and against the self-sufficiency of the text, but in the course of it the text becomes more and more powerful, and rather than being liberated, the reader finds himself more constrained in his new prominence than he was before.'[57]

It is difficult to see in what respect the reader is constrained in Fish's article, which revolves around three basic arguments: 1. the meaning of a text is not objectively given, as the New Critics would have it, but develops in the course of the reading process; 2. the critique of the so called *affective fallacy* (cf. chap. 2) is itself a fallacy, precisely because the response of the reader is decisive in the formation of literary meaning; 3. readers do not respond to the text as static totality, but adjust and re-adjust their interpretations from verse to verse, from narrative sequence to narrative sequence, from sentence to sentence. Meaning as a dynamic component of the reading process thus appears as being in permanent flux: as an open process which cannot be pinned down to a conceptual system or a logical definition. So far Fish's particular version of the Kantian maxim 'without concept'.

However, this 'extreme Kantianism' suffers from a major flaw which seems to have escaped Fish's attention. He focuses almost exclusively on the non-professional reader without ever analysing the institutionally and theoretically relevant difference between the literary scholar, the literary critic, and informed readers at large. For him the experience of the average informed reader is decisive and seems to have become the norm for the constitution of meaning: 'The system of correspondences yielded by a structuralist analysis are not necessarily perceived or attended by the reader (. . .).'[58] But this means neither that structural analysis is impossible or irrelevant nor that readers do not perceive and understand texts along structural lines. They simply do it in an unsystematic, spontaneous manner, observed by both semioticians and phenomenologists like Greimas and Ingarden.[59]

A similar argument applies to the distinction between professionals and non-professionals in medicine, geology, linguistics, and anthropology. No matter how long they peer into an electronic microscope, non-professionals will not recognise viruses or bacteria (they may appear to them as spots, dots or stripes but not as the specific objects a medical scientist is interested in). The tourist will admire the colours of rocks and stones without being able to decipher their geological meaning. Closer to literature, the linguist will recognise grammatical or discursive structures which most readers are not aware of. And finally, the average tourist will merely perceive a colourful dance where the anthropologist recognises a mourning ritual.

These examples show that the informed reader around whose experience Fish builds his theory is not the relevant instance. Naturally, Fish would disagree, simply because he has long since given up the idea of a scientific literary theory which also elicits scathing remarks from deconstructionists (cf. chap. 7), some of whom (e.g. G. H. Hartman) would like to dissolve theory in creative writing. However, such fashionable extremisms should not distract from the fact that many forms of literary theory (literary semiotics, sociology of literature, literary anthropology) clearly belong to the social sciences spectrum and can be treated accordingly.

Implicitly even Fish seems to recognise this fact when he puts forward his crucial argument: namely the idea that the reading process is being permanently shielded against arbitrariness by virtue of the reader's membership in an *interpretive community*, i.e. in a collective with shared norms and values: 'Indeed, it is the interpretive communities, rather than either the text or the reader, that produce meanings and are responsible for the emergence of formal features.'[60] In other words, the stability of meaning is guaranteed by the latter's origin in social collectives. Fish (naively) believes that their collective nature puts meanings beyond arbitrariness and subjectivism, 'because they do not proceed from an isolated individual but from a public and conventional point of view'.[61]

This argument is unsatisfactory for two reasons: 1. the fact that certain meanings do not proceed from an individual but from a group, does not make them less subjective, or less arbitrary, for it is a well-known fact that collectives such as political parties or religious sects are quite capable of propagating the most absurd ideas and of having reasonable individuals eliminated who query these ideas. The public or conventional character of a point of view does not make it plausible or rational, as Galileo's plight with the Church shows. 2. The second reason is closely related to the first: if interpretation and the resulting meaning are based on collective positions, then there will be as many meanings (interpretations) as there are groups.

Fish casually dismisses the second argument, saying that it is both 'unassailable' and 'irrelevant': 'So that while it is generally true that to have many standards is to have none at all, it is not true for anyone in particular (for there is no one in a position to speak "generally"), and it is a truth of which one can say "it doesn't matter".'[62] But if this truth doesn't matter, one begins to wonder what the whole discussion was about. How are we to understand Fish's initial argument that the reader 'supplies *everything*', if there is nothing to supply, because collective meanings are as subjective and arbitrary as individual ones? At the end of the day, everything seems to dissolve in arbitrariness and relativism: for each liberal, each Marxist, and each feminist belongs to a particular readership and will simply adhere to her or his particular and relatively arbitrary truth. It becomes clear at this stage that Fish's theory – if it is one – does not solve any of the most pressing problems. However, the problem of *scientific collectivities* is important and will be discussed again in the last chapter.

CHAPTER 5
From Marxism to Critical Theory and Postmodernism

More often than not the Critical Theory (*Kritische Theorie*) of the so-called Frankfurt School is associated or simply identified with Marxism.[1] Although nobody will deny that certain essential similarities exist, because the authors of Critical Theory use some of the key Marxist concepts, such as late capitalism, reification, alienation, exchange value, and domination, crucial differences ought not to be overlooked. Critical Theory in general and Theodor W. Adorno's brand in particular contain numerous elements which are quite incompatible with Hegelian Marxism: the idea that history, far from being a process of emancipation from class domination, is a fatal progression towards catastrophe; the complementary idea that a critical theory of society should not become involved in the ongoing class struggle (unity of theory and practice), but should stay aloof from particular interests and express the global negativity of capitalism; finally the idea that it is not the revolutionary class (the proletariat) that articulates true, unalienated consciousness, but the isolated intellectual. From a Marxist or Marxist-Leninist point of view, this is of course heresy – a heresy, however, which has turned out to be a lot more realistic and open to new insights than the official Marxist creed.

So far, capitalism has survived Marxism, and the bankruptcy of official Marxism-Leninism confirms Adorno's idea that the latter was just another ideology. This also applies to Socialist Realism which Adorno always rejected, arguing that before he accepted the style of Socialist Realism he would prefer art to disappear altogether. However, it does not apply to the Marxist theories of the Hungarian philosopher and politician György Lukács (1885-1971) and to his Romanian-French disciple Lucien Goldmann (1915-1970). Both thinkers have the crucial merit of having contributed to the development of a Marxist aesthetic (sociology of literature) which Marx and Engels had mapped out in scattered writings in a rudimentary and somewhat unsatisfactory form. It is by and large a Hegelian aesthetic which foregrounds the conceptual aspects of art, neglecting its ambiguity, its polysemic openness.

Unlike the Hegelians Lukács and Goldmann, Adorno and his friend Walter Benjamin are very critical of aesthetic conceptualisation and tend to emphasise the irreducible ambiguity of art. They analyse the mimetic, non-conceptual aspects of language and show to what extent the latter resists integration into theoretical discourse. Although their positions differ in many respects, both Adorno and Benjamin oscillate between the Hegelian urge to define the conceptual *truth content* (*Wahrheitsgehalt*, Adorno) of art and the Kantian refusal to conceptualise. This is indeed a paradoxical stance, and the whole of Adorno's discourse is geared towards the figure of the paradox. It is nonetheless incompatible with the aporias of Deconstruction (as will be shown in the seventh chapter), because it never renounces the search for truth. In spite of this Hegelian slant, Adorno's aesthetics can be read as a permanent polemic against Hegel, especially against Hegel's idea that artistic truth can be subsumed under the conceptual truth of philosophy (science) which will, in the course of history, supersede artistic production altogether. Adorno turns this doctrine upside down, arguing that art is the ultimate repository of truth in a media society marked by distorted communication.

Like Benjamin and Adorno, the Russian theoretician Mikhail M. Bakhtin ought to be understood as a critic of Hegelian aesthetics in their Marxist-Leninist guise. In this sense he can be read as a follower of the Young Hegelians (Vischer, Feuerbach, Stirner) who challenged the authority of Hegel's system in the second half of the 19th century. In what follows, it will be shown that Bakhtin's revolt against the Neohegelian aesthetics of Socialist Realism accounts, at least in part, for the Young Hegelian bias in his thought and for the typological affinities (analogies) between his philosophy and the philosophies of Friedrich Theodor Vischer, Max Stirner, and Ludwig Feuerbach. However, Bakhtin's 'Young Hegeliansm' is not simply based on analogies or similarities, for it is a well-known fact that the Russian author was familiar with Vischer's theory of the grotesque, the theological work of David

Friedrich Strauss, and other Young Hegelian writings which are more or less overt critiques of religion, official philosophy, and the Prussian state.

This Young Hegelian context, which will be outlined later on, is also relevant to the understanding of Walter Benjamin's theory of society and artistic production. Like the Young Hegelians and Bakhtin he realised that the classical and romantic periods had come to an end and that – after 1848, the year of the French July-Revolution – the contours of a new artistic paradigm were discernible: the contours of modern art which could no longer be understood within Hegel's classicist conception of the harmonious totality. On the contrary, Baudelairian and avant-garde art, which Benjamin focused on, was fiercely opposed to totality, synthesis, harmony, conceptual unity, and other Hegelian notions. It was geared towards disharmony, disruption, fragmentation, and the experience of shock.

Benjamin's attempt to relate all of these phenomena to the every day experience of modern industrial society is one of the salient features of his modernist aesthetics, which is comparable to Bakhtin's by virtue of its emphasis on disharmony, ambivalence, and plurality.

The discussion of Jameson's, Eagleton's, and Callinicos' Marxist critique of postmodern art at the end of this chapter has a contrastive function. It is a – relatively modest – attempt to explain how Marxist aesthetics and literary theory have changed within the postmodern constellation. It will become clear that the humanist, critical or revolutionary functions of art which were paramount in Lukács', Goldmann's, Adorno's, and Benjamin's writings have lost most of their credibility in a postmodern set-up where art is increasingly becoming integrated into what Adorno and Horkheimer used to call the *culture industry* (*Kulturindustrie*).

1 Marx, Lukács, and Goldmann: Hegelian Aesthetics
In spite of the fact that Althusser and his disciples have tried to dissociate Marx's work from Hegel's dialectic, arguing that *Capital* founded a new scientific (historical) paradigm in the sense of Galileo's physics, Marx's and Engels' Hegelian heritage is a commonplace of Marxist philosophy.[2] Considering the numerous links between Hegel and the Young Hegelian Marx, who was

supposed to review Friedrich Theodor Vischer's *Ästhetik* in 1857, the Hegelian or Neohegelian character of Marx's theory of art is not surprising. It develops three fundamental ideas of Hegel's *Aesthetics*: the *historical perspective*, the emphasis on artistic *production*, and the definition of the work of art as a *sensuous articulation of the idea*.

Although they are embedded in a materialist context in Marx's work, all three ideas retain their Hegelian character insofar as they converge in the assumption that works of art can be conceptualised as univocal expressions of different types of historical consciousness. However, like Hegel, Marx and Engels are anxious to point out that literary works are not conceptual systems and hence ought not to be confused with philosophy or science. In the famous *Sickingen Debate* (1859) for example, in the course of which Marx and Engels blame the writer and politician Ferdinand Lassale for having transformed his hero Franz von Sickingen into a mouthpiece of his own social theory, it becomes quite clear that Marx's and Engels' aesthetic follows Hegel's postulate that art should primarily address the *senses* (*sinnliches Scheinen der Idee*).

This postulate is further developed by Friedrich Engels in a well-known letter to Minna Kautsky (26th November 1885), which praises Minna Kautsky's novel *Die Alten und die Neuen* for creating *typical characters*, i.e. characters which are typical of a particular socio-historical situation: 'Each of them is a type'[3], he observes and explains that this kind of synthesis between the general and the particular in the *type* is exactly what Hegel had always demanded. It will be shown later on that the typical as synthesis between the general and the particular, between essence and appearance is to be found at the center of Lukács' aesthetic theory. What S. S. Prawer writes about the typical or representative character in Marx's theory is also valid in the case of Lukács: 'Above all: the critic must ask himself whether a given fictional character is at once individual and representative.'[4]

Marx believes that the notary Jacques Ferrand in Eugène Sue's *Les Mystères de Paris* is a social type because he combines some individual features with the general characteristics of the Paris notary of the nineteenth century: a corrupt mentality behind a moral façade. Criticising Franz Zychlin's interpretation of *Les Mystères de Paris*, he explains that Zychlin naively mistakes the moral appearance for the real thing and considers Jacques Ferrand as a guardian of the moral order. He aptly points out that as a social type Sue's notary is simply an ideological device or mask which hides and justifies the money machine of capitalism.[5]

As a critique of ideology and of an abstract moralising idealism, Marx's theory has considerable merits that have not been diminished by the collapse of Marxism-Leninism – which in the course of time was also turned into an ideological façade by the ruling Nomenklatura. However, Marx's approach to literature reveals a crucial weakness of Hegelian aesthetics: the tendency to translate texts into conceptual statements and to reduce them subsequently to their denotative function. 'Marx', S. S. Prawer remarks, 'does not pay much attention to form and structure, but all the more to the novelist's and dramatist's evocation of character.'[6] One could specify that Marx is primarily interested in fictional characters as types because they help us understand a socio-historical context as a meaningful totality. In other words, he emphasises – like Hegel – the cognitive, not the aesthetic or *poetic* (Jakobson) function of literature.

This aspect of Marx's theory clearly comes to the fore in some of his comments on Balzac's *Comédie humaine* which he and Engels preferred to most theoretical texts as a source of socio-economic information. In this context Balzac's novel *Les Paysans* is read denotatively as an historical document which reveals the dependence of the average peasant on the usurer. Although it would be somewhat unfair to criticise Marx's literary comments in *Capital* (a treatise on capitalist economy, not on aesthetic theory), it is certainly true that all of these comments tend to conceptualise literature and to reduce it to its referential function. Art is perceived as a barometer of social change, not as a polysemic source of interpretation and reinterpretation.

Although it is difficult to find out whether Marx had actually read Hegel's lectures on aesthetics or how well he knew this posthumously published work[7], it can be assumed that he was familiar with Hegel's ideas on aesthetics and applied them in his own comments on art and literature. The following satirical verses (quoted by S. S. Prawer, p. 22) show to what extent Marx himself was aware of the Hegelian slant in his approach to aesthetics:

Verzeiht uns Epigrammendingen,
Wenn wir fatale Weisen singen,
Wir haben uns nach Hegel einstudiert,
Und sein' Ästhetik noch nicht – abgeführt.

(Pardon us creatures of epigram
If we sing unpleasant tunes;
We have learnt our lesson of Hegel
And are not purged of his aesthetic.)

In the case of György Lukács, the Hegelian bias is even more pronounced – and it is not mitigated by the ironical and satirical attitude which was dictated to Marx by his anti-Hegelian materialism. The most important work of the young Lukács, the *Theory of the Novel* (1920), is Hegelian insofar as it considers the break between subject and object, between consciousness and being as the central issue of the modern novel. Like Hegel, Lukács begins with the question how the alienated subject can bridge the gap between itself and the world. Unlike Hegel he refuses to bring about a reconciliation between subject and object by an apology of the real (an apology of the political system of the Prussian state), but projects it into a utopian future. In a critical preface written in the 1960s he points out that the fragmentary *Theory of the Novel* was the first work 'in which the findings of Hegelian Philosophy were concretely applied to aesthetic problems'.[8]

Unfortunately, the applications are not very concrete because the author tends to identify individual novels – such as Cervantes' *Don Quixote* and Flaubert's *Education sentimentale* – with types of consciousness that can ultimately be defined in terms of conceptual systems. In very much the same way as Hegel, he thus tends to equate the polysemic literary text with a univocally defined historical process.

In spite of his conversion to dialectical materialism in *History and Class Consciousness* (1923), Lukács remains a Hegelian at heart. For most of the articles published in this book converge towards the Hegelian idea that all social and historical phenomena ought to be understood as imbricated totalities forming one meaningful whole which evolves in the course of history. Unlike his disciple Lucien Goldmann who believes in a dialectic between the parts and the whole, arguing that they should elucidate each other mutually, the young Lukács remains faithful to Hegel's idea that the parts are subordinate to the totality and can only be understood within the latter.

This point of view implies – among other things – that social phenomena such as morals and art cannot claim any kind of autonomy but are part and parcel of a socio-historical totality defined by the philosopher. In *Der junge Hegel* (1948), possibly his most important work on Hegel, Lukács criticises the Kantian conception of ethical autonomy, according to which ethical postulates may contradict historical trends or political truths. As a Hegelian Marxist he believes that, far from being an autonomous realm, ethics are integrated in the socio-historical totality of the class struggle and hence part of politics. Within the aesthetic context he holds that art cannot be understood as an autonomous entity which pleases without concept, but has to be conceived of as an historical fact which signifies within a social totality. In his *Aesthetic* (*Die Eigenart des Ästhetischen*) he criticises Kant's philosophy, arguing that '*with its idea "without concept" it eliminates all rationality from aesthetics*' ('*daß sie (. . .) – mit der Konzeption "ohne Begriff" – aus der Ästhetik jede Ratio austreibt*'.).[9]

Unlike Kantians and Neokantians who believe that Kant acted very sensibly when he attempted to draw the limits of conceptual thought, postulating the autonomy of the aesthetic realm *vis-à-vis* the concept, Lukács blames him for banning reason from aesthetics, thus opening the door to irrationalism. In this controversy a great deal depends on how irrationalism is defined: should it be defined with Hegel and Lukács as a limitation of reason, as an attempt to restrict conceptual thought, or with Kant and the Kantians as conceptual totalitarianism which brutally annexes whatever it cannot understand? – This question points far beyond the problems of aesthetics and will be dealt with in some detail in the chapter on deconstruction.

In order to understand Lukács' theory of literary *reflexion* (*Widerspiegelung*) it is important to know, however, that he refuses to admit phenomena into his discourse which cannot be dealt with on a conceptual level. Like Hegel he distinguishes art and literature from philosophy by emphasising their sensuous aspects or, as he prefers to put it, their *anthropomorphic* character.

What he means is that art primarily addresses the senses, not that it cannot be translated into conceptual language. Literature, for example, addresses our senses by representing characters, their actions, emotions, and words; nevertheless, it can be translated into the conceptual discourse of philosophy: for it merely represents by non-conceptual means what the philosopher explains on a theoretical level. Literature thus appears as an *ancilla philosophiae*, especially since the incongruence between its *expression plane* and its *content plane* (discussed in chapter 1) is glossed over.

Lukács' theory of *realism* and of *realistic reflexion* is based on the assumption that good ('progressive') literature reveals the essence or truth of a particular socio-historical situation by creating typical characters, actions, and events: by *showing* the reader what the Marxist philosopher *explains* in theory. In his *Werther*-novel, Lukács says, Goethe does not simply create a problematic character who falls prey to his passions, but simultaneously represents the tragic situation of the German bourgeoisie towards the end of the eighteenth century. Like Werther, the unfortunate hero of the epistolary novel, this class appears incapable of extricating itself from its contradictions and fails to follow the emancipation movements of the British, the American, and the French bourgeoisie. In this light, the figure of Werther is defined as *typical* because it makes the aporias of the German bourgeoisie visible.

Similarly, Lukács considers Lucien de Rubempré, the hero of Balzac's novel *Illusions perdues* (1837-1839), as a typical example of the French writer of the early nineteenth century: 'With considerable finesse and audacity Balzac depicts the new, specifically bourgeois type of the poet (. . .).'[10] What is so specifically bourgeois about Lucien de Rubempré? The fact, explains Lukács, that he illustrates the commercialisation or 'commodification' of literature in a culture dominated by journalism and increasingly oriented towards market-mechanisms.

An analogous case in Lukács' work is Adrian Leverkühn, the hero of Thomas Mann's postwar novel *Doktor Faustus*: his fate – often compared with Nietzsche's – illustrates the isolation of the modern artist in the twentieth century. Far from being a simple eccentric, he exemplifies the fatal marginality of modern artists such as Schönberg, Van Gogh, Rimbaud, Joyce, and Kafka. The typical, as defined by Lukács, is therefore not the most frequently occurring phenomenon (the statistical average), but the general rule or trend made visible in a particular case. In his *Aesthetic*, Lukács explains: 'for only if the detail acquires a symptomatic character which marks and reveals the essential, is the object, as a rationally organised totality of details, projected onto the level of the Particular, the Typical.'[11]

The crucial concepts here are: *essence (Wesen)*, *rational (vernünftig)*, *totality (Totalität)*, and *typical (das Typische)*. Inevitably, the question crops up *who decides* whether a literary representation reveals the totality, the essence, and the typical or rational aspects of reality. What is reality and who defines it? These are decisive questions concerning all theories of realism. Lukács does not answer these questions explicitly, he answers them by a semiotic trick: by implicitly postulating an identity between his Marxist discourse and the real world.

This implicit postulate which also marks the discourse of Hegelian philosophy has far-reaching consequences: only litera-ture which can be interpreted as rational, essential, 'typical', and realistic *within* the semantic system of this discourse is acceptable. All other forms of literature are disqualified by Lukács as 'natu-ralistic' and 'abstract'. The word naturalistic is chosen to indicate that, with Zola's Naturalism, a literary style evolved which reproduces appearances without ever penetrating to the core, the essence of the matter, and without representing the typical within a rational totality that makes reality comprehensible and transparent. According to Lukács, Expressionism and modernism (Kafka, Proust, Joyce)[12] have inherited this 'naturalist' tendency towards appearance and incoherence which makes a concrete, i.e. totality-based understanding of reality impossible and remains entirely abstract. This is why he repeatedly accuses modernists and avant-garde authors of 'Naturalism'.

It will have become clear by now that Lukács can only be so dogmatic about modernism and the avant-garde (calling both literary currents 'decadent'), because he fails to perceive his own theory of realism as merely a *possible construction* based on a *particular discourse*. Assuming – with Hegel – that his own discourse faithfully reproduces the real, he is virtually compelled to condemn everything which does not conform to his own discursive practice. At the same time he canonises certain authors – Goethe, Sir Walter

Scott, Balzac, Thomas Mann – as founders of realism, tacitly assuming that his interpretations of these authors are the only possible ones. However, they are merely constructions (*aesthetic objects* or *concretisations* in the sense of Mukařovský and Ingarden), and it is perfectly possible – within the framework of a different discourse and a different construction – to interpret Thomas Mann as a modernist similar to Proust, Kafka, and Joyce. (The relationship between discourse, construction, and literary polysemy will be discussed in some detail in the last chapter.)

Time and again Lucien Goldmann has defined himself and has been defined as a disciple of Lukács.[13] This attempt to describe Goldmann's approach within a humanist Marxism should not be misunderstood. Although it is true that Goldmann's work is inspired by that of the Hungarian philosopher, it has to be specified that only the texts of the young Lukács (*The Soul and the Forms*, 1913, *The Theory of the Novel*, 1920, and *History and Class Consciousness*, 1923) have been acknowledged by Goldmann as having had an impact on his own thought, and not the publications of the 'old' Lukács which, as has been shown, develop a prescriptive and rather dogmatic aesthetic theory. Unlike this theory, Goldmann's brand of Marxism which he called *genetic structuralism* (*structuralisme génétique*) prescribes neither a realist reflexion nor a representation of types revealing the essence of the socio-historical context. Unlike the old Lukács, Goldmann never explicitly condemned the contemporary avant-garde nor the modernist tradition.

However, it would be somewhat naive to assume – as some of Goldmann's disciples seem to do[14] – that Goldmann's approach is a continuation of Lukács' early work and has little or nothing to do with his later writings and his theory of realism. For it is not difficult to discern the common denominator which links the works of the two authors: the Hegelian *category of totality*. In very much the same way as Lukács' and Marx's *type* (*Typus*), Goldmann's concept of *signifying structure* (*structure significative, structure mentale*) is a totality in both the Hegelian and the hermeneutic sense: it is meant to explain each individual part of a text in conjunction with the global context and understand the latter as a coherent whole mirrored partly or integrally by each of its elements. The meaning of an element, remarks Goldmann in *The Hidden God*, depends on the coherent structure of the work as a whole.[15] Unlike Hegel and Lukács (in *History and Class Consciousness*), who tend to subordinate the parts to the whole, Goldmann pleads in favour of a dialectical reciprocity in which the whole is explained by the parts and vice versa.

In his monumental study *The Hidden God* (Paris, 1955), Goldmann attempts to show that the *structure significative* underlying Blaise Pascal's *Pensées* and Jean Racine's tragedies is a paradoxical and tragic *innerworldly refusal* (*refus intramondain*) which makes the acting subjects of the *Pensées* and of Racine's tragedies (*Andromaque, Bérénice, Phèdre*) consciously reject a world in which they are compelled to live. He believes that each of Pascal's maxims is geared towards this structure and that each of Racine's tragedies obeys its laws. In Racine's tragedy *Phèdre*, where a compromise with the worldly authorities seems possible and imminent at one point, the heroine soon recognises the futility of such a solution and adheres to the tragic refusal that leads to her death. Her life – like that of other Racinian characters – is a life torn apart by the demands of the gods and those of a depraved social world.

Goldmann explains this tragic structure of Racinian drama by relating it to a conceptual, theological discourse: the Jansenist doctrine propounded by the Flemish theologian Jansenius (Jansen) and later on adoped and developed by the theologians and philosophers of the monastery of Port-Royal (Saint-Cyran, Arnauld d'Andilly, Antoine Le Maître) whose thought had a considerable impact on that of Pascal and Racine. Jansenist theology as a *world vision* (*vision du monde, Weltanschauung*) thus appears to be at the origin of the tragic structure, the *innerworldly refusal* underlying Pascal's *Pensées* and most of Racine's theatre.

The importance and function of Jansenist theology as a *vision du monde* is in turn explained in conjunction with the political marginalisation of a social group in seventeenth century French society: the *noblesse de robe*. This group of bourgeois origin whose support was vital for the survival of the French monarchy while it was engaged in a perilous struggle against the feudal lords, lost its importance and its power (anchored in the provincial parliaments) as soon as Louis XIV gained the upper hand in his conflict with the nobility and no longer needed his bourgeois allies. At this point, tragic Jansenism came to fulfil a crucial function: it justified the withdrawal of the *noblesse de robe* from public life and the concomitant *innerworldly refusal* of the social world as a whole. The latter was considered corrupt by thinkers such as Pascal, Saint-Cyran, and Martin de Barcos and its laws incompatible with the beliefs and principles of a true Christian. However, all of the radical Jansenists were compelled by the sheer factuality of their existence to recognise the inevitability of life in a world inacceptable to them.

Goldmann believes that this paradoxical and tragic situation is expressed in a particularly coherent manner by Pascal's *Pensées* and Racine's tragedies. 'Expressed' is here the key word, for the interpretations in *The Hidden God* are based on the assumption that literary works ought to be read as coherent totalities in the Hegelian sense and that especially 'great' works express univocally *world visions* (*visions du monde*), i.e. conceptual systems that are responsible for their coherence.

At the same time Goldmann postulates a *functional homology* between the structure of a work and the world vision on the one hand and the socio-historical position of a group such as the *noblesse de robe* on the other. In *The Hidden God* the *noblesse de robe* adopts so to speak the tragic vision of Jansenism in order to explain the world and to justify its action: its withdrawal from the political scene. This withdrawal is enacted in Racine's theatre whenever the hero acting under the eye of the gods, prefers death to a compromise with the corrupt world.

According to Goldmann, great works of philosophy and art, which have the merit of expressing the world visions of social groups in a particularly coherent form, thus contribute to the capacity of these groups to interpret reality in accordance with their problems and needs. In other words, a work of art fulfils, in very much the same way as a philosophical text, an orienting function which is mainly due to its drive towards coherence and totality. It is not by chance that in his major work Goldmann reads philosophical and literary texts as comparable expressions of Jansenist theology without asking himself to what extent polysemic literature emancipates itself in the course of history from the biographical or social context of its production. Has Racine not been applauded in the course of the eighteenth, nineteenth, and twentieth centuries by generations of spectators who have never heard of Jensenist theology? Has Planchon not enacted *Bérénice* as a modern play?

None of these questions seem to matter in Goldmann's approach which – like Hegel's and Lukács' aesthetics – is geared towards the *genetic* problems of art. This is why he decided to call his method *'genetic structuralism'* (*'structuralisme génétique'*) in order to distinguish it from the a-historical, synchronic perspective of the Saussurians, who – according to his critique – are quite unable to answer the question *why* certain forms of art appear (are produced) in a particular socio-historical context. Although Goldmann's critique is not beside the point (unlike Saussure, Claude Lévi-Strauss has explicitly rejected the genetic approach)[16], his own brand of structuralism tends to reduce literary texts to conceptual systems, to univocal messages and to disregard their capacity to generate new and contradictory meanings in the course of time: a capacity analysed by Russian Formalists, Czech Structuralists, and reader-response criticism all over the world.

The idea that Goldmann's theory apparently contradicts Lukács' prescriptive, neo-classicist aesthetic should not divert our attention from the fact that his somewhat uncritical adoption of Hegel's and Lukács' category of totality is incompatible with the experiments of modernism and the European avant-garde movements. What he has to say about Samuel Beckett's work shows to what extent he continues to apply Hegelian and classicist concepts to an experimental discourse which turned against the classical and the Hegelian traditions: 'I shall probably succeed in demonstrating that this work, if it is great, integrates the antagonisms, the difficulties, and the ruptures in a global vision of the world which can be reduced to a system.'[17] Coherence may be the ideal of all Hegelians; it was certainly not Beckett's ideal.

But how, one may ask, would Goldmann have reacted if in the course of textual analysis he had discovered that Beckett's dramas and prose do not integrate antagonisms, difficulties, and ruptures, because the author and his narrators modestly choose to enact their modernist or postmodernist agnosticism? He may have been compelled to follow Lukács and to condemn Beckett as an incoherent or even decadent writer . . . The Hegelian category of totality does not leave much room for aesthetic manoeuvering.

*2 Benjamin and Adorno between Kant and Hegel: Avant-Garde,
Ambiguity, and Truth*

At the beginning of this chapter, it was already pointed out that
Critical Theory in the sense of Walter Benjamin and Theodor W.
Adorno cannot be dealt with under the label 'Marxism'. While
Benjamin in his later writings develops a materialist theory of
history and art inspired by Jewish Messianism, Adorno cautiously
oscillates between Kant and Hegel whenever he deals with the
relationship between art and philosophy and with the conceptual
aspects of art. Unlike Hegel, Marx, Lukács, and Goldmann, Benjamin and Adorno never really believed in history as a process of
cumulative emancipation. On the contrary, they tended to regard
history as a progression towards disaster. Their sceptical attitude
towards human evolution was not only inspired by the First and the
Second World War, Fascism, and National Socialism, but – in the
case of Adorno – also by the political stalemate which marked the
confrontation between the capitalist and the Stalinist blocs after the
Second World War. In this situation, Adorno found it impossible
to believe in a revolutionary liberation of humanity by the working
class. Instead of searching for a revolutionary consciousness in
post-war consumer society (as Herbert Marcuse tirelessly did)[18],
he retreated into the aesthetic realm. In the Sixties art appeared
to him as the guardian of a type of reason that had not yet been
usurped and instrumentalised by power-seeking technocrats.

Adorno owes this type of thought to his older friend Walter
Benjamin, who turned against all Hegelian and Marxist attempts
to dominate nature and to assimilate the objective world to the
discourse of the thinking subject. One of his main philosophical
pursuits was to study the *'language of things'* (*'Sprache der Dinge'*)[19],
thus revealing the subjective dimension of the objective world, a
dimension completely neglected by Hegel who tended to reduce
the object to the concepts of the philosophical subject. Rolf
Tiedemann is quite clear on this point: 'Unlike Hegel, who
identifies the concept and its object, deducing the latter from
the former, Benjamin insists on the dignity of phenomena.'[20] In
other words: the discourse of philosophy must be prevented from
equating the objective world with its concepts; it should respect the
particularity of things.

In this context, it is hardly surprising that – like the Young

Hegelian F. Th. Vischer before him (chap. 1.2) – he seeks counsel in Kant's philosophy in order to avoid the identifying mechanisms of Hegel's discourse. In his important essay 'Über das Programm der kommenden Philosophie' ('The Programme of Future Philosophy'), he sketches a philosophical theory which takes into account the unbridgeable gap between subject and object, between thought and reality, revealed by Kant and glossed over by Hegel.

In the linguistic realm these attempts to preserve the autonomy of the object lead to a strong emphasis on the *expression plane* (Hjelmslev) or the *signifier*, as Saussurians would say. According to Benjamin, even in language there is a rest which escapes conceptualisation and which only thinking in 'configurations', 'constellations', '*thought images*' ('*Denkbildern*') or allegories may hope to capture. This mode of thought had a lasting influence on Adorno who later appropriated Benjamin's word 'configuration'. Less rational than Adorno, Benjamin blames Humboldt and Hegel for overlooking the '*magic aspect of language*' ('*die magische Seite der Sprache*').[21]

Although it will never be quite clear what he means by this, it is probably correct to assume that he aims at the non-conceptual residues in language and in human life as a whole. For in an article 'About the Mimetic Ability' ('Über das mimetische Vermögen') he stresses the mimetic origin of human actions (in ritual dance, in painting and hunting) in order to reveal a mimetic alternative to the conceptual domination of the world propagated by rationalists and Hegelians alike. Hence *mimesis* is not conceived as imitation or reflexion of the real (as in Lukács' case), but as an *assimilation to the object*, as becoming similar to the thing itself. It should be emphasised, however, that neither Benjamin nor Adorno ever envisaged an irrational abandonment of conceptual thought; they simply believed that it is irrational to negate the non-conceptual and non-rational elements of language and of life in a rationalist manner.

Within this philosophical perspective it is easier to understand why Benjamin's aesthetic theory combines three elements, all of which are anti-Hegelian: rejection of classicism (of classical harmony), rejection of conceptualism (literary texts as coherent totalities in the sense of Lukács and Goldmann), and a revolutionary orientation towards the experiment of the European avant-garde. It becomes clear at this stage that Benjamin's materialism which in later writings is often substantiated by quotations from Marx, has little to do with Lukács' Hegelian Marxism, which is so hostile to modernism and the avant-garde movements.

Benjamin's rejection of the classical ideal of a harmonious totality marks virtually all of his writings on Baudelaire and what he calls 'die Moderne' (early modernist art and literature). What are the salient traits of the modern era in literature, in art? According to Benjamin, one of them is the experience of *shock*: a sudden coincidence of elements that are usually kept apart. It is a coincidence which, as will be shown later on, is comparable to M. M. Bakhtin's description of carnival: an event in the course of which the noble and the vile, the holy and the profane, the tragic and the comic, life and death are brought together in explosive mixtures causing shock, laughter or both at the same time.

Analysing Baudelaire's style, Benjamin shows, for example, that the poet combines Romantic features with those of Realism and that he introduces an urban, mundane, and technical vocabulary into the discourse of lyrical poetry, a vocabulary scrupulously avoided by Romantics such as Lamartine: *quinquet, wagon, omnibus*. The sudden coincidence of apparently incompatible aspects of life is considered to be another characteristic of Baudelaire's poetry and of his work as a whole:

> Analyse des contre-religions, exemple: la prostitution sacrée.
> Qu'est-ce que la prostitution sacrée?
> Excitation nerveuse.
> Mysticité du paganisme.
> Le mysticisme, trait d'union entre le paganisme et le christianisme.
> Le paganisme et le christianisme se prouvent réciproquement.
> La révolution et le culte de la Raison prouvent l'idée du sacrifice.
> La superstition est le réservoir de toutes les vérités.[22]

The Nietzschean idea (conceived independently of Nietzsche) that 'superstition is the reservoir of all truths' brings about a sudden coincidence of opposites which shocks the reader who is used to the institutionalised separation of 'superstition' and 'truth'. A similar shock comes about in the Surrealist *collage* which frequently combines heterogeneous contexts, rigidly kept apart, separated in daily life; or in Bertolt Brecht's Epic Theatre where the course of action is suddenly interrupted by an actor's commentary or by a gesture quite unforeseen by the spectators.

In all of these cases Benjamin recognises symptoms of a modern era: an era which tends to destroy the harmonious totality of the Classical and the Romantic periods. The radical critique of holistic harmony in Baudelaire's poetry, Breton's Surrealism, and Brecht's drama implies a break with Lukács' and Goldmann's Hegelian ideal of an aesthetic totality that can be translated into a conceptual system. Goldmann's idea (mentioned above) that Beckett's work 'integrates the antagonisms, the difficulties, and the ruptures in a global vision of the world which can be reduced to a system' is diametrically opposed to Benjamin's avant-garde aesthetics. Benjamin would have emphasised the incongruencies, ruptures, and shocks in Beckett's texts.

In his theory of art, modernist and avant-garde *shock* (*Schock-erlebnis*) entails what he calls the *destruction of aura*. In his well-known essay on 'The Work of Art in the Age of Mechanical Reproduction' (1933), he distinguishes *auratic* and *mechanical* art arguing that the former is traditional in character and closely linked to the sacred object of religious rituals. Such an object combines two essential features: it is *unique* and kept at a *distance* from the onlooker, pilgrim or worshipper. Good examples are certain Russian icons, such as the Black Madonna of Vladimir, or the Polish Black Madonna of Częstochowa. They are unique as originals and only accessible to those who are not daunted by long and cumbersome travel. This combination of uniqueness and distance which constitutes what Benjamin calls *aura* is destroyed in mechanical modern art such as photography and film, which are entirely based on reproduction, repetition, and a *rapprochement* between the aesthetic object and a mass public.

This elimination of uniqueness and distance can also be under-stood metaphorically and applied to literature. Classical, Romantic, and even High Modernist literature preserved a certain *aura* by virtue of excluding the masses and addressing a cultural elite. One could also say that this kind of literature stayed at an auratic distance from the masses. What fascinates Benjamin in the avant-garde movements, especially in Surrealism, is their attempt to close the gap between art and society and to project artistic experience into everyday life. About Breton's Nadja, Benjamin writes: 'Nadja is an exponent of these masses and of that which inspires them in a revolutionary sense.'[23] In other words: Benjamin believes that Breton's experimental text eliminates the distance that separates traditional literature from everyday life. It is difficult to share this belief in a society which has institutionalised Surrealism in museums, libraries, and university seminars as a somewhat esoteric and elitist practice.

Nevertheless, some theoreticians of postmodernism such as Scott Lash consider Benjamin and the Surrealists as precursors of a postmodern art which absorbs 'popular' elements, thus trying to bridge the gap between 'high brow' and 'popular' aesthetics. Scott Lash writes: 'Benjamin's valuation of popular cultural products, which can envisage critique from an aesthetic dimension that is integral to the social, is consistent with a *post*modernist aesthetic.'[24]

Unfortunately he overlooks the fact that the 'popularisation' of art had a certain meaning in the Thirties that is no longer valid in our Fin-de-siècle. Benjamin could still hope that an artistic production (Epic Theatre, film) geared towards mass reception would function as a catalyst in the revolutionary process both he and Brecht believed in: it would help to trigger off the proletarian revolution Benjamin was hoping for in a messianic spirit. Any attempt at resuscitating this hope in a postmodern market society is bound to fail. At present, the 'popularisation' of art has a rather different meaning: far from being revolutionary it merely accelerates the integration of art into commerce, into what Adorno and Horkheimer call *Kulturindustrie*. It is not by chance that Adorno criticised Benjamin's theory of the 'destruction of aura' and of artistic 'reproduction' as a potential concession to the market forces of late capitalism.[25]

Unlike Benjamin who combined Kantian with messianic and avant-garde elements in an aesthetic theory marked by the experiments of the Expressionist and Surrealist movements, Adorno attacked Hegelian classicism and conceptualism by a partial return to Kant and Croce. Martin Zenck sums up Adorno's aesthetic position in one sentence when he remarks: 'One could argue that

Adorno's *Aesthetic Theory* is a mobilisation of Kant against Hegel.'[26] This means primarily that Adorno rejects the Hegelian (Lukácsian, Goldmannian) attempt to conceptualise reality, thus subjecting it to the domination of the knowing subject. He follows Kant by tracing the limits of knowledge and subjectivity: the limits to conceptual appropriation of reality by the subject.

He criticises Hegel for having attempted a reconciliation between the philosophical subject and objective reality by *identifying* the latter with conceptual knowledge, i.e. with his own philosophical system which becomes a substitute for the real. Like the Young Hegelians Vischer, Feuerbach, and Ruge, Adorno protests that this *identification of thought and reality* (*Identitätsdenken*, Adorno, Horkheimer) is characteristic of a repressive idealism which presumptuously negates the contradictions, idiosyncrasies, and polysemies of the real world.

The syntheses of the Hegelian system which are meant to *overcome* (*aufheben*) the contradictions of society are pseudo-syntheses, according to Adorno, that merely conceal social antagonisms instead of resolving them. Although he approves of the Young Hegelian and Marxian criticism of Hegel's conception of history as a permanent progression towards freedom and the self-realisation of the human subject, he nevertheless blames Marx and Engels for having 'deified' History ('*Vergottung der Geschichte*')[27] in spite of their atheism.

Adorno's alternative to Hegel's and Marx's models of a historical dialectic based on the idea of progressive human emancipation is a *negative dialectic*: 'Such dialectics is negative. Its idea names the difference from Hegel. In Hegel there was coincidence of identity and positivity; the inclusion of all nonidentical and objective things in a subjectivity expanded and exalted into an absolute spirit was to effect the reconcilement.'[28] To this repressive reconciliation of subject and object Adorno opposes a negative dialectic, the essential elements of which were sketched at the beginning of this chapter: a refusal to identify subject and object (*Nichtidentität*); a rejection of the Marxist 'unity of theory and practice'; a refusal to consider history as a process of emancipation.

It is above all the refusal to identify the subject of philosophical knowledge with the objective world that brings forth a philosophical discourse similar to Benjamin's: a discourse sceptical of conceptualisation and inspired by *mimesis*, by the non-conceptual elements in language. The non-conceptual, mimetic moment is inherent in art and literature which in Adorno's and Horkheimer's *Dialectic of Reason* (1947) are considered as alternatives to the conceptual domination of rationalist discourse, especially to the discourse of Enlightenment (*Aufklärung*).

If one were to express Adorno's project of a negative dialectic as succinctly as possible, one could say that he envisaged a 'non-theoretical' theory: a theory inspired by music and literature, in particular by the mature poetry of Friedrich Hölderlin, which gave birth to Adorno's concept of *parataxis*.[29] Other key concepts such as *constellation* and *configuration* which Adorno owes to Benjamin (see above) are meant to reinforce the mimetic impulse of theoretical discourse, so that the particularity of the analysed phenomena is not dissolved in conceptual abstraction. In his early works Adorno believed, as did Benjamin, that a *constellation* (*configuration*) of arguments and perspectives is more suitable for understanding particular phenomena than a conceptual system in the sense of Hegel.

Later on he sought to model his discourse on intermediate forms situated between theory and literature such as the essay, hoping to do justice to the particular feature and the individual being, both of which were threatened by the streamlining effects of the (Comtian, Hegelian) system. In order to counter these effects, Adorno devised a thought based on the particular *model* which he developed in the *Negative Dialectic* (1966) and which at one time he considered as the best way of approaching reality without reducing its particularities to the abstractions of the subjective concept. Eventually, he decided to abandon the idea of the model and replaced it by *parataxis*: by a paratactic (i.e. non-hypotactic, non-hierarchical) way of writing which he developed in his posthumously published *Aesthetic Theory* (1970) and which in some respects is a return to the early idea of *constellation* or *configuration*. Parataxis is a configurative discourse that groups arguments in an associative, essayistic manner instead of organising them inductively or deductively within a hierarchical system.

The sketches of Benjamin's and Adorno's conceptions of theory show to what extent both authors are strangers within the Marxist debate. Benjamin's messianic and avant-garde aspirations have always irritated Marxists who turned out to be even more hostile to Adorno's attempts to use literary models (especially Hölderlin's poetry) for a new foundation and re-orientation of theoretical discourse.

It is essential to take this re-orientation into account in order to grasp Adorno's literary essays and his *Aesthetic Theory*. For the latter should be read parallel to his writings on the theory of knowledge: like other phenomena, the work of art cannot be univocally defined by concepts, as Hegel, Lukács, and Goldmann would have it. In this respect Adorno sides with Kant against Hegel whom he criticises for his aesthetic 'intolerance of ambiguity'[30] (he uses the English expression in *Ästhetische Theorie*).

In spite of this Kantian scepticism towards the conceptualisation of art, Adorno refuses to acknowledge Kant's maxim 'without concept', for he expects art to criticise society and express truth in what he calls *truth content* or *Wahrheitsgehalt*. In this respect he remains a Hegelian, albeit in the Young Hegelian tradition, which began to doubt the validity of Hegel's aesthetic system. Adorno resumes some of the Young Hegelian arguments when he praises Friedrich Theodor Vischer (one of Hegel's disciples, cf. chap. 1) for having realised that art does 'not reduce without remainder into the idea'[31] and that the aesthetic 'residue' which defies conceptualisation is essential.

Situated between Kant and Hegel, Adorno's conception of art is ambivalent and paradoxical, for it seeks to combine Kant's 'without concept' with Hegel's conceptual quest for truth. Adorno himself is well aware of the paradox when he points out in *Aesthetic Theory*: 'The paradox that art says it and at the same time does not say it, is because the mimetic element by which it says it, the opaque and particular, at the same time resists speaking.'[32] In other words, the mimetic, non-conceptual aspect of art and literature accounts for the impossibility of their conceptual definition in the rationalist or Hegelian sense. But how is this ambivalent and paradoxical nature of literature to be imagined?

In a first step one could argue that Adorno stresses the importance of the *expression plane* of the literary text (without using Hjelmslev's concept, of course) and the impossibility to reduce the latter to the *content plane*. This is undoubtedly correct, but Adorno's concepts of *paradox* and *ambiguity* mean a lot more. They involve what he calls '*art's double character*' ('*der Doppelcharakter der Kunst*')[33], i.e. the fact that art is at the same time autonomous and a social phenomenon, a *fait social* in the sense of the Durkheim school.[34] It is autonomous because it resists translation into conceptual systems (into ideologies, moral philosophies or metaphysics) and it is a social fact because aesthetic autonomy itself is the result of socio-historical processes (of secularisation and the rise of individualism which gradually divorce the aesthetic realm from the religious). Precisely because art is social and can at any moment be usurped by its political, moral, cognitive or commercial functions, Adorno pleads for a militant autonomy that resists the integration of art and literature into the commercialised communication systems and its ideologies: into the '*culture industry*' ('*Kulturindustrie*', Adorno, Horkheimer).

This negative conception of art is exemplified by his analyses of Samuel Beckett's work, in particular by his essay on *Endgame*. It is one of the most important essays written by Adorno and an attempt to define art negatively as a negation of ideological meaning and as a *critique of ideology* (*Ideologiekritik*). Far from being a manifesto of the existentialist creed, as some interpreters would have it, *Endgame* is read by Adorno negatively as a parody and a refutation of the existentialist ideology that was popular between the wars (Heidegger) and reappeared in France and Germany after the Second World War, in the 1950s and 1960s. He thinks that Beckett's so-called absurd theatre ought to be seen as a parody of traditional theatre that has long since become integrated into the culture industry. In Beckett's plays most categories of traditional drama are exposed to parody and irony.

In *Endgame*, for example, the two heroes Hamm and Clov are non-heroes or anti-heroes: instead of acting like heroic figures (in the Classical or Romantic sense), they remain passive; their dialogue is all but dramatic and regularly degenerates into small talk and trivial squabble. Finally, the catastrophe which usually announces the *dénouement* of a tragedy, degenerates into the trivial news that the two protagonists have run out of sleeping tablets. In other words: Beckett's *Endgame* cannot be used in any positive, meaningful way, neither for ideological, nor for commercial purposes. Its absurdity coincides with its negative character, with its rejection of ideology and commercial communication.

The case of Stefan George's aestheticism is somewhat different. Adorno reveals two contradictory aspects of George's lyrical work which is torn between an ideological and a critical impulse: on the one hand the poet seems unable to resist the penchant for an elitist ideology which degrades his language, on the other hand he succeeds in developing a style, the negativity and purity of which enables him to write poems beyond or outside the commercialised communication system of his time. Unlike Lukács or Goldmann who would like to define the ideologies expressed by literary texts, Adorno reveals the precarious position of literature between ideology and its critical negation.[35]

In an essay on Valéry published under the title 'The Artist as Deputy' (1953), he attempts to show to what extent Valéry's hermetic poems resist the commercialised communication of the culture industry. The poet, he argues, refuses to address the senses, to write 'sensuous' poems in the romantic, symbolist or impressionist style. 'For him', he explains, 'to construct works of art means to refuse the opiate that great sensuous art has become since Wagner, Baudelaire, and Manet; to fend off the humiliation that makes works of art media and makes consumers victims of psychotechnical manipulation.'[36] Valéry's art is ascetic insofar as it rejects the images of the culture industry, insofar as it defines itself primarily as a *rational construct*, not as a product of intuition and the senses which are being exploited by the media. Valéry's art is hermetic and esoteric at the same time. Here one of the main problems of contemporary art comes to the fore: the works of art which resist integration into commercialised culture tend to become marginal in a society whose mass culture is marked by what Adorno calls 'psychotechnical manipulation'.

However, their marginality and negativity are part and parcel of the *truth content* (*Wahrheitsgehalt*), and Adorno insists on the fact that in this respect the aesthetic negation of meaning continues to be meaningful. It expresses negatively the critical truth about society, a truth that can no longer be found in the consciousness of the proletariat (Marx, Lukács) but recedes into the aesthetic enclave where the artist becomes a *deputy* (*Statthalter*) of critical knowledge. This retreat into the aesthetic realm marks the whole of post-war Critical Theory (especially Adorno's) and distinguishes it from Neomarxism. In the case of Critical Theory the integration of the working class into consumer society leads to an aesthetic turn within the critical discourse. This discourse turns to art as the last repository of critical consciousness.

In postmodern debates, Adorno has frequently been criticised as 'elitist' or 'aristocratic'. Linda Hutcheon for example writes: 'To rage, as many do, following Adorno, against mass culture as only a negative force may be, as one architect/critic has remarked, "simply continuing to use an aristocratic viewpoint" (. . .).'[37]

To this Adorno would probably have answered that, far from being democratic, mass art is imposed on the people by the ruling trusts and cartels: in very much the same way as commercialised food. While mass food and drugs destroy their bodies, the stultifying practices of commercial texts and films make their intellects wither. Critics like Linda Hutcheon fail to see that without a revolutionary movement, mass culture loses the critical impulse which Walter Benjamin never forgot to associate with the idea of revolution and emancipation.

3 Mikhail M. Bakhtin's Young Hegelian Aesthetics

Like Walter Benjamin and Theodor W. Adorno, Mikhail M. Bakhtin cannot be understood as an exponent of Marxist aesthetics in the sense of Lukács or Goldmann. However, his literary theory is closely associated with the Hegelian tradition which it tries to subvert by challenging its classicist premises and by focusing on the role of the grotesque, the ugly, the incongruous, and the ambivalent in literary texts.

In the first chapter Bakhtin's hostility towards Hegelian classicism and his proximity to the Young Hegelian aesthetics of F. Th. Vischer already came to the fore. It was claimed, among other things, that by emphasising the grotesque and the comic the Russian critic challenges Hegelian aesthetic discourse, marked by the classicist ideals of harmony, seriousness, and a monological structure. As an alternative to Hegel's classicism, Vischer's theory is particularly important for Bakhtin, because it attempts to integrate the grotesque and the comic into an aesthetic system that announces the ambivalences of modernism: 'Hegel completely ignores the role of the comic in the structure of the grotesque, and indeed examines the grotesque quite indepenedently of the comic. F. Th. Vischer differs from Hegel.'[38]

Bakhtin's comments on Hegel's and Vischer's theories of the grotesque, of laughter, and popular culture, of carnival and carnivalisation are important because they reveal the thrust of his argument. It takes the same direction as the anti-Hegelian discourses of the Young Hegelians Vischer, Feuerbach, and Ruge whenever the latter object to the aristocratic tone, the monologue, and the repressive aspects of the Hegelian system, proposing alternatives in the realm of laughter (Vischer), materialism (Feuerbach), and partisan politics (Ruge). It is these affinities between Bakhtin and the rebellious disciples of Hegel, which seem decisive here, not the fact that Bakhtin mentions Vischer's theory of the grotesque, Kierkegaard, Belinsky, and Nietzsche in several of his writings.

Nietzsche's importance for Bakhtin ought not to be underestimated because of various negative remarks dropped here and there by the Russian author.[39] Rainer Grübel quite rightly dwells upon the affinity between the two thinkers, pointing out the similarity between Nietzsche's myth of the 'eternal return' and Bakhtin's idea of 'reincarnation' in the world of carnival: 'The *moment of reincarnation* (. . .) which according to Bakhtin is essential to the aesthetics of the grotesque is reminiscent of Nietzsche's principle of the "eternal return" (. . .).'[40] He stresses the ambivalent character of Bakhtin's notion of the grotesque: 'As an aesthetic category the grotesque is by no means a counterpart of the beautiful, but a transgression of the antinomy between the beautiful and the ugly into the ambivalent ugly-beautiful.'[41]

These remarks about the aesthetics of the grotesque make it clear that this extreme, irreducible ambivalence relates Bakhtin to Nietzsche (cf. chap. 1.2) and the Young Hegelians Vischer, Feuerbach, and Stirner. Like these thinkers, he starts from the dialectical unity of opposites, but no longer believes in the possibility of a Hegelian *synthesis* (*Aufhebung*) and the construction of the historical system. The latter is abandoned along with the postulate of a subject-object-identity, Hegelian monologue, and Hegel's notion of truth, as a relic of classicism.

The affinity with Nietzsche and the Young Hegelians is further strengthened by Bakhtin's discovery of the non-rational, the Dionysian, which is no longer denied or suppressed – as is the case in Hegel's aesthetics – but greeted as a liberating and critical principle which brings about a fusion between the conscious and the unconscious, between wake and dream. Rabelais' conceptions of time and space are to be understood in this context, where the image of a phallic spire fertilising a woman transgresses the logic of everyday thought into the realm of oneiric associations: 'The belfry', writes Bakhtin, 'has a topographic character, the tower pointing upward, to heaven, is transformed into the *phallus* (the bodily lower stratum) and impregnates women (again the body's lower parts).'[42]

However, Bakhtin's 'Young Hegelianism' should not be limited to the question concerning Vischer's, Kierkegaard's or Nietzsche's influence; nor should it be reduced to a simple analogy between theories. It should be considered in relation to the strong affinity between Bakhtin and Dostoevskij, the main representative of aesthetic polyphony and the inventor – as it were – of the polyphonic novel. Not only was Dostoevskij a contemporary of the Young Hegelians, all of whom were born in the first ten or fifteen years of the 19th century, but he also became acquainted with the works of Ludwig Feuerbach, Max Stirner, and David Strauss through the Russian Hegelian Visarion G. Belinskij. Bakhtin himself underlines the importance of Max Stirner for his book on Dostoevskij: 'Thus the prototypes for Raskolnikov's ideas, for example, were the ideas of Max Stirner as expounded by him in his treatise *Der Einzige und sein Eigentum*, and the ideas of Napoleon III as developed by him in *Histoire de Jules César* (1865).'[43] Here it becomes clear that Dostoevskij who, until his conversion to Christianity, wrote under Belinksij's influence, lived in a social and linguistic situation that might be described as 'Young Hegelian'.

The aesthetic elements which Bakhtin admires most in Dostoevskij's novels – carnivalisation, ambivalence, and polyphony – can be considered as a challenge to the Hegelian system: to its classicism, its systematic syntheses, and its monologue. In Dostoevskij's texts, Bakhtin argues, not a single voice, not even that of the narrator, dominates or integrates the other voices which are autonomous and capable of defending their independence. In this context, the polyphonic novel is read by Bakhtin as a democratic and revolutionary genre which anticipates the development of literature as a whole: 'The novel has become the leading hero in the drama of literary development. (. . .) In many respects the novel has anticipated

and continues to anticipate, the future development of liter.
a whole.'⁴⁴

It goes without saying that such statements only apply in the case
of certain novels: the critical and polyphonic texts Bakhtin focuses
on. Here it becomes obvious that, far from being a simple generic
notion, his concept of the novel is the metonymic expression of
an avant-garde aesthetic that challenges the monologic aesthetics
of Hegel, of Socialist Realism, and of all other dominant discourses,
past and present. Not all novels are polyphonic, and Bakhtin who
criticised Tolstoj's work for being monological was well aware
of this. The reason why he emphasised literary polyphony and
attached such importance to Dostoevskij's novels was political: his
rejection of classicism, monologue and aristocratic seriousness was
not only directed against Hegel, but also and above all against the
classicist – i.e. Hegelian – doctrines of official Marxism-Leninism
and its aesthetics of Socialist Realism.

Unless this political context is taken into account, it is virtually
impossible to explain the anti-Hegelian or Young Hegelian bias
of Bakhtin's aesthetics and poetics. For they both defy a Marxist-
Leninist discourse which in many respects can be considered a
materialist continuation of Hegelianism: of systematic thought,
identification of subject and object, monologue and classicism.
This is the reason why Bakhtin was ostracised under Stalinism
and permanently exposed to the threat of deportation. (His disciple
and colleague V. N. Vološinov actually perished in one of Stalin's
concentration camps.)

Various scholars of Slavic philology, such as Renate Lachmann
and Hans Günther, quite rightly believe that Bakhtin's terminology
and aesthetic theory cannot be understood adequately as long as
they are isolated from the dominant aesthetic ideology and the
political situation of the Twenties and Thirties. Lachmann is
correct in pointing out that Bakhtin's concept of *ambivalence*,
for example, acquires a critical value as it is opposed to the
Socialist-Realist postulate of aesthetic univocity – a postulate
Socialist Realism shares with Hegelianism and Hegelian Marxism. Bakhtin's concept, argues Lachmann, should be seen 'as a
fundamental critique of the dominant ideology's claim to possess
the one and only truth'.⁴⁵

Hans Günther is even more specific when dealing with Bakhtin's latent polemics against Socialist Realism, for he shows that the key concepts of Marxist-Leninist aesthetics are being systematically challenged by Bakhtin's alternative. Apart from authoritarian seriousness, monologue, and hierarchically prescribed popularity, the aesthetic notion of the *typical* is questioned: 'Bakhtin's grotesque realism also implies a critique of the concept of the typical which is particularly characteristic of Socialist Realism and which was canonised in the early Thirties in reaction to the publication of Friedrich Engels' letter to Minna Kautsky.'[46] As a Hegelian concept (linked to Hegel's notion of totality), the typical cannot be understood independently of the dialectic between appearance and essence, the part and the whole.

It is precisely the category of totality, linked in Hegel's (Lukács', Goldmann's) philosophy to monosemic reductions of art and to aesthetic closure, which is globally challenged by the idea of ambivalence. Very much like the Young Hegelians and Nietzsche, Bakhtin chooses ambivalence, the openness of which cannot be curbed by Hegel's syntheses. He thus undermines Hegel's systematic dialectic, whose aspiration towards total knowledge was inherited by Marxism-Leninism, and develops an open, negative dialectic that admits the unity of the opposites but no positive synthesis in the sense of Hegel's *Aufhebung*.

In some respects he anticipates Walter Benjamin's and Theodor W. Adorno's Critical Theory which is also a critique of Hegelian systematic thought and of Hegelian Marxism. The crucial difference between Bakhtin and the founders of Critical Theory (especially Adorno) consists primarily in Bakhtin's democratic belief that the popular culture of carnivalisation, ambivalence, and laughter would eventually prevail and lead to the fall of all authoritarian systems. Unlike Bakhtin, who was too much fixated upon the Soviet situation, Adorno realised that there were forms of domination which were far more sophisticated than Stalinist or Fascist dictatorships: trusts and cartels operating in a postmodern market economy defined as social, liberal or simply 'open'.

4 Marxist Aesthetics in a Postmodern World: Alex Callinicos, Terry Eagleton, Fredric Jameson

Although Bakhtin has never defined himself as a Marxist in the sense of Lukács, Goldmann or Jameson, Bakhtin's and Jameson's positions can be shown to be complementary within the Hegelian-Marxist debate. They are complementary insofar as Bakhtin's critique is primarily directed against the Hegelian ideology of Marxism-Leninism.[47], whereas Jameson has to grapple with a postmodern social reality in which ideologies – especially the Marxist ones – seem to be running out of steam.

Unlike Benjamin and Bakhtin who could still believe, each in his particular way, in the critical capacity of the people, in the synthesis of popular resistance and avant-garde practice or in the carnevalesque culture of laughter and its democratic potential, Jameson is confronted by a late-capitalist reality that seems to have integrated all of these critical practices by commercialising them in the media, thus transforming them into instruments of what Adorno and Horkheimer called *Kulturindustrie*. The carnivalisation of culture in films such as Monty Python's *Life of Brian* has no critical effect in the sense of Benjamin or Bakhtin: far from undermining the established order, it merely consolidates the power of the culture-producing trusts, all of which tell the consumers to 'have fun'.

In this situation two incompatible strategies are conceivable: an outright rejection of all postmodern practices which can be viewed as concessions to commercialisation, consumer society, and culture industry, and an attempt to save and adapt the critical discourse of Marxism to a society where discussions about alternatives to the capitalist order are increasingly being dismissed as irrelevant.

Authors such as Alex Callinicos and Terry Eagleton have opted for the first strategy, rejecting all attempts to reconcile Marxism with postmodern consumer culture. Callinicos sketches the present situation from a Marxist point of view: 'Not only does belief in a postmodern epoch generally go along with rejection of socialist revolution as either feasible or desirable, but it is the perceived failure of revolution which has helped to gain widespread acceptance of this belief.'[48] The specifically Marxist problem seems to be the disappearance of what Herbert Marcuse called the 'second dimension': the historical dimension of a revolutionary overcoming of the established order and the critical ability to *perceive* this dimension.

According to Eagleton this ability has all but vanished from

postmodern aesthetic consciousness. The very concept of alienation which has always been fundamental to Marxist critique seems
to have become unthinkable:

> The depthless, styleless, dehistoricised, decathected surfaces of
> postmodernist culture are not meant to signify an alienation,
> for the very concept of alienation must secretly posit a dream
> of authenticity which postmodernism finds quite unintelligible.
> (. . .) Postmodernism is thus a grisly parody of socialist utopia,
> having abolished all alienation at a stroke.[49]

It is a parody of socialist utopia inasmuch as it pretends that all
of our wishes can be realised by financial, scientific or technical
means, thus insinuating that all kinds of revolutionary aspirations
have become obsolete.

Continuing to adhere to the great Marxist meta-narrative (in
spite of the collapse of official Marxism in Eastern Europe),
Eagleton believes that postmodernism is just another phase in
the evolution of capitalism, i.e. the 'pre-history' of humanity in
the Marxist sense. In his book *The Illusions of Postmodernism*, he
explains:

> And this 'pre-history' is akin in some ways to the postmodernist's
> History. It is, as both Marx and Joyce's Stephen Dedalus com-
> ment, a 'nightmare' from which we are trying to awaken; but
> to dream that one has awoken only to discover that one hasn't
> is just more of the nightmare and a suitable image of postmodern
> prematurity. For socialism, the death of History is still to arrive
> (. . .).[50]

It seems difficult to criticise postmodernism effectively by simply
perpetuating the teleological discourse of Hegelian Marxism.

Unlike Callinicos and Eagleton, Jameson opts for the second
strategy, trying to develop Marxist discourse without globally
rejecting postmodern culture. His remarks about the inevitability
of a postmodern situation are well balanced and lack the polemical
undertone which accompanies Eagleton's critique: 'The point is
that we are *within* the culture of postmodernism to the point where
its facile repudiation is as impossible as any equally facile celebration
of it is complacent and corrupt.'[51]

Developing this twofold diagnosis, Jameson adopts a rather

conciliatory attitude when dealing with postmodern literature: 'Culturally I write as a relatively enthusiastic consumer of postmodernism, at least of some parts of it: I like the architecture and a lot of the newer visual work, in particular the newer photography. The music is not bad to listen to, or the poetry to read (. . .).'[52] From the point of view of Critical Theory the conciliatory discourse is verging on sheer complacency when Jameson goes on to say: 'Food and fashion have also greatly improved, as has the life world generally.'[53] This diagnosis may be correct as long as it is applied to the life on Jameson's campus (although one may wonder about the fashion), but it instantly turns into a cynical caricature if applied to the 'life world' of working class (or unemployed) suburbs in New York, Chicago or Los Angeles, usually referred to as 'run down' by American estate agents.

There is a striking contrast between Jameson's postmodern Marxist discourse on the one hand and the discourse of Critical Theory on the other. Jameson leans over backwards in order to avoid radical criticism of commercialised culture which might make him sound 'old fashioned' or simply Marxist. However, the price he has to pay for making overtures to the postmodernists is relatively high: he renounces the revolutionary perspective of Hegelian Marxists such as Lukács and Goldmann and the negative stance of Critical Theory which makes a radical approach (beyond Marxism) possible.

It is not surpising therefore that Jameson's critique of postmodern culture and society is rather bland and non-descript. On the one hand, he concedes that all of aesthetic production has become part and parcel of commodity production (if this is the case, how can he declare himself to be an 'enthusiastic consumer'?); on the other hand, he insists on the necessity to go beyond commodity production and the reification it entails by devising critical strategies adaptable to the techniques of media communication. In order to attain a certain degree of emancipation in a society dominated by commercialised media, he proposes a 'pedagogic-political' model based on Brecht's Epic Theatre. Adapted to the media and systematically developed, this model is expected to fulfil the function of an educational and political 'cartography' (as Jameson puts it)[54], a cartography that will strengthen the individual's sense of orientation within the complex and fragmented world of late capitalism.

As in the case of Lukács and Goldmann, the Hegelian category of totality is the key to Jameson's critique of postmodernism and to his aesthetic and didactic model. For only if the individual catches a glimpse of the global context of alienation, is there a chance that critical consciousness will develop. 'It has not escaped anyone's attention', Jameson explains towards the end of his book on postmodernism, 'that my approach to postmodernism is a "totalizing" one.'[55]

However, a 'totalising' perspective has also been adopted by Niklas Luhmann in his theory of social systems which is quite hostile to Hegelianism and Marxism – both considered by Luhmann as ideologies of the nineteenth century.[56] It is by no means certain therefore that a totalising approach will be successful as a social critique in late capitalist media society.

The alternative appears to be – especially within the context of this chapter – Adorno's negative dialectic based on the assumption that the totalising approach has lost its critical bite, because the social system as a whole is false ('the whole is the false').[57] This negative perspective is re-opened in a postmodern context by Jean-François Lyotard's aesthetic theory of the *sublime* which no longer draws on Hegel's dialectics but on Kant's aesthetic aporias. It will be discussed in detail in the eighth chapter.

CHAPTER 6
The Aesthetics of Semiotics: Greimas, Eco, Barthes

Like Marxism and reader-response criticism, semiotics can best be understood as a rather heterogeneous theoretical compound which is not held together by an aesthetic framework in the Kantian, Hegelian or Nietzschean sense. It is therefore misleading to identify literary semiotics with a particular approach (Greimas', Eco's or Barthes') or to assume that the concept of *sign* and the related concepts of *signifier* and *signified* in the Saussurian sense guarantee some kind of terminological and methodological homogeneity. For the Saussurian and Hjelmslevian heritage which underlies European semiotics and supplies most of its terminology does not provide a clearly identifiable aesthetic orientation. On the contrary, the common terminology which semioticians such as Greimas, Eco, and Barthes use (*discourse, sign, signifier, signified*) merely conceals the aesthetic disparity of their approaches and theoretical intentions.

It is the task of this chapter to reveal the aesthetic heterogeneity of semiotics and to demonstrate to what extent Greimas develops a semantic theory of the *content plane*, while Roland Barthes emphasises the autonomy of the *expression plane* in an attempt to deliver the signifier from its semantic and metaphysical constraints. Unlike Greimas who is a rationalist at heart and in some respects a Hegelian in search of textual monosemy, Barthes develops a *sémiologie* which starts from rationalist, Cartesian premises, but eventually turns into a Nietzschean celebration of the *polysemic signifier*. The section on Barthes concludes this chapter, announcing the problems and proposals of deconstruction: a theory which questions the validity of distinctions such as *signifier/signified* or *expression plane/content plane*. It turns Barthes' polysemic signifier and figurative language against theoretical discourse itself, i.e. against its conceptual foundations (cf. chap. 7.4).

Situated between Greimas and Barthes, between a rationalist

and a Nietzschean perspective, the semiotic theory of Umberto Eco owes much of its perspicacity and versatility to Kant and his idea that 'the Beautiful' (i.e. art and literature) addresses the intellect by non-conceptual means. In spite of the fact that Eco borrows some of Greimas' concepts and time and again quotes Barthes with approval, he makes it quite plain, especially in his later works, that although literary texts cannot be identified with a particular conceptual meaning, they are not meaningless, because they encourage certain meanings and discourage others. For this reason, he quite plausibly argues, interpretation has limits, because it cannot impose meanings which are manifestly being discouraged by the interpreted text.

Although the three semiotic models – of Greimas, Eco, and Barthes – are complementary in some respects, it will become clear in what follows that the realm of semiotics is as heterogeneous as *philosophical* aesthetics. Although semiotic theories are genetically related to the linguistic paradigm that evolved partly as a reaction to philosophical speculations on language, they have inherited the fundamental philosophical controversies regarding the nature of aesthetic objects. Their scientific aspirations have not provided an answer to the fundamental aesthetic question which is at the centre of this book: Can the meaning of literary texts be defined on a theoretical (conceptual) level and, if so, how?

Like Hegel and philosophers of the Enlightenment period before him, Greimas believes that all texts (literary and non-literary) are accessible to conceptual thought and can be interpreted or defined univocally within the conceptual framework of a theoretical discourse. Like Kant, Eco cautiously scans the limits of conceptualisation in the aesthetic realm, but nevertheless insists on the possibility of theoretical analysis. Having abandoned Saussurian rationalism, Barthes, the Nietzschean critic, turns his back on the rationalist or Hegelian concept and proclaims the freedom of the signifier, the phonetic unit not tainted by meaning. However, the knowledge that semiotic theories set out from very different aesthetic premises and may pursue incompatible aesthetic goals, should not lead to the rash conclusion that the language of semiotics is simply a new jargon dealing with old philosophical problems. It is one of the aims of this chapter and indeed of the book as a whole to explain why and how new terminologies and new discourses can open up new theoretical perspectives. They make old problems appear in a new light, thus transforming them into new problems and new objects of knowledge. Eco's idea, for example, that the aesthetic object imposes limits on conceptual knowledge is (remotely) Kantian; but, far from being a simple repetition of the *Critique of Judgement*, it is a new construction. Similarly, Barthes' aesthetics of the signifier does not simply repeat Nietzsche's critique of rationalist and Hegelian conceptualisation, but heralds the radicalism of deconstruction.

1 Greimas or the Search for Meaning

In very much the same way, Greimas' *structural semiotics* is not simply a repetition of rationalist or Hegelian tenets, but a systematic attempt to define with utmost precision the meaning of literary and non-literary texts. The fact that Greimas concentrates on the identification of meaning in *texts* and not (like the New Critics, Jakobson or Barthes) on the specific character of *literary texts*, on their *literariness* (Jakobson), is a symptom of his *conceptual* approach. Like Goldmann, the Hegelian Marxist, who believed that philosophical *and* literary texts are organised by underlying semantic structures, Greimas is convinced that political, philo-sophical, commercial, and literary texts are accessible to semiotic analysis, which reveals their semantic and narrative foundations. A striking analogy will appear between what Goldmann calls the *structure significative* or *mentale* and what Greimas defines as the *deep structure* or *structure profonde*. In both cases it is a structure which organises the totality of the text.

We are reminded of Goldmann's *genetic structuralism* when Greimas insists on the global, totalising approach of the literary universe and demands 'that we have knowledge of the totality of the universe analyzed, or at least of a representative sample'.[1] Although Greimas' totality is a rationalist rather than a dialectical or Hegelian concept, we are nevertheless reminded of Hegel's way of looking at things, when the French semiotician sets out to define the semantic structures and the *deep structures* of literary texts, dismissing their polysemy as the result of superficial or fragmentary reading. He believes that it is possible 'to overcome the obstacles which the polysemic character of the surface text puts in the way of the reading process'.[2] Far from celebrating with Barthes and the deconstructionists the 'open' character of texts and the infinity of the reading process (in *'l'infini du langage'* as Barthes puts it), Greimas is convinced, like Goldmann, that a systematic analysis will yield the one and only meaning science can grasp.

Naturally Greimas is aware of the peculiarities and the specific character of literature. Especially in his early publications, for example in 'La Linguistique structurale et la poétique' (1967), or in his introduction to the collective volume *Essais de sémiotique poétique* (1972), he seeks to define the specificity of poetic texts in a Hjelmslevian perspective, by emphasising the isomorphism between the expression and the content plane: 'the isomorphism between expression and content'.[3] Especially lyrical texts, he argues, are marked by a correspondence between phonetic and semantic units. We find this kind of correspondence in Shakespeare's second sonnet:

> When forty winters shall besiege thy brow
> And dig deep trenches in thy beauty's field . . .

On the one hand, the alliteration of *besiege* and *brow*, which links the two lexical units on the phonetic level, evokes at the same time the circular movement of a siege which in some cases may resemble the shape of a brow; on the other hand, the alliteration of *dig* and *deep* may be heard as reproducing the sound of digging, thus tying together the expression and the content of the verse.

However, in his later works Greimas abandons this kind of Hjelmslevian and Jakobsonian inquiry into the idiosyncrasies of poetic discourse and concentrates on the relationship between semantic and narrative structures in literary, political, juridical, and scientific texts. The fact that these very different textual types are grouped together bears witness to a universalist approach which neglects the specific character of the individual types, putting their common features in the foreground. This universalism is comparable to that of the Hegelians and the Hegelian Marxists who tend to look for the ideologies or world visions articulated by philosophical, scientific, and literary texts, neglecting the specific features of each of them. In this respect, the semiotician and linguist Greimas is closer to the Marxists than to the linguistically inspired New Critics and Formalists.

In other words, Greimas is to be understood as a theoretician of the *content plane* (Hjelmslev) who gives priority on all levels to the semantic structures which he calls *isotopies*. What exactly are *isotopies*? According to Greimas and his disciples (Joseph Courtés, Jean-Claude Coquet) isotopies exist both on the phonetic and on the semantic level, on the expression and on the content plane. Both kinds of *isotopies* can be defined in a first step as *repetitions or recurrencies of certain phonetic or semantic features*. Alliterations, for example, such as *besiege-brow* or *dig-deep* can be considered as phonetic isotopies – in spite of the fact that they are made up of only two elements. (The minimum requirement for the existence of an isotopy are phonetic or semantic features common to *at least two* textual units.) In this context the *semantic isotopy* which is at the centre of structural semiotics (phonetic istopies are neglected by Greimas) is defined by Greimas and Courtés as: '*iterativity (recurrence) on a syntagmatic level of classemes which guarantee the homogeneity of a discourse as utterance*' ('*l'itérativité, le long d'une chaîne syntagmatique, de classèmes qui assurent au discours-énoncé son homogénéité*').[4]

It is important to note – especially in view of the deconstructionist problems dealt with in chapter seven – that, according to Greimas, *iterativity* or *recurrence* of semantic units does not destroy the homogeneity of a text, but contributes to its coherence. One could also say that variations of a (literary) theme do not lead to the disintegration of the theme but to its development and its concretisation.

However, let us return to the definition of *isotopy*. In order to define this concept systematically, it is necessary to take into account the related concepts of *seme, sememe*, and *classeme*. For we can only speak of an *isotopy* if in a text at least two *sememes* (or words in context) have a common *seme* (or dominant concept). A sentence like 'Mary and John are in love and intend to get married' is semantically coherent, because *sememes* such as *Mary, John, love, intend*, and *get married* have the *seme* 'human' in common. At the same time the two *sememes* 'John' and 'Mary' are held together by the complementary *semes* 'masculine' and 'feminine' which, along with the *seme* 'sexuality' (contained in the *sememes* 'love' and 'marry'), can be subsumed under the most general and dominant *seme* 'human'.

The latter is the dominant concept of the *isotopy* (the sentence) and is defined by Greimas as the *contextual seme* or *classeme*. The word *classeme* has been introduced in order to remind us of the fact that it forms a class of words or *sememes* in discourse and that the recurrence of *classemes* implies the formation of an indefinite number of classes (such as organic/inorganic, natural/cultural, human/animal, etc.) which are called *semantic isotopies*. Hence an isotopy comes into existence whenever a *classeme* or general concept is introduced by a speaking subject who subsumes all the words or *sememes* belonging to a particular class under the corresponding *classeme*.

In the first two lines of Shakespeare's sonnet 'When forty winters . . . ' the *classeme* 'military' is inherent in the *sememes* 'besiege', 'dig', 'deep', 'trenches', and 'field'. It thus forms a *class* of words or a *semantic isotopy* which has a *metaphoric* character and dominates the beginning of the sonnet. However, this sonnet is certainly not a poem about strategy, but merely uses the 'strategic' or 'military' metaphor in order to make us imagine the complex – and ultimately inexplicable – relationship between youth and old age, beauty and decay, life and death. Its semantic isotopies form an intricate network of metonymies and metaphors which cannot be reduced to one encompassing *seme* such as 'marriage' in the case of 'John and Mary' or 'victory' in the case of a 1945 article narrating German or Japanese surrender.

In other words, poems and other literary texts are not *monosemic*, but *polysemic* structures that cannot be reduced to one *classeme* and the corresponding *isotopy*, but have to be read on different semantic levels or *isotopies* which do not necessarily form a homogeneous system. Especially modernist or avant-garde poems combine heterogeneous *isotopies* which, far from being univocal messages, defy all attempts at conceptual translation. The seventh stanza of Wallace Stevens's enigmatic poem *A Primitive like an Orb* illustrates what is meant:

> The central poem is the poem of the whole,
> The poem of the composition of the whole,
> The composition of blue sea and of green,
> Of blue light and of green, as lesser poems,
> And the miraculous multiplex of lesser poems,
> Not merely into a whole, but a poem of
> The whole, the essential compact of the parts,
> The roundness that pulls tight the final ring.

Although the meaning of the whole seems to be within arm's reach in this text, it recedes and becomes almost unintelligible as soon as we have a closer look at it. For the stanza and the entire poem leave open the question whether a totality (of nature, for example) is being *described* or created in a poetic sense. The phrase 'composition of blue sea and of green' may refer to both, the spontaneous collusion of colours in nature or to the creative composition of the poet. In other words, the stanza can be read simultaneously on the *isotopy* of 'nature' and of 'poetry'. Greimas would use the term *pluri-isotopie* in order to take into account the possibility that the text cannot be subsumed under a single meaning or an encompassing *isotopy*.[5]

He tends to believe, however, that in most cases even polysemic or 'pluri-isotope' poems are held together by an encompassing semantic structure. François Rastier, a disciple of Greimas, set out to show in an article entitled 'Systématique des isotopies' (1972) that Stéphane Mallarmé's poem *Salut* can be read on three semantic levels or *isotopies*: 1. as 'cheers' at the beginning of a banquet; 2. as a sailor's 'greeting', and 3. as a metaphoric expression of 'writing', of 'écriture'. For Rastier, as for Greimas, it is important that these three isotopies are not equivalent, because, as Rastier points out, the first two isotopies are metaphors of 'writing' (the voyage for example as a metaphoric description of the vicissitudes of writing) and hence subordinate to the encompassing meaning of 'écriture': 'In any case there is a reflexivity in Mallarme's text, for the latter is marked by a metaphoric orientation towards the isotopy of writing (. . .).'[6]

One may assume that Greimas and his disciples would also have attempted a hierarchical and systematic reading of Stevens's *A Primitive like an Orb*, reading it as a poem on poetry: as autoreflexivity of 'writing'. It is by no means certain, however, that meaning can be defined as easily as that, and J. Hillis Miller may be right in pointing out the unresolvable ambiguity of Stevens's text (cf. chap. 7). Undaunted by the ambiguities, contradictions, and imponderables of modernism, Jean-Claude Coquet remarks about Rimbaud's *Illuminations*: 'The whole constitutes a "linguistic object" which it is easy to translate univocally. We call this translation the *linguistic meaning (sens linguistique)* of a work.'[7] Like the Hegelians and Marxists, Greimas, Rastier, and Coquet seem to believe that semantic analysis can reveal the hidden meaning or 'linguistic meaning' of a literary text. Literature thus appears as an aesthetic object that can be univocally defined by conceptual means.

In his analyses of narrative texts, of Georges Bernanos' (1888–1948) novels and Guy de Maupassant's (1850-1893) short story *Deux Amis*, Greimas calls this 'hidden meaning' the *deep structure* which – from 1968 onwards – he illustrates by a *semiotic square*. In his analyses of Bernanos' works he distinguishes four semantic elements which together form the encompassing *isotopy* of 'existence'. Apart from *Life* and *Death*, considered by Greimas as secondary isotopies, 'existence' also includes elements or *sememes* which can logically be grouped under *non-Life* and *non-Death*. The global formula for the deep structure of Bernanos' literary universe is presented in Greimas' *Sémantique structurale* (1966):

$$\frac{L}{\text{non-L}} \approx \frac{D}{\text{non-D}}$$

In this formula wherein L(ife) and D(eath) form *opposites (contraires)* L(ife) and non-L(ife), D(eath) and non-D(eath) form *contradictions*. Whenever L refers to the positive definitions of Life (*change, clarity, warmth*) and non-L to the negative definitions of Death (*identity, darkness, cold*), D refers to the positive definitions of Death (*heaviness, lack of colour, monotony*) and non-D to the negative definitions of Life (*purity, airiness, colour*). Between 1968 and 1976 Greimas formalised this deep structure of Bernanos' work by constructing a *semiotic square* which, in his analysis of Maupassant's *Deux Amis*, he superimposes on the semiotic square constructed in conjunction with Maupassant's short story. The superposition reveals both similarities and differences between Bernanos' and Maupassant's worlds. In spite of the fact that Maupassant's text is also structured by a fundamental *opposition (deep structure)* between Life and Death, his symbols differ quite substantially from those of Bernanos, and the difference indicates that a *deep structure* such as *Life/Death* can undergo endless variations from author to author.

Before we have a closer look at these variations and Greimas' comparative semiotic square (Bernanos' and Maupassant's worlds superimposed), let us return to Maupassant's *Deux Amis*. It is a story about two friends, Sauvage and Morissot, who meet by chance in the streets of Paris during the Prussian siege of 1870. They are fanatical fishermen and decide to obtain a special permit from the local commander in order to be able to fish behind the French lines. They arrive at the river and in spite of the artillery thunder on top of Mont-Valérien they enjoy a good catch. However, they are caught by Prussian soldiers whose commanding officer accuses them of espionage and threatens to have them shot if they don't tell him the password of the French defences. They refuse, are shot, thrown into the water, and the Prussian soldiers eat their fish.

As in the case of Bernanos, Greimas starts from the *opposites Life/Death* (*Vie/Mort*). He then goes on to show that the different elements of the semiotic square which are derived from this fundamental opposition, are associated in Maupassant's text with symbols that differ substantially from those used by Bernanos. Unlike Bernanos who associates *Death* with *water* (heaviness, cold) and *non-Death* with *air*, Maupassant associates *Death* with the *earth* (Mont-Valérien) and *non-Death* with *water*. Both authors establish a link between *life* and *fire* (the sun in the case of Maupassant). In Bernanos' work, however, *non-Life* is associated with the *earth*, whereas in *Deux Amis* it is linked to the *sky* and the *air*. A comparison of the two fictional worlds yields the following semiotic square which illustrates the *deep structures* of Bernanos' and Maupassant's texts:

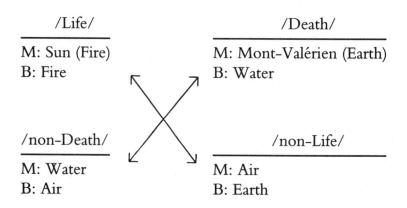

/Life/	/Death/
M: Sun (Fire)	M: Mont-Valérien (Earth)
B: Fire	B: Water

/non-Death/	/non-Life/
M: Water	M: Air
B: Air	B: Earth

In the *Sémantique structurale* and in *Maupassant*, Greimas considers the *semiotic square* or *deep structure* as the basis or source of all narrative structures of a text. Life and Death are not simply semantic units, but also units of action or actants: 'But, at the same time, because they are capable of receiving qualifications, their syntactical status is that of actants.'[8] This argument is based on the assumption that the semantic structures of a literary or non-literary text determine its narrative processes: both on the level of narration and on that of narrative action. In this context one could postulate a *homology* between the narrative dynamics of discourse and its semantic foundations. This homology appears clearly in Greimas' analysis of *Deux Amis* where the symbols of Life and Death (*sun, Mont-Valérien, water, sky*) are transformed into *actants* which operate within certain *isotopies* ('life', 'death', 'fire', 'water', 'earth'), thus developing the semantics of the text on the level of narrative action.

Before we return to the analysis of *Deux Amis*, it is necessary to clarify the notion of *actant*. An *actant* is a narrative function with a subjective and an objective aspect, which means that we can distinguish *subject-actants* from *object-actants*. The former can be heroes or villains, individuals or collectives (e.g. political parties or institutions); the latter can be human beings or material objects (e.g. the princess, the treasure, the truth) which subject-actants set out to conquer, appropriate, and possess. It is important to note that, in Greimas' semiotics, objects, symbols or concepts can also be *actants*. It is a well-known fact that the sun or the moon can act in fairy-tales or poems, but we do not always realise that in theoretical texts concepts can be made to act and that materialism can defeat idealism or vice versa. In this case truth can become an *object-actant*.

Apart from distinguishing *subject* and *object-actants*, Greimas distinguishes *actants of enunciation or communication* (e.g. narrators) and *actants of narration* (e.g. characters in novels). The former are external to the text (in most cases, e.g. in *Deux Amis*, the narrator does not act in the text), whereas the latter are *actors* (protagonists). On this level Greimas distinguishes: the *Addresser* (*Destinateur*), the *anti-Addresser* (*anti-Destinateur*), the *Addressee* (*Destinataire*), the *anti-Addressee* (*anti-Destinataire*), the *Subject* (*Sujet*), the *anti-Subject* (*anti-Sujet*), and the *Object* (*Objet*). In fairy-tales, for example, the king acts as *Addresser* when he sends out a prince asking him to deliver a princess who has been abducted by a magician acting on behalf of an enemy king. In this particular case the prince is the *Subject* (or *Addressee*), the magician is the *anti-Subject*, the enemy king is the *anti-Addresser* and the princess the *Object*.

Applying this scheme to Maupassant's *Deux Amis*, Greimas shows how the semantic opposition between the two *isotopies* 'Life' and 'Death' engenders a narrative sequence (a sequence of actions) in which the sun fulfils the function of an *Addresser* responsible for the actions of the *collective Subject* Sauvage and Morissot; symmetrically, the Prussians are defined as a *collective anti-Subject* undergoing the influence of Mont-Valérien which fulfils the function of *anti-Addresser*. The complexity of the model is increased by the fact that *Subject* and *anti-Subject* have each a second(ary) *Addresser*: in the case of the two friends it is the water; in the case of the Prussians it is the sky. These secondary *Addressers* (called *non-anti-Destinateur* and *non-Destinateur* by Greimas) represent the items *non-Death* and *non-Life* respectively (cf. semiotic square). Greimas explains: 'If we take into account the polemical structure of narration, then the two narrative subjects – the subject "two friends" and the anti-subject "Prussians" – would each be endowed with a dual Addresser.'[9] (By polemical structure Greimas means the conflictual situation which opposes *actants* and *anti-actants*.)

In the end, argues Greimas, the defeat of the two friends is only apparent, because in their death they are united with one of their *Addressers*, namely the water (they are thrown into the river). Symmetrically, the victory of the Prussian soldiers cannot be considered as real, because the two friends manage to escape into 'their' element. Greimas reasons as follows: 'With respect to its results, S2's [i.e. the Prussians] Narrative Programme could be read as a victory on the plane of seeming and as a failure on that of being and, inversely, S1's [the two friends] Narrative Programme ended in an apparent failure and a real victory.'[10]

At this stage some critical remarks seem appropriate. The first remark concerns what Coquet calls 'linguistic meaning' or 'sense linguistique', for Greimas does not make it quite clear whether the semantic and narrative structures he analyses are such 'linguistic meanings' on which other (psychological, sociological or Marxist) interpretations should be based or whether they are meant to be 'final' interpretations themselves which exclude alternative attributions of meaning.

The second remark concerns Greimas' analysis as such. For all its thoroughness and precision it does not include factors that would considerably modify it if they were taken into account. After Claude Bremond[11], Ann Jefferson quite rightly points out that 'surface features'[12] do not seem to count in Greimas' investigations. What would the text look like, one might ask, if not only the sequences of actions (*narrative programmes*, Greimas) were dealt with but also the point of view of the narrator, which is so important for F. K. Stanzel and G. Genette[13], and the dialogues between the characters? Would a narratological description in this particular sense not yield a completely different picture, i.e. theoretical object of *Deux Amis*? In other words: how 'objective' or 'reliable' are Greimas' descriptions of *deep structures*?

This brings us to the last remark. How can Greimas compare the world of Bernanos' novels (*Sémantique structurale*, 1966) with a six-page-story by Maupassant without raising the question of the text corpus? How can he pretend to superimpose two models ('Bernanos', 'Maupassant') without having analysed the rest of Maupassant's work? For it is hard to see how the opposition sun–water/Mont-Valérien–sky could explain other novels or short novels by Maupassant (e.g. his short stories *Misti* or *Blanc et bleu* or his novels *Pierre et Jean* or *Le Horla*).

Although Greimas and his disciples have done a lot to elucidate the semantic and narrative structures of texts[14], they have done little to establish a link between these structures and what Ann Jefferson calls the 'surface features': the narrator's perspective, the dialogues, the notions of time and chronology (which Genette focuses on), as well as the ambiguities, ambivalences, and polysemies of texts. It seems that they left the analysis of these aspects of literature to Eco, Barthes, and the deconstructionists . . .

2 Umberto Eco: From the Avant-Garde to Postmodernism

In many respects Umberto Eco occupies an intermediate position between Greimas and Barthes. Unlike Greimas who relentlessly seeks to define the global meaning of a text, thus renewing some of the Hegelian-Marxist endeavours in a semiotic context, the early

Eco emphasises the *open* character of literature, i.e. the possibility of endless re-interpretation. Unlike Barthes who radicalises this openness by insisting on the unlimited polysemy of the signifier, Eco, especially in his later works, traces the *limits of interpretation*, arguing that some interpretations are encouraged, whereas others are discouraged by texts.

The early Eco's aesthetic point of view is rather close to that of early Russian Formalism (cf. chap. 2) and of Roman Jakobson. Like Roman Jakobson, the Kantian linguist, the author of *L'opera aperta* (1962) believes in the *autoreflexivity* of art and literature. His concept of *autoreflexivity* is akin to Jakobson's idea that the 'poetic message' (predominantly) refers to itself, not to the author, nor to the reader, nor to social reality. This conception of art is Kantian insofar as it rejects all attempts to define the aesthetic sign primarily as a social, economic (useful), didactic or philosophical (conceptual) fact.

However, the early Eco cannot simply be understood as a Neo-Kantian; for like the Russian Formalists and the young Roman Jakobson whose texts he knew, his defence of artistic autonomy is motivated by an avant-garde view of the world. Like the Russian Formalists and Futurists, the Italian semiotician pleads at the beginning of the Sixties – and six years before the student revolt of 1968 – in favour of the avant-garde technique of *de-familiarisation* which he considers as a possible response to social *alienation* in capitalism: 'One can only make alientation appear by de-familiarising it (. . .).'[15] Like Adorno (cf. chap. 5), he envisages *de-familiarisation* as a predominantly *formal* process, for like Adorno he thinks that social critique can optimally articulate itself on a formal level.

In the Sixties, the work of James Joyce appears to him as the most convincing model of social critique: a model which questions the narrative stereotypes of traditional novels. Considered as an alternative to Aristotelian poetics (marked by a causal link-up of actions and narrative sequences), Joyce offers a type of novel which is not structured by linear narrativity, but by a paradigmatic, associative principle. Towards the end of *Opera aperta*, Joyce appears in an avant-garde perspective as an author who dissolves language, thus reacting to the disorders and fragmentations of the modern age.

In contrast to Adorno whose negative critique implies a rejection of revolutionary action, Eco seems to regard the de-mystifying and de-familiarising techniques of the avant-garde as catalysts in the revolutionary process. As in the case of Surrealism and Futurism, form – or rather the destruction of it – appears to him as a kind of political *engagement* that may be conducive to the de-mystification of ideologies, stereotypes, and clichés. Unfortunately, Eco does not attempt to relate these avant-garde practices to a critical theory of society capable of assessing the impact of such aesthetic practices in a late-capitalist world which is being increasingly dominated by a utilitarian and technocratic outlook. It could very well be that in such a world aesthetic revolts have very little effect indeed. In this respect Eco differs substantially from the Marxists and the authors of Critical Theory who were well aware of the political limits of avant-garde rebellion.

Eco's early approach does overlap with Adorno's aesthetics of negativity insofar as the Italian semiotician also holds that the work of art is marked by a fundamental ambivalence because it is meaningful without being definable on a conceptual level. Polysemy and conceptuality, openness and closure are interrelated, and their close coexistence excludes a unilateral or one-dimensional approach to art. In this context, Eco distinguishes two kinds of openness: 'openness of the first degree', which depends on the creativity of the reader, and an 'openness of the second degree' which is an aspect of the work's structure as such and is systematically developed by avant-garde movements. (It is interesting to note to what extent Eco is in agreement with Ingarden (cf. chap. 4.2) on this point. Openness can mean two things: the freedom of the reader's imagination and the polysemies or *blanks*, as Ingarden and Iser would say, inherent in the text structure.)

In later publications Eco redefines *openness* by using Hjelmslev's distinction between *denotation* and *connotation*. The literary text, he argues, transforms the primary or *denotative* meanings of natural language into secondary or *connotative* meanings by creating a system of new linguistic (especially semantic) conventions within which the words of everyday life acquire new (i.e. secondary) meanings: '*In this way the literary work permanently transforms its denotations into connotations and its signifieds into signifiers of other signifieds.*'[16] In other words: the primary codes of natural language, which are anchored in conventions and fulfil communicative functions (e.g.

in political, economic or scientific languages), are transformed by literary practice into secondary codes within which words assume new, unusual or *de-familiarised* meanings.

Eco calls these *secondary codes* private codes or *idiolects* of writers: 'Such a type of private code is usually called an "idiolect"'.[17] The *idiolect* of a writer could also be considered as the totality of semantic shifts that come about whenever secondary or *connotative* meanings are superimposed on the meanings of every day communicative language. In Kafka's parable *Before the Law*, for example, the word 'law' acquires new connotations and a new meaning that are specific for Kafka's *idiolect* and also occur in the rest of the fragmentary novel *The Trial*. It is neither the 'Law' of the lawyer nor the 'law' of the physicist, nor that of the theologian: it is a new word which evokes all the meanings of the primary system (of natural language), but at the same time defies all attempts to pin it down to one of them.

In an attempt to establish a link between *polysemy* or *openness* and *aesthetic value*, Eco argues that a work is really valuable or great if the polysemies of its signifiers resist all efforts to reduce it to a particular (religious, ideological, metaphysical) meaning. This aesthetic postulate comes very close to that of Jan Mukařovský who also believes that the *aesthetic value* of a literary text depends on its capacity to resist interpretation (monosemisation). It is interesting to observe how both conceptions of aesthetic value contradict Goldmann's Hegelian criteria which identify value with conceptually definable coherence.

In spite of this Kantian refusal to consider the literary text as the equivalent of a conceptual totality in the Hegelian sense, Eco is convinced that the text is 'something which *must have a structure*, for otherwise there would be no communication, but merely a random stimulation of aleatory reactions'.[18] In a more recent work, *I limiti dell'interpretazione* (1990), he specifies his stance by including the external context of literary works which also limits the freedom of interpretation, thus excluding arbitrariness: '(. . .) But if I decide to interpret Wordsworth's text, I have to respect its cultural and linguistic background.'[19] Globally, Eco's theory of literary interpretation can be described as a dialectic between the freedom of interpretation and the fidelity to the structured context of the message: 'Medieval interpreters', he explains, 'were wrong in taking the world as a univocal text; modern interpreters are wrong in taking every text as an unshaped world.'[20]

Commenting on *Un drame bien parisien* (1890), a short story by the French author Alphonse Allais (1855-1905), Eco tries to illustrate the dialectic between freedom and fidelity, analysing systematically the coexistence of determinacy and indeterminacy. To begin with, he argues, the reading process tends towards the construction of an *interpretative coherence* which he calls the *topic*, comparing it to Greimas' concept of *isotopy* (cf. above). Returning to Kafka's parable *Before the Law*, one could say that a reader could decide that the *topic* of this text is the 'law' in the juridical sense (thus misreading its polysemy); however, other readers could decide that the topic is a religious or a metaphysical one, etc. In Alphonse Allais' text, Eco explains, at least two *topics* coexist, both of which are related to the jealousy of the young couple acting at the centre of the scene. For the text can be read simultaneously as a story about an act of adultery *and* as a story about a misunderstanding (concerning adultery).

The naive reader is likely to decide in favour of one of the two *topics* (*isotopies* in the sense of Greimas) and to ignore the other one along with the ambiguity or polysemy of the text. From a semiotic point of view, Eco explains, at least three stories coexist: the story of the two characters Raoul and Marguerite, the story of the naive reader who is aware of only one *topic*, and the story of the critical reader who relates the two topics to one another, thus reflecting the role of the naive reader whose limited horizon (*horizon of expectation, Erwartungshorizont,* Jauss would say) is observed with hidden irony by Allais' narrator.

Here it becomes clearer what Eco means by a dialectic between freedom and fidelity to the text, between indeterminacy and determinacy. Unlike the naive reader who spontaneously decides in favour of certain semantic structures, neglecting all the others, the critical reader becomes aware of the complexity of the text, i.e. of it determinacies *and* its indeterminacies, of its relative openness *and* the limits of interpretative freedom. Within this context Eco distinguishes the *usage* (*uso*) of a text from its *interpretation* (*interpretazione*). Unlike the naive reader who spontaneously 'uses' Allais' story in order to satisfy various aesthetic, emotional or ideological needs, the critical reader takes into account all aspects of the structure, thus interpreting it – and the role of the reader(s) – in a totalising perspective. It is interesting to observe how in Eco's carefully argued theory the Kantian and the Hegelian impulses check each other: while the Kantian impulse tends towards an emphasis on openness and ambiguity (coexistence of heterogeneous or incompatible *topics*), the Hegelian impulse tends towards determinacy, limitation, and totalisation. The critical reader follows both impulses controlling them by semiotic means.

According to Eco the possibility of a reflexive and critical reading process depends on the capacity of the reader's *encyclopedia*. What exactly does he mean by this term? He means the reader's global knowledge: the acquired literary and non-literary culture. In *Lector in fabula* he speaks of a 'global system' which can be considered as *encyclopedic competence*.[21] Hence the encyclopedia could be conceived of as a linguistic and cultural competence used by the reader in order to define the *topic(s)* and the narrative structures of a text. (In Eco's later works the notion of *encyclopedia* replaces the notion of *code* which Eco finds too restrictive.)

The reader's response to historical novels, for example, illustrates what is meant by *encyclopedia* and *encyclopedic competence*; for in order to understand and enjoy this type of novel it is necessary to have at one's disposal a considerable amount of historical and geographic knowledge. In order to understand, for example, Sir Walter Scott's novel *Kenilworth* (1821) or his *St. Ronan's Well* (1823), it is indispensable to have some knowledge of Scottish history, geography, and culture. It goes without saying that literary competence is also part and parcel of the reader's encyclopedia: 'The encyclopedia', Eco explains, 'does not only register the "historical" truth that Napoleon died in St. Helena, but also the "literary" truth that Julia died in Verona.'[22]

The 'openness' of the text in the sense of Kant's 'without concept' (i.e. without the possibility of univocal definition) is therefore limited both on the semantic and on the pragmatic level. It is limited on the semantic level insofar as the *topics* or *isotopies* cannot be arbitrarily chosen or defined by the reader whose freedom of interpretation is constantly being restrained by semantic and narrative structures. It is also limited on the pragmatic level (i.e. on the level of social experience) because most readers only have a limited encyclopedia at their disposal, which makes it difficult for them to take into account all semantic elements, all meanings of the text. Some of these meanings remain hidden forever: for example in ancient Greek or Roman texts referring to other texts, some of which have long since disappeared, or to customs quite unknown to philologists and to the average reader. As in the case of Jauss' and Iser's reader-response criticism both 'openness' and 'closure' of a text are due to the interaction between the semantic and narrative structures on the one hand and the *horizon of expectations* (Jauss) or the *encyclopedia* (Eco) on the other.

It is clear therefore that a text encourages certain interpretations and discourages others within a certain *encyclopedic context* or *horizon of expectations*. 'In this sense', Eco points out, 'the internal textual coherence controls the otherwise uncontrollable drives of the reader.'[23] This is roughly what Ingarden says – albeit in a phenomenological context – about the relationship between text and reader (cf. chap. 6).

Eco's approach is slightly more concrete when he distinguishes between an *intentio operis* and an *intentio lectoris*:

> The problem is that, if one perhaps knows what is meant by 'intention of the reader', it seems more difficult to define abstractly what is meant by 'intention of the text'. The text's intention is not displayed by the textual surface. (. . .) One has to decide to 'see' it. Thus it is possible to speak of the text's intention only as the result of a conjecture on the part of the reader.[24]

As far as this dialectic goes, Eco's theory is more dynamic and more flexible than that of Greimas and his disciples who seek to give an 'objective' account of textual structures, forgetting that this account is always the result of subjective conjectures. In the last chapter the question to what extent the text is always the construction of a subject will be dealt with more thoroughly.

From what has been said so far, it will have appeared that Eco's theory moves from the radical avant-garde postulate about the *openness* of literary texts to a more modest and cautious stance which makes the text appear as an ambiguous entity that encourages some interpretations and discourages others. Within the framework of this dialectic between *openness* and *closure*, Eco criticises what he calls *overinterpretation*: the attempt of – mainly deconstructionist critics – to project certain meanings into a work of literature which the latter does not warrant, which it neither encourages nor discourages. Eco's critique of Geoffrey H. Hartman's deconstructive readings will be referred to in the next chapter where a certain arbitrariness of deconstructive analyses will be revealed.

However, Eco's move away from the experimental *openness* of the avant-garde to a more moderate hermeneutic of semantic limitation is not only relevant within the semiotic context, but also important from an aesthetic point of view. For with the publication in 1980 of his bestseller *Il nome della rosa* (Engl. 1983) he renounces his avant-garde critique of commercial literature in capitalist society and adopts a *postmodern* aesthetic tending to reconcile some experimental practices with a readable, consumer-friendly narration. *The Name of the Rose* is, as Werner Hüllen points out, 'certainly an open novel in Eco's sense. However, in contrast with other works which Eco describes as being typical for openness – especially the works of James Joyce – it has a very conventional form'.[25]

This return to literary convention and to a plot characteristic of the detective novel (at the end of the day Jorge appears as the villain) corresponds to a trend within postmodernism: to the revaluation of popular and commercial forms which are no longer condemned in the name of negativity and of avant-garde radicalism. This radicalism, Eco argues, has become sterile, because its repertoire of experiments and innovations is exhausted:

> But the moment comes when the avant-garde (the modern) can go no further, because it has produced a metalanguage that speaks of its impossible texts (conceptual art). The postmodern reply to the modern consists of recognizing that the past, since it cannot really be destroyed, because its destruction leads to silence, must be revisited: but with irony, not innocently.[26]

The Name of the Rose illustrates better than any other text this postmodern creed adopted by the Italian semiotician.

The ninth chapter will reveal, however, that Eco's is not the only postmodern aesthetic. Lyotard, turning to Kant's theory of the Sublime, develops an aesthetic of radical negativity which, although it is reminiscent of Critical Theory, differs substantially from the latter by its unidimensional destructiveness. Unlike

Adorno who was anxious to preserve the utopian moment by defending the autonomy of the individual, Lyotard abandons the complementary ideas of subjectivity and utopia. His only aim is to represent the negativity of late capitalism.

The postmodern Eco's problem seems to be that – unlike the early Eco of the avant-garde period – he does not seem to be aware of this negativity: of the destructive forces of capitalist production. By simply ignoring them in his later writings, by pleading in favour of a postmodern aesthetics of consumer-friendly literature, he abandons his own critical stance of the Sixties. In this respect his intellectual itinerary runs parallel to that of Hans Robert Jauss who eventually tried to combine aesthetic distance with aesthetic identification and catharsis. Both authors seem to act in accordance with the signs of the times. After the crippling defeats of socialism, it no longer seems opportune to expose the negativity of late capitalism and of its commercialised culture.

3 Roland Barthes' Nietzschean Aesthetics

In contrast to Greimas and Eco, Barthes – at least in his later writings – finds it hard to believe in any kind of semantic structure that would restrict the openness of texts and the metamorphoses of meaning. He appears as a semiotic antipodes of Greimas who subordinates the conceptual elements of the *content plane* to the *polysemies* of the *expression plane* and the autonomy of the *signifier*. Insofar as his aesthetic approach is inspired by Nietzsche's critique of metaphysics (cf. chap. 1.2), he announces the problems and arguments of the deconstructionists. This is why his model concludes this chapter. For it also bridges the gap between semiotics and deconstruction, an approach which can be considered as Nietzschean in most respects.

The shift from Kant and Hegel to Nietzsche that can be observed in Barthes' work is a paradigmatic shift from the *content* to the *expression plane* and from a strong (Cartesian, Hegelian) or a weak (Kantian) conceptualisation to a radical negation of the concept and its applicability to literature. Barthes himself tries to explain and justify this shift in a commentary on his intellectual development which moved from a systematic conceptual approach to a Nietzschean celebration of the *polysemic signifier*. He distinguishes three phases, the first of which is dominated by the critique of ideology in the Neomarxist sense and in the sense of Critical Theory: 'Semiology appeared to me, then, in its program and its tasks, as the fundamental method of an ideological critique.'[27] *Le Degré zéro de l'écriture* (1953) and *Mythologies* (1957) were written in this first period. The second period, explains Barthes, 'was that of science, or at least of scientificity'.[28] At this point he developed a systematic approach towards the semiotics of fashion (*Système de la mode*, 1967) that was inspired – among other things – by Lévi-Strauss' structural anthropology: 'The pleasure of system', Barthes comments, 'replaced the superego of science: this was already a preparation for the third phase of this adventure: finally indifferent to an indifferent science (an *adiaphoric* science, as Nietzsche had said), I entered by "pleasure" into the Signifier, into the Text.'[29]

In other words, the third phase which this analysis focuses on is marked by a playful adherence to the polysemy of the signifier. It is also marked by Nietzsche's philosophy which doubts the authority of the concept, revealing the dependence of metaphysical truth on the collusion of tropes, of rhetorical figures, and the illusory character of subjective identity. Although this should not be taken to mean that Barthes' Nietzschean critique is restricted to this phase of his intellectual development, it is particularly important in the last ten years of his life (1970-1980).

In the course of this decade Barthes abandons the concept of *structure* (this is why he is often referred to as a 'post-structuralist') and replaces it with (non-)concepts such as *signifying practice (pratique signifiante)* and *play (jeu)*. For Barthes, the Nietzschean critic, the aesthetic link between *text* and *signifier* is crucial: 'The instance of the text is not signification but the signifier, in the semiotic and the psychoanalytic acceptation of that term (. . .).'[30] In *S/Z*, a thorough analysis of Balzac's short novel *Sarrasine*, he holds that the ideal text is not a meaningful structure of *signifieds*, but '*a galaxy of signifiers*': '*une galaxie de signifiants, non une structure de signifiés*'.[31] But what exactly is the role of the *signifier* in Barthes' theory of the text and in his aesthetics?

If the concept of *signifier* in the sense of Barthes is to be defined or described with some precision, it has to be made clear that it is being used metaphorically and hence cannot be read as a synonym of Saussure's *signifiant*. For Barthes' signifier is a lot more than the phonetic side of the sign: it is the sound of music, the image in all meanings of this word; it is the graphic sign and the generalised polysemic sign that is not reducible to the concept. One could also argue that it is a metaphoric reference to the *expression plane* and that Barthes is the theoretician par excellence of this linguistic plane.

In an attempt to upgrade the variable, polymorphic, and polysemic graphic sign, Barthes sets out to demonstrate in 'Erté ou à la lettre' (1973), an analysis of Erté's famous alphabet of letters composed of erotic figures, to what extent the letter as a graphic unit defies communication and conceptualisation. Barthes challenges the rationalist creed according to which the graphic sign is no more than a simple instrument of communication. To him Erté's alphabet appears as a subversive transformation of the communicative sign into an erotic image which gives us pleasure.

Divested of all communicative functions, the pure *phoné* of music, viewed by Nietzsche as the highest of all arts, appeals to those who do not search for meaning; it can be considered as analogous to the free-floating graphic sign: 'Music is that which the text expresses and leaves implicit: whatever is being expressed, but not articulated: whatever is outside meaning and the meaningless, whatever belongs to *signifiance* which contemporary textual theory postulates and tries to define'.[32] It is not by chance that towards the end of his article 'La Musique, la voix, la langue', which was quoted here, Barthes praises music for '*being a good metaphor*' ('*d'être une bonne métaphore*'). The link which he tries to establish between music and language reappears in his essay on Schumann where both, music and text, are presented as open-ended processes of signification, as *signifiance*: 'Thanks to music we understand the text as signifiance better.'[33] In spite of these exploratory incursions into the graphic and the acoustic world, Barthes tends to concentrate on the linguistic signifier which he rediscovers (in a *de-familiarised* form, the Formalists would say) in Chinese and Japanese, in two languages whose *signifiers* have detached themselves from their *signifieds* – at least from the point of view of a 'speechless' European. Watching Antonioni's film about China, Barthes is overcome by the feeling of listening to the buzz of language: '*le bruissement de la langue*', its music that speaks to us without articulating any *signifieds* or concepts. He describes a similar experience in *L'Empire des signes*

(1970), which is not so much a book about Japan, but a book about pure language sound which – to the European – seems delivered from conceptual meaning.

Barthes feels at home in this empire of pure sound, in a world where the domination of conceptual thought has been superseded by the freedom of imagination. It is the world of the French historian Michelet whom Barthes admires for having preserved and expanded the polysemy of language and its figures. He calls him the 'prince of the signifier'[34], thus conferring upon him the greatest honour the semantics of Barthian discourse allow for. Stéphane Mallarmé is the other ally in Barthes' unrelenting struggle against the rule of the concept, against *logocentrism*: 'We had to wait till Mallarmé for our literature to conceive a free signifier no longer burdened by the censure of the false signified, and to attempt a writing finally rid of the historical repression in which the privileges of "thought" imprison it.'[35]

Barthes' critique of the signified which throughout his work accompanies his struggle for openness or polysemy, is to be understood globally as a sustained polemic against semiotic theories that are geared primarily towards the *content plane* and neglect the *expression plane*. His rejection of these theories, blamed for their Cartesian rationalism, implies a rejection of Saussure's and Greimas' rationalist systems. For Saussure, Barthes explains, the signified meaning is the linguistic equivalent of the gold standard in economics: like gold which is meant to form the basis of economic value, the signified is regarded by rationalists of all origins as the foundation of linguistic meaning. Coining the expression '*the Gold of the Signified*'[36], Barthes traces a parallel between language and finance: between the communicated concept and the exchange value imposed by the markets.

At the same time, however, he opposes the Saussure of the *anagrams* to Saussure the rationalist, the Cartesian. For he believes that Saussure's theory of the anagrams which is not based on rational inductions or deductions but on hidden phonetic and graphic associations (e.g. plum-lump; amor-Roma; aimer-Marie), contradicts and subverts the rationalist's conception of language as a system of logically structured functions.[37]

In the next chapter it will become clear to what extent deconstruction can also be regarded as a radical Nietzschean critique of linguistic rationalism and Hegelian conceptualism. It will be shown that the deconstructionists – like Barthes – follow Nietzsche by insisting on the *particularity* of the sign (its graphic, phonetic aspect) and by subordinating its *universal* components (the *signified*, the *concept*) to this particularity. Globally speaking, 'post-structuralism' in its Barthian and its deconstructionist form could therefore be considered as a strong tendency towards particularisation and a move away from universalist rationalism.

This general tendency is common to Barthes (who published several of his articles in the avant-garde review *Tel Quel*) and other *Tel Quel* authors such as Derrida, Julia Kristeva, and Jean-Joseph Goux. Following Nietzsche, they established a link between the domination of the concept, the metaphysical tradition, and the domination of society by the *exchange value*, the market laws. 'From Aristotle to Martinet', Goux argues, 'the accent is put unanimously on the *exchange value* of signs.'[38] In his struggle against the *signified* ('*ce monstre: le Dernier Signifié*')[39] and ultimate meaning, Barthes – like the other *Tel Quel* authors – defends whatever cannot be universally exchanged: the *particular*, that which has *no equivalent*.

Along with signified, exchangeable meaning Barthes and his friends challenge the notion of author: of an identifiable subject responsible for a homogeneous meaning. Where meaning as a totality in the hermeneutic and the Hegelian-Marxist sense is radically criticised and superseded by *openness* or *signifiance*, the subject as a guarantor of coherence is also sacrificed. From a Barthian point of view, the notion of author is inseparable from the *signified*, the *signifié*: 'We expect the *author* to move from signified to signifier, from content to form, from project to text (. . .).'[40] Rejecting this priority of conceptual content over form, Barthes imagines the text as an open collusion of signifiers, as a *signifiance* or a process of meaning that cannot be arrested by a semantic definition in the sense of Greimas' *deep structure*.

In short: Barthes' idea of the text corresponds to that of the European avant-garde of the 1950s and 1960s. It is similar to that of the *Tel Quel* group, of the Nouveau Roman (Robbe-Grillet, Butor), and of the Nouveau Nouveau Roman (Ricardou, Sollers). However, its origins can be traced back to the French Surrealists, to Bataille, Brecht, Mallarmé, and – Nietzsche. The importance of Robbe-Grillet for Barthes' aesthetics comes to the fore in the early

Essais critiques (1964), where, quoting the *nouveau romancier*, Barthes explains why he intends to renounce the concepts of subjectivity, intentionality, and meaning and why '*literature is by definition formal*' ('*la littérature est par définition formelle*').[41] Apart from projecting literature – and indeed all texts – onto the *expression plane*, he places it in the avant-garde context which has been particularly important for literary theory ever since it was launched as a theory of innovation and a norm-breaking practice by the Russian Formalists and Futurists.

His avant-garde aesthetic does not only emphasise the signifier but also the *desire* (*désir*) and the *pleasure* (*plaisir*) which are inherent in texts and which are both of Nietzschean origin. In an interview published in 1981 he comments on the relationship between sensuality and avant-garde practice: 'Whenever it's the *body* which writes, and not ideology, there's a chance the text will join us in our modernity.'[42] In this respect, he argues, Sade, Fourier, and Loyola, whose discourses he compares systematically[43], have created '*languages of desire*' ('*des langues du désir*').[44] Not their philosophies or ideologies are important – Sade's ideas about sexuality, Fourier's socialism or Loyola's theology – but their discursive practices aiming at *classification* (of sexual acts, social or religious practices, rituals). For all of these practices are invested by desire.

However, this desire can only thrive if texts are conceived of as open constructs which do not limit the reader's imagination. Barthes' own somewhat extravagant reading of Sade, Fourier, and Loyola illustrates what he means by textual openness: it is the freedom of readers to read texts against the grain and to associate – within a completely new context – authors whom one would normally not bring together. Their texts become comparable only when projected onto the formal level of the *signifier*, the *expression plane*.

On this level Barthes distinguishes the *readable* (*lisible*) from the *writable* (*scriptible*) text. In contrast with the *writable* text which reflects the practice of the contemporary avant-garde and which contemporary authors can go on writing, the *readable* text has lost all of its practical relevance: it can still be read, but cannot be used as a model of writing, of *écriture*. Barthes explains: 'The writable text *is us writing*, before the never ending game of the world (the world as game) has been paced, cut, crossed and manipulated by a particular system (ideology, genre, critique) (. . .).'[45] Barthes, the Nietzschean and avant-garde writer, then turns against the *readable*, the classical, the dead text: 'As the *vis-à-vis* of the writable text there is the negative, reactive value, its countervalue: that which can be read but not written: the *readable*. Every readable text we call a classical text.'[46] Vincent Jouve has found an even more radical notion of textuality in Barthes' work: the *texte recevable*. It is the radically avant-garde text that cannot *yet* be written; it is the text to come, the text of the future.[47]

Barthes believes that Balzac's short story *Sarrasine* exemplifies the *readable* or classical text that can be actualised or re-activated by a polysemic reading in the course of which its ambiguity and its different levels of meaning become apparent. It is the story of the French painter Sarrasine told by the narrator-hero to Madame de Rochefide. The main topic of the story is Sarrasine's love for the castrato Zambinella whom the painter mistakes for a beautiful woman. The title *S/Z* which brings together the abbreviated names of Sarrasine and Zambinella contains a fundamental ambiguity which seems to undermine – together with the phonetic relevance criteria (S=voiceless, Z=voiced) – the semantically relevant opposition between *masculine* and *feminine*. This opposition is put in question by the presence of Zambinella who is *neither* masculine *nor* feminine. In an interview Barthes comments on the ambiguity of the title: 'It is a title which contains several meanings and in this respect it announces one of the projects underlying the book: the attempt to demonstrate the possibilities of a pluralist criticism which attributes several meanings to a text.'[48]

In order to reveal these meanings and the plural, polysemic character of Balzac's text, Barthes uses two key concepts: *connotation* and *code*. The first (Hjelmslevian) concept which was introduced here in conjunction with Eco's semiotics (see above) is defined by Barthes in accordance with Hjelmslev and Eco as *secondary meaning*: 'Itself constituted by an encounter of signifiers and signifieds, the first message becomes the simple signifier of the second message, according to a kind of disconnected movement, since a single element of the second message (its signifier) is extensive with the totality of the first message.'[49] Thus a secondary or connotated signified comes about.

In his 'pluralist' analysis of Balzac's *Sarrasine*, Barthes sets out to show how the reader reconstructs different meanings (signifieds) in the text by becoming aware of the corresponding textual codes. By *code* Barthes simply means a way of reading or as Louis-Jean Calvet puts it: '*direction potentielle de lecture*'.[50] The *code* directs and regulates the reading process which results in a *lexie* (one of the several textual meanings). By revealing the coexistence of several *lexies* in Balzac's text, Barthes hopes to demonstrate its irreducibly plural character.

In his analysis he distinguishes five *codes* which make five different 'readings' or attributions of meaning possible: 1. a code of *action* which presents the text as a causal sequence; 2. a *hermeneutic* code which revolves around Zambinella's ambiguous identity; 3. a *semic* code which contains the semantic elements – mainly the opposition *masculine/feminine* – marking the protagonists and their actions; 4. the *symbolic* code which articulates the polysemy of the text; 5. finally the *referential* code which Barthes describes (rather vaguely) as consisting of 'the quotations from the thesaurus of knowledge and wisdom'.[51]

Although Barthes may genuinely believe that by offering this kind of semiotic analysis, he has demonstrated the plural character of the text, it is by no means certain that he has refuted the existence of *deep structures* or at least *semantic structures* underlying Balzac's story as a whole. When he argues, for example, that the story is globally structured by the semantic opposition between *active* and *passive*, *castrating* and *castrated* characters[52], he comes very close to a structural analysis in the sense of Greimas. And Greimas is not altogether wrong when he points out that 'Barthes only discovers deep structures in order to condemn them'.[53] There is a certain amount of truth in this ironical remark: for it shows that Barthes' radical pluralism is as one-sided as Greimas' rigorous monism or semanticism. The text is neither a univocal message nor an undefinable plurality in the sense of *signifiance*; it is a dynamic synthesis of openness and closure that cannot be reduced to a static *deep structure* or to a plurality of readings. Therefore Eco is right in arguing that the reader's response is always a response to something that is *structured*.

In the next chapter it will be shown to what extent this statement is neglected by the deconstructionists who, following

Nietzsche's playful 'linguistics' and aesthetics, radicalise Barthes' stance, denying the very existence of semantic structures. They adopt – rather uncritically – Nietzsche's idea that all concepts ultimately depend on tropes (rhetorical figures) whose polysemy makes all attempts to fix or define meaning appear futile.

CHAPTER 7
The Nietzschean Aesthetics of Deconstruction

The 'Nietzschean turn' which was announced in the last section of the preceding chapter is at the centre of the deconstructionist scene. Unlike the theories of Jauss, Benjamin, Adorno or Eco, the deconstructionist approach cannot be understood as an aesthetic situated between Kant and Hegel, as a theory oscillating between openness ('without concept') and systematic, conceptual closure, between *signifier* and *signified*. For Derrida and his American followers attack the very notion of concept, the idea that it is possible to distinguish an *expression plane*, which varies from language to language, from a *content plane* consisting of invariable concepts or pure forms common to all languages and human beings.

This Platonic idea is rejected and replaced by a radical Nietzschean critique based on the assumption that all concepts are pseudo-concepts because they depend on rhetorical figures or tropes: on metaphors, metonymies, synecdoches. Even such apparently scientific concepts like *isotopy* (Greimas), *deep structure* (Greimas) or *content plane* (Hjelmslev), they would argue, are latent metaphors inextricably tied up with the rhetorical images of 'place' (*topos*), 'depth', 'content', and 'plane' (= flat surface).

In other words, deconstruction – like Nietzsche's theory of language – eliminates the metaphysical, conceptual dimension which Plato's, Aristotle's, Descartes', Hegel's, and even Kant's philosophies thrive on: the dimension of logic or pure form (Plato) which all idealist philosophy considers as fundamental and superior to the 'variable' aspects of language such as rhetorical figures, homonyms, and entire phonetic systems that distinguish languages from one another. Deconstruction is one-dimensional insofar as it follows Nietzsche in denying the autonomy of the conceptual (ideal) world and the very possibility of distinguishing concept and phonetic form, *signified* and *signifier*, *content* and *expression*.

Considering language in a perspective that is quite similar to

Barthes', Derrida refuses to derive the *signifier* from the *signified*, arguing that meaning can never be fixed by relating synonyms or synonymous words from different languages to an apparently invariable concept, because this concept is an illusion based on our idealist prejudice that 'behind' the varying and volatile linguistic expressions there is something constant and stable these expressions can be related to. In reality, explains Derrida, concepts are no more than illusory effects brought about by the never-ending interplay of signifiers. Like Barthes' semiology, his theory of language and his aesthetics are oriented towards the expression plane and strongly opposed to the Platonic, rationalist (Cartesian), and Hegelian domination of the concept, referred to by Derrida as *logocentrism*. Adopting a Barthian perspective, one could define Derrida's brand of deconstruction as a theory of *signifiance*, an open-ended *process of meaning*.

So far this theory has been characterised mainly negatively in contrast to Platonism, rationalism, and Hegelianism. In what follows it will be shown, however, that it was not only influenced by Nietzsche's critique of metaphysics, but also by Heidegger's continuation of this critique and by German Romantic philosophy. Especially Geoffrey H. Hartman's conception of literary criticism bears all the marks of Romantic poetics in the sense of Friedrich Schlegel, whom Hartman quotes on several occasions. Hartman is a particularly typical representative of American deconstruction insofar as he combines the influences of Romantic and of Nietzschean philosophy.

Although Romantic influence is not immediately discernible in Derrida's work, the philosophically-minded reader is struck by the affinity between Friedrich Schlegel's and Derrida's theories of language. Both theories oppose the rationalist tenet that language is an instrument of communication and a vehicle of conceptualisation, explanation, and definition. Romantics and deconstructionists stand the rationalist argument on its head by pointing out that the polysemic, metaphoric word, far from being a means of communication and comprehension, is an obstacle to both.

Finally, Derrida's radical critique of Hegel is often reminiscent of certain Young Hegelian polemics against the Hegelian system. On several occasions it will become clear in this chapter that deconstruction is not only a Nietzschean, but also a Young

Hegelian approach that challenges Hegel's systematic conceptual thought by a philosophical anarchism, some of which reminds us of Stirner, Feuerbach, Ruge, and other rebellious disciples of Hegel.

1 The Philosophical Origins of Deconstruction: From Platonism and Hegelianism to Nietzsche and Heidegger

In order to understand Derrida's philosophy it is necessary to remember that he associates *logocentrism* or the domination of the concept (see above) with the idea that this domination was made possible in European metaphysics by a systematic subordination of the *written* to the *spoken* word. Plato, Derrida believes, was among the first to degrade the written word, which he compared to a drug – a *pharmakon* – designed to assist our memory in its struggle against oblivion. Like all drugs, *writing* or *écriture* combines certain immediate advantages with disastrous side-effects. On the one hand, it offers crucial points of reference to our memory; on the other hand it may cause memory to atrophy by preventing us from using it regularly. Like all his idealist heirs, Plato eventually condemns the written word (*écriture*) accusing it of being hostile to life and living thought. Moreover, it is unstable and unreliable, because it can be read and interpreted in many different contexts prone to permanent change. Far from safeguarding the immediate *presence of conceptual truth* – as does the spoken word, the *parole* – the written text, according to Plato, depends on changeable *opinion*.

It is interesting to note that in Derrida's interpretation of Plato *writing* is not condemned for technical reasons (as an inadequate aid for example), but on moral grounds, because it leads to the instability of *meaning*. It tends to call into question the presence of truth which can only be brought about by the univocity of the spoken word, the *parole*. According to Derrida, most idealist philosophers prefer the *parole* to the *écriture* which they consider with suspicion, although they depend on it as *writers*.

This ambivalent love–hate attitude towards the written word, Derrida argues, is characteristic of European philosophers such as Rousseau, Condillac, Hegel, Heidegger, and even Nietzsche. Rousseau appears to him as a representative of the Platonic tradition 'which determines literary writing in terms of the speech present in the story or song (. . .).'[1] Within this *phonocentric* perspective, writing is envisaged as secondary or derived: as an irritating *supplement* that detracts from the univocity and purity of speech, of the *phoné*.

Far from being a *supplement*, Derrida points out in his critique of Rousseau, the written word as *archi-écriture* is inherent in all acts of speech. This should not be taken to mean that Derrida naively presupposes the historical precedence of writing; he does believe, however, that the seemingly univocal *parole* is not immune to the effects of polysemy which haunt the written message as it moves from context to context. Logocentrism, Derrida adds, is no guarantee of immunity in spite of all its efforts to ban ambiguity and polysemy with the help of conceptual systems and definitions.

Even more suspicious of writing than Rousseau, Etienne Bonnot de Condillac appears to Derrida as a rationalist guardian of the *presence of meaning* (*présence du sens*) guaranteed by the spoken word. According to Condillac, Derrida explains, there is a close link between writing and a frivolous way of life, between *écriture* and *frivolité*: 'The source of all evil is writing. The frivolous style is the – written style. (. . .) It is enough to be methodical in order to avoid being frivolous.'[2] A paternal authority, a Father, is therefore needed who will keep a close eye on the frivolous writing of the philosopher. This father is the *logocentrism* or *phallogocentrism* (logos + phallus) of idealist philosophers such as Hegel, Husserl, and even Heidegger whose thought had a lasting impact on Derrida's deconstruction.

The case of Hegel – as presented by Derrida – is particularly interesting because of its ambivalence. On the one hand, Derrida reads Hegel as the main representative of *phono-* and *logocentrism*, as the systematic thinker of social and historical totality, as the philosopher of conceptualisation; on the other hand, he discerns in Hegel's discourse a global tendency which subverts the domination of the concept, a tendency which announces the openness of writing.

Derrida sets out to demonstrate that Hegel follows the rules of the metaphysical tradition by favouring the spoken word to which he had to 'subordinate writing'[3] In the first chapter it has already been pointed out that Hegel's *logocentrism* leads to a strong emphasis on the *content plane* in aesthetics at the expense of the *expression plane* (Hjelmslev) and of artistic polysemy. 'Nevertheless', remarks Derrida, 'all that Hegel thought within this horizon, all, that is, except eschatology, may be reread as a meditation on writing.'[4]

One is struck by the Young Hegelian diction of this sentence. Like Feuerbach, Marx, and Engels who perceive in Hegel's all-encompassing idealism the contours of a revolutionary theory which will put an end to the idealist tradition as such, Derrida believes that Hegel's extreme form of logocentrism anticipates the writing of deconstruction or deconstructive writing. How are we to imagine this mutation or transformation of systematic philosophy into deconstruction? Is it possible to read Hegel as a deconstructionist?

In *La Dissémination* and other texts, Derrida quotes numerous passages from Hegel's work in order to show to what extent the aspiration towards total and absolute knowledge turns against itself, as it were, vitiating the presence of meaning and the domination of the concept. He insists on Hegel's idea that dialectical thought which aspires towards total knowledge cannot be summarised in a *preface*. For Hegel himself explains in his *Science of Logic* why dialectical logic cannot be presented in a short summary: the global context can only be understood when it is finished, when the dialectical movement has come to an end (*Vollendung*). But this movement cannot come to an end, argues Derrida, because history continues, because language and discourse continue, because life itself continues.

Hence completion or *Vollendung* in the Hegelian sense is an idealist, logocentric illusion, says Derrida. Following the Young Hegelians and Nietzsche, he doubts the possibility of Hegelian syntheses which are made possible by the concept of *Aufhebung* and are responsible for the closure, the completion of Hegel's system. In *Glas*, an experimental text which juxtaposes and interprets extracts from Hegel's and Jean Genet's (a rebellious writer's) works, he seeks to demonstrate that *Aufhebung* is simply a *tour de force* imposed by conceptual domination: 'Thus *Aufhebung* is also a suppressive counterpressure, a counterforce, a *Hemmung* (. . .).'[5] From a semiotic point of view it appears as a metaphysical idealisation: 'The concept relieves the sign that relieves the thing.'[6] In other words: the object is dissolved in the concept (it is identified, Adorno would say, with the conceptual thought of the subject).

Rewording Adorno's negativity, Derrida suggests that we should cease to envisage the unity of opposites as a *synthesis* or *Aufhebung* and instead rediscover the negativity of Hegel's dialectics. For in German, *aufheben* does not only mean to *retrieve* or *preserve*, but also to *cancel* or *nullify* (a decision is nullified: *ein Beschluss wird aufgehoben*). Having exposed the ambivalence of this key Hegelian concept, Derrida attempts to derive his own anti-concept of *différance* from this deconstructive negativity of Hegelian dialectics. For it is perfectly possible to envisage the unity of opposites without synthesis, without *Aufhebung*: as a *radical ambivalence* or *aporia*. (Opposites such as good and evil, essence and appearance, truth and falsehood may be considered as belonging together without forming dialectical syntheses and a coherent whole as is the case in Hegel's system.) In this context the idea of synthesis is superseded by the deconstructive idea of *aporia* which – as will be shown later on – is at the centre of Paul de Man's aesthetics. Derrida mentions 'that singular aporia called "deconstruction"'.[7]

It will become clear, especially in conjunction with the American deconstructionists, that deconstruction is a systematic attempt to reveal the negativity of a text: its ambiguities, aporias, and polysemies – all that escapes conceptualisation or conceptual definition. In this respect, the deconstructionists can indeed be considered as the antipodes of Hegel and the Hegelian Marxists.

Their main sources of inspiration are Nietzsche and Heidegger. Since Nietzsche's role in Derrida's philosophy will be discussed in more detail in the next section, it seems crucial to consider Husserl's and Heidegger's deconstructive potential at this stage. It is not altogether surprising that, having found a penchant for logocentrism in the philosophies of Plato, Rousseau, and Hegel, Derrida finds traces of *phono-* and *logocentrism* in Husserl's phenomenology and Heidegger's existentialist ontology.

Husserl, the founder of modern phenomenology, is accused by Derrida of having consolidated the domination of the spoken word and the concept within the metaphysical tradition. In *La Voix et le phénomène*, Husserl appears as one of the staunchest exponents of this tradition: 'Husserl radicalises the necessary privilege of the *phoné* which is inherent in the entire history of metaphysics, by exploiting all the available resources with the greatest critical refinement.'[8] Husserl, explains Derrida, undertakes everything in order to restrict the 'excesses of meaning' due to philosophical *writing* (*écriture*) and to the uncontrollable polysemy of the signifier. He goes out of his way to safeguard 'the pre-expressive layer of meaning' and 'the conceptual and universal form'.[9] In other words, he is determined to finish Plato's metaphysical project designed to isolate the pure idea (not contaminated by material expressions) and to bring about the *presence of meaning* (*présence du sens*). In spite of all these metaphysical efforts, says Derrida, Husserl is finally obliged to recognise the irreducible autonomy of the signifier and to deconstruct his own discourse.

Although Martin Heidegger is far more critical than Husserl of the metaphysical tradition which he associates with the Nietzschean *will to power* and the technological domination of the human Subject over nature, he is nevertheless a philosopher of the spoken word, of *phonocentrism* and *logocentrism*: 'Implicitly or explicitly, the valorization of spoken language is constant and massive in Heidegger.'[10] Despite this strong metaphysical tendency, Derrida discovers traces of negativity in Heidegger's philosophy. As in the case of Husserl, Hegel, and other representatives of *logocentrism*, Derrida sets out to show to what extent even Heidegger's defence of the concept (as spoken word, as presence of meaning) is subverted by the philosopher's own discourse.

In his attempts to think the difference between Being and Existence, Heidegger discovers that the two cannot be identified (defined) outside their *difference*. He therefore tries to think the difference as such: that which cannot be fixed or identified outside the differing process: '*das Differente aus der Differenz*'.[11] For Derrida this discovery of difference as a process which does not lead to identification and definition is decisive, because it enables him to formulate his own anti-concept of *différance*, a neologism derived from the French words *différence* (difference) and *différer* (to differ, to postpone). In a first step, *différance* could be described as a *process of meaning* which no attempt at conceptualisation or definition can put an end to. It is a perpetual negation of what Derrida calls the *presence of meaning* or *présence du sens*; it could be compared to Barthes' *signifiance* (cf. chap. 6.3).

Considered within the context of this book, Derrida's position appears not only as a radical negation of rationalist and Hegelian attempts at conceptualisation (of literature, of the text), but also as a challenge to the more moderate position of Kantians like Mukařovský and Eco who believe that in spite of its relative openness and interpretability a text has structures accessible to conceptual analysis. Derrida denies this, arguing that the very concept of *structure* is a *logocentrist* myth which dissolves in the process of *différance*.

Although he owes the notion of *différance* to Heidegger's *Differenz*, Derrida is primarily a Nietzschean thinker who sets out to show how the metaphysical search for truth – from Plato to Heidegger – has failed. This assessment is confirmed by Christopher Norris:

> Thus when Heidegger puts forward a reading of Nietzsche as 'the last metaphysician', Derrida can shrewdly turn back his argument by pointing out that Nietzsche has anticipated any such critique through rhetorically deconstructing all claims to knowledge, his own included. It is Heidegger's quest for meaning and authenticity – his entire philosophical hermeneutic – which thus becomes the target of Derrida's Nietzschean critique.[12]

It was the aim of this introductory section to show that Derrida's Nietzschean critique is not only directed against Heidegger, but against virtually all metaphysical thinkers. The argument put forward by the deconstructionists thrives on a paradox: in trying to consolidate the domination of the concept (the *presence of meaning*), the metaphysicians achieve the very opposite, thus *deconstructing* their own project.

In what follows, the philosophical argument will be completed by a semiotic and a literary one. It will be shown what the expression 'Nietzschean critique' means within a linguistic (semiotic) context and why this context is relevant for the understanding of *différance* and of the related anti-concepts of *iterability* (*itérabilité*) and *dissemination* (*dissémination*).

2 Derrida's Romantic and Nietzschean Heritage: écriture, itérabilité, différance
Derrida, Nietzsche, and the German Romantics (especially Friedrich Schlegel) are related to one another by their common refusal of the rationalist and Hegelian idea that language is primarily

an instrument of knowledge and a means of communication. 'There are no mysteries in language'[13], remarks Greimas, the unrepentant rationalist, the thinker of the *content plane*. Projecting the discussion onto the *expression plane*, the Romantics, Nietzsche, and Derrida reject the rationalist idea that there exists a one-to-one correspondence between *signifier* and *signified*, that synonyms can be treated as equivalents, and that phonetic differences between languages can safely be neglected as long as 'we know what we are talking about'.

Friedrich Schlegel has already been quoted in the first chapter as saying to the rationalist critics of Romanticism that they would be 'thoroughly distressed if the whole world were made quite comprehensible in accordance with (their) wishes'.[14] Schlegel and Derrida not only believe that the rationalist utopia of total linguistic transparence is impossible; they also hold that it is not desirable to bring about a utopian situation in which the one-to-one correspondence of *signifier* and *signified*, of phonetic unit and concept puts an end to linguistic and literary creativity. Anyone who has experienced the constraints of technical translations, constraints emanating from semantic conventions fixed by technical dictionaries and manuals, will feel a certain amount of sympathy for the Romantics and deconstructionists.

However, both Romantics and deconstructionists are one-sided inasmuch as they completely disregard the fact that meaning can very well be fixed (by convention) in mathematical, technical, and other artificial languages. Although such languages are extreme cases which apply neither to natural language nor to literature, they do illustrate the *possibility* of what Derrida calls the *presence of meaning*. And this possibility as such sheds new light on the whole problematic: for it shows that univocity and *presence of meaning* are at least theoretically conceivable and that Greimas' rationalist or Goldmann's Hegelian arguments are not sheer illusions, although they may be overly optimistic. (Cf. the end of this chapter where the problem of *universals* is dealt with.)

Far from sharing this optimism, Derrida returns to Nietzsche's theory of an ambivalent world and of language as rhetoric. In Nietzsche's philosophy Good and Evil become indistinguishable: 'Is Good not Evil? and is God not a simple invention, a ruse of the devil? Is it conceivable that in the end everything is false?'[15] In

Nietzsche's discourse, which is structured by a radical ambivalence, it is not possible to synthesise these opposites in a Hegelian manner in order to obtain encompassing units on a higher level. What is more, it is not even possible to tell them apart, to define their *difference*.

In this respect, Nietzsche appears as a forerunner of Derrida, de Man, and Hillis Miller all of whom insist on the ambivalent and aporetic character of philosophical, linguistic, and literary problems. Derrida for example argues that Yahwé (YHWH), the God of the *Old Testament*, made impossible the task of the translator who has been haunted by aporia ever since the mythical events of Babylon occurred: 'YHWH simultaneously demands and forbids in his deconstructive gesture, that one understand his proper name within language, he mandates and crosses out the translation, he dooms us to impossible and necessary translation.'[16]

There is no transcending this contradiction in a post-Hegelian situation marked by extreme ambivalence and aporia. The whole of Franco-American deconstruction could be envisaged against the backdrop of this post-Hegelian, i.e. Young Hegelian and Nietzschean, scenario in which truth appears as dependent on the volatile figures of rhetoric. 'What then is truth?' asks Nietzsche and gives an answer which links truth to rhetoric: 'a mobile army of metaphors, metonymies, anthropomorphisms.'[17] This definition – if it is one – is ruled by ambivalence insofar as the metaphysical concept of truth is virtually identified with its opposite: with the language of rhetoric, spoken by the Sophists and abhorred by Plato.

In *L'Ecriture et la différence*, Derrida draws his inspiration from Nietzsche when he decides to replace the metaphysical concepts of *Being* and *Truth* with the notion of *play*: 'We doubtless would have to cite the Nietzschean critique of metaphysics, the critique of the concepts of Being and truth, for which were substituted the concepts of play, interpretation, and sign (sign without present truth) (. . .).'[18] Derrida resumes Nietzsche's critique of truth when he imagines the history of philosophy as a rhetorical process of metaphorisation. Metaphors cannot be contained or defined by concepts, he argues, because they are at the very source of conceptualisation. The concept of metaphor as such (*meta-pherein* = to transpose) is itself metaphorical and hence cannot be used as a device for defining rhetorical figures.

Following Nietzsche, Derrida develops a playful, rhetorical *écriture* which replaces the metaphysical concepts of *Truth* and *Being* with polysemic figures or anti-concepts such as *iterability (itérablité)*, *différance*, and *dissemination (dissémination)*. All of these figures have one common denominator: they are designed to subvert the idea of a *present meaning* and the complementary idea of *truth*. At the same time they are metaphors of an open-ended process of *significance* or *signifiance*, as Barthes would say.

Iterability is possibly the key figure of Derridean deconstruction: not only because Derrida uses it in his radical critique of Austin's Speech Act Theory, but also because it can be treated as an antonym of Greimas' *iterativity* and the related concept of *isotopy* (cf. chap. 6.1). What exactly is *iterability* or *itérabilité* and why can it be considered as a link between linguistic philosophy, semiotics, and aesthetics?

Let us return for a moment to Greimas' concepts of *iterativity* and *isotopy* and recall that *isotopy* is defined in structural semiotics as 'iterativity (recurrence) on a syntagmatic level of classemes which guarantee the homogeneity of a discourse as utterance.' This means, as was already pointed out in the previous chapter, that repetition or iterativity of semantic units (words, expressions, actants) enhances the semantic cohesion of discourse by actualising or foregrounding different aspects of its content. Derrida inverts this argument, turning it against the rationalist tenets of structural semiotics and Austin's Speech Act Theory. He holds that the repetition of one and the same word – within a discourse and between discourses – cannot be viewed as a reproduction of the same, the identical or the synonymous. For whenever a sign is repeated it (re-)appears in a different context and the contextual shift invariably alters its meaning. He calls this process *iterability* and tries to show how repetition in the sense of *iterability* leads not to the consolidation, but to the disintegration of textual meaning. (We shall see in the fourth section of this chapter – in conjunction with Hillis Miller's literary theory – how this argument can be applied to literature.)

At this stage it is important to note that the opposition between *iterativity* and *iterability* is a construction of this chapter which Derrida, who never dealt with Greimas' semiotics, does not mention. However, it seems to be a useful construction because *iterability* is the antonym par excellence of *iterativity* and because it illustrates as concretely as possible the contrast between Nietzschean deconstruction and rationalist semiotics. Derrida himself originally used the *iterability*-argument against Austin's Speech Act Theory.

According to Derrida, Speech Act Theory – like all logocentrist thought – presupposes the *presence of meaning* which, in the case of John L. Austin, implies the univocal presence and reception of a speech act or utterance. This kind of univocal presence, says Derrida, cannot exist, because the repetition of a speech act may at any point cause a shift in its meaning. If somebody says about his friend: 'He is not a fool!' he can imply that his friend is a very wise, prudent, and reliable person and hence extremely unlikely to commit a foolish act. However, if I report the conversation to this friend, telling him: 'He said, he is not a fool!', the implications may change to such an extent that the recipient of the message is led to believe that his wisdom and his prudence are in doubt or that his friend simply hopes that he will not commit the foolish act in question: 'He is not a fool, I hope.' We all know that everyday language is riddled with misunderstandings which crop up whenever a semantic shift occurs in a new context of communication.

This is exactly what Derrida means when in his critique of Austin's approach he speaks 'of unities of iterability, of unities separable from their internal or external context, and separable from themselves, to the extent that the very iterability which constitutes their identity never permits them to be a unity of self-identity.'[19] In other words, *iterability* in the sense of repetition or recurrence of a sign eventually leads to the disintegration of the sign's identity: for *pragmatic* reasons (because of the heterogeneity of communication contexts) and for *semantic* reasons (because the semantic context of a discourse may change from sequence to sequence). Derrida does not explicitly distinguish these two contexts, but it is essential to do it here, because Austin's Speech Act Theory is mainly geared towards the pragmatics of language (the communication context) whereas Greimas' theory deals primarily (although not exclusively) with the semantics of discourse.

Derrida's article provoked a sharp critique by John R. Searle (one of Austin's disciples) who was shocked mainly by Derrida's assertion that the intention of a speaker is never fully present in his text and that Austin has developed a theory based on abstractions and illusions. In fact Derrida criticises Austin for not taking into account the linguistic functions of quotation, parody, pastiche, and irony which can change the meaning of a speech act. The utterance 'he is not a fool' can also acquire an ironical meaning or be parodied whenever it is repeated. Finally, Derrida blames Austin for presupposing the presence of the total context of semantic and pragmatic (communicational) meaning.

However, this total context – we are once again confronted with the Hegelian problem of total knowledge – is never 'given', because all contexts are open or incomplete (and so is our knowledge). Derrida, who believes (quite rightly) that all depends on open and inexhaustible contexts, explains in his article on Austin: 'For a context to be exhaustively determinable, in the sense demanded by Austin, it at least would be necessary for the conscious intention to be totally present and actually transparent for itself and others (. . .).'[20] One could turn this argument around, saying that the conscious intention (of a speech act) cannot be entirely present and transparent to itself unless the total context is exhaustively determined. In short, for Derrida, Austin's and Searle's Speech Act Theory is a continuation of philosophical *phono-* and *logocentrism*: it can only postulate the presence of an author's intention and the identity of a repeated speech act by abstracting from the openness of contexts and from the phenomenon of *iterability* which is partly due to this openness.

The idea that all contexts or totalities are open and hence cannot be exhaustively described ('made present') also plays an important part in Derrida's critique of Saussure which gives birth to the figure of *différance* (already commented on in the first section). The common denominator of *iterability* and *différance* is the idea that meaning cannot be made present or identified: either because changes in context lead to changes in meaning or because only differences between semantic units can be described, but never the actual identity of a unit.

In an attempt to make his figure of *différance* plausible, Derrida tries to avail himself of Saussure's rationalist conception of the language system. From Saussure's point of view, difference appears as the key to our understanding of language. For its functions cannot be defined as independent units, but only in relation to one another or as *differing* from one another. This is why Saussure can hold that in language there are only differences:

> Within the same language, all words used to express related ideas limit each other reciprocally; synonyms like French *redouter* 'dread', *craindre* 'fear', and *avoir peur* 'be afraid' have value only through their opposition: if *redouter* did not exist, all its content would go to its competitors. (. . .) The value of just any term is accordingly determined by its environment; it is impossible to fix even the value of the word signifying 'sun' without first considering its surroundings: in some languages it is not possible to say 'sit in the sun'.[21]

For Derrida this passage becomes a crucial starting point of de-construction. Although he accepts Saussure's idea that meaning in language depends on the interaction and differentiation of the units involved, he rejects Saussure's postulate that the semantic value of a word can be univocally determined in conjunction with the differences which make up its semantic context. Any attempt at a univocal definition appears to him as a *logocentrist* manoeuvre designed to assure the *presence of meaning* or a *transcendental signifier* (an equivalent of Plato's pure form).

Meaning, argues Derrida, cannot ever be present, because it is always being *differred* (postponed) in a movement which he calls *différance*. This *différance* is inherent in every single difference, in every opposition which deconstructs itself as soon as we realise that the difference between the terms involved cannot be fixed, but has to be *differred*, because each of the two terms – *signifier* and *signified*, *concept* and *figure*, *man* and *woman* – is partly identical with the opposite term. 'Hence the differences are produced – differred – by *différance*'[22], explains Derrida. Figure and concept, metaphor and concept, for example, cannot be neatly distinguished, because concepts themselves (e.g. metaphor, definition, isotopy) are meta-phorical, figurative. Therefore attempts to fix the difference between metaphor and concept fall prey to the movement of *différance* which is comparable to the movement of *iterability*.

Both movements subvert conceptualisation by weakening the signified and reinforcing the role of the *signifier* and of the *expression plane*. From a semiotic and aesthetic point of view, *différance* could be envisaged as an uninterrupted collusion of signifiers, to which Derrida refers in *L'Ecriture et la différence*: 'But is it by chance that the book is, first and foremost, volume? And that the meaning of meaning (in the general sense of meaning and not in the sense of signalization) is infinite implication, the indefinite referral of signifier to signifier?'[23]

This would indeed be the end of meaning in the structuralist (Saussurian, Greimasian) sense. Fortunately, Derrida's position is so extreme that it becomes self-contradictory: whenever the deconstructionist protests (as Derrida very often does) that he has been misunderstood or misinterpreted, whenever he relies on an English translation of one of his works, he presupposes a definable meaning.

3 Derrida on Mallarmé and Jean-Pierre Richard

'Except in the *Livre irréalisé* by Mallarmé, that which is written is never identical to itself'[24], concludes Derrida in the passage quoted above. In a chapter of *La Dissémination* (1972) ('La Double séance'), he criticises Jean-Pierre Richard's thematological interpretation of Stéphane Mallarmé's work which was published in 1962 under the title *L'Univers imaginaire de Mallarmé* and presented by the author himself as a unifying project geared towards the 'identity of the written word'. In contrast to Richard who sets out to demonstrate the thematic coherence of Mallarmé's poetry, Derrida seeks to reveal the *iterabilities* and incongruencies of the poet's text. The following confrontation of the two literary critics is not devoid of irony: for both – Jean-Pierre Richard and Derrida – invoke the authority of the great poet in order to prove their point.

Although Jean-Pierre Richard cannot be considered as a structuralist in the sense of Greimas, he uses the term *iteration* (*itération*) in order to describe the thematic coherence of Mallarmé's work which he relates to Hegel's totalising project in philosophy. In his thematological perspective this work appears as a meaningful *totality* consisting of mutually interdependent parts.

In this context, inspired, as a German critic aptly points out, by the search for a 'unitary vision'[25], Richard uses – several years before Derrida – the word *dissémination*, which he finds in Mallarmé's 'Préface à *Vathek*'. Commenting on the anglicisms in William Beckford's French novel *Vathek* (1778), Mallarmé mentions the writer's characteristic sentence which '*is disseminated in shadowy vagueness*' ('*se dissémine en l'ombre et le vague*'). Mallarmé describes his alternative as '*shedding light on words*' ('*la mise en lumière des mots*').[26]

In *L'Univers imaginaire de Mallarmé*, Richard refers to this contrast between shadow and light and introduces the substantive *dissémination* later on taken over by Derrida: 'Against the dissemination of meaning', he explains Mallarmé's point of view, 'the well-chosen word will surround truth with hard contours'. ('*Contre la dissémination du sens, le mot heureux campera donc la vérité d'un dur relief*.')[27] The disputed concept or figure appears for the first time in a *logocentric*, unifying, and totalising context with Hegelian connotations. For one of J.-P. Richard's chapters carries the title 'Towards a dialectics of totality'.

But what exactly does J.-P. Richard's Hegelianism consist in? Mainly in his attempt to read Mallarmé as a poet who defends meaning against '*the verbal incursions of chance*' ('*les invasions verbales du hasard*')[28] and who therefore constructs a meaningful totality emanating from a subjective grand design. Richard is quite explicit about the Hegelian context when he mentions Mallarmé's references to the German philosopher ('Mallarmé might have remembered Véra's comments on Hegel')[29] and when he insists on the poet's synthesis of the 'sensous' and the 'abstract concept' in the idea.

In other words, Richard sees Mallarmé as a poet of synthesis who, in *Le Mort vivant*, for example, seeks to reconcile 'hostile elements' such as night and day, death and life, etc. In order to bring about this reconciliation, says Richard, he uses the metaphor as a stylistic means of dialectical synthesisation: 'For Mallarmé the ideal equilibrium is that which comes about between two conflicting elements. The metaphor is thus a bringing together and the synthesis a dialectical reduction of the double to the one.'[30] Some of Richard's arguments remind us of Lucien Goldmann's *genetic structuralism*, especially of the idea that it is necessary to understand the totality in order to understand the parts and vice versa. Richard seems to follow this hermeneutic movement when he speaks of 'the dialectical proof of the whole by the part and of the part by the whole'.[31]

On the semantic level he uses concepts such as *iteration* and *recurrence* which are reminiscent of Greimas' terminology: 'The iteration of motives guarantees the rigour of thematic development'.[32] In Mallarmé's poetry, he argues, the image of a glacier is associated with metaphors of chastity in order to evoke the 'coldness of virginity'.[33] This is both a Hegelian and structuralist approach governed by the idea of totality.

After what has been said about Derrida's critique of Hegel and structuralism, it is not altogether surprising that the deconstructionist was irritated by Richard's totalising vision. In *La Dissémination* he accuses Richard of logocentrism, Platonism, and Neohegelianism. To begin with, he doubts the very possibility of 'thematic analysis' and of its central thesis according to which Mallarmé intends to contain and control *dissemination* in order to bring about unity. In his critical remarks he tries to deliver the word *dissemination* from its Platonic-Hegelian yoke and to transform it into a figure of deconstruction.

He sets out to demonstrate, as might have been expected, that there is no ultimate meaning (*'signifié en dernière instance'*)[34] in Mallarmé's poetry. In order to prove his point he quotes extensively all the ambiguities and polysemies of Mallarmé's poems and insists on the fact that a thorough reading of these poems transforms Richard's *iteration* (*itération*) into *iterability* (cf. above) and semantic dispersion: *dissemination*. Thus the figure of *dissemination*, which was burdened by negative connotations both in Mallarmé's and Richard's text, turns into a euphoric concept of deconstruction.

How do *iterability* and *dissemination* work in Derrida's analyses? The word *pli* (*fold, crease, line,* etc.) which occurs frequently in Mallarmé's poems (e.g. in *Hommage*: '*Le silence déjà funèbre d'une moire/Dispose plus qu'un pli seul sur le mobilier*') and which Richard subsumes under a semantic totality governed by the concept of 'intimacy', is deconstructed by Derrida who draws our attention to all those elements which in Mallarmé's *pli* also express 'dehiscence, dissemination, spacing, temporization etc.'[35] He criticises Jean-Pierre Richard's Hegelian approach, adding: 'This confirms the classical reading of Mallarmé and confines his text within an atmosphere of intimism, symbolism, and neo-Hegelianism.'[36]

Although Derrida does not deny the existence of certain themes found by Richard in Mallarmé's poems (such as *pli, blanc, azur*), he categorically rejects the idea that these themes can be grouped together in a conceptualised totality in the Hegelian sense. In contrast to Richard's totalising hermeneutic, Derrida's figure of *dissemination* is closely related to the figures of *iterability* and *différance* and does not admit any kind of conceptual fixation. It even excludes the traditional distinction between 'original' and 'metaphorical' meaning. In a situation in which truth is reduced by Nietzsche (and Derrida) to a 'swarming multitude of metaphors' (Nietzsche), any attempt to define or explain metaphor by conceptual means is a priori condemned to failure.

Only figurative meaning exists and philosophy turns into rhetorics in the sense of Nietzsche: 'Since everything becomes metaphorical', argues Derrida, 'there is no longer any literal meaning and, hence, no longer any metaphor either.'[37] Mallarmé's *pli* is irreducible to the concept of metaphor: not only because original or actual meaning does not exist, but also because this polysemic signifier acquires contradictory meanings. Derrida tries to show that *pli* means at the same time '*virginity*' and that '*which rapes it*' ('*ce qui la viole*') and that in other instances its meaning is ambivalent and undecidable.

It may have become clear at this stage that *dissemination* in Derrida's sense cannot be identified with the concept of *polysemy* or *pluri-isotopy* as defined by Greimas (cf. chap. 6.1): i.e. as coexistence of heterogeneous isotopies. For in the context of polysemy, meaning can be defined insofar as a word (*sememe*, Greimas) can be collocated on a particular isotopy or on several isotopies. Therefore it is not undecidable. Deconstruction differs radically from semiotics by introducing a radical, Nietzschean ambivalence which makes a univocal definition of linguistic units impossible. This ambivalence can lead to *aporias* which play an important part in the discourse of the American deconstructionists Paul de Man and J. Hillis Miller.

4 Paul de Man: Allegory and Aporia

It is probably not wrong to consider the representatives of American deconstruction as the academic successors of the New Critics (cf. chap. 2). For the institutional hegemony which the New Criticism enjoyed before the Second World War was replaced in the 1970s and 1980s by a hegemony of deconstruction built around the University of Yale, where the most prominent deconstructionists taught. Writing at the beginning of the 1990s, David Lehman remarks: 'The deconstructors of "hegemony" are observed to be working toward their own hegemony (. . .).' He adds with respect to Paul de Man that he 'is generally considered to be the guiding light of literary deconstruction.'[38]

However, the new approach has not simply replaced New Criticism; it has also reinstated and renewed some of its methodological principles such as *close reading* along with the emphasis on the reader and the reading process. Following Kant, Paul de Man adopts the point of view of the reader or spectator and opposes all Hegelian attempts to explain the work of art as a conceptual system. Renewing the Kantian bias of the New Critics (e.g. Ransom's, cf. chap. 2), he refuses to consider literary criticism as a science: 'The semantics of interpretation have no epistemological consistency and can therefore not be scientific.'[39]

He goes a lot further than Kant and the New Critics, however, when, following Nietzsche, he stresses the predominance in discourse of the rhetorical figure, pointing out in *The Resistance to Theory* that the real difficulties crop up as soon as we become aware of 'the epistemological thrust of the rhetorical dimension of discourse.'[40] This dimension, formerly analysed by Nietzsche, makes systematic conceptualisation impossible and explains – according to de Man – the formidable obstacles all theories of literature are confronted with. For the literary text 'foregrounds the rhetorical over the grammatical and the logical function'.[41]

Inasmuch as de Man's rhetorical conception of discourse does not stop at the borders of the literary domain, but extends into the realm of theory, the very notion of theory undergoes a drastic particularisation. As a kind of rhetoric, as a figurative discourse dominated by tropes, theory vitiates its own efforts at systematisation and conceptualisation: 'Nothing can overcome the resistance to theory since theory *is* itself this resistance.'[42] Nietzschean paradox and Romantic irony resound in this sentence which announces and explains the aporias of de Man's thought.

In contrast to Hegel who insists on the conceptual character of dead or automatised metaphors (e.g. *field of research* or *magnetic field*), reducing metaphor to its '*abstract meaning*' ('*abstrakte Bedeutung*')[43], de Man insists on the figurative or rhetorical character of key theoretical concepts. If his appraisal were correct, one would also have to accept the complementary thesis put forward by another American deconstructionist, Jonathan Culler: 'There is, for example, no question of escaping from the pitfalls of rhetoric by becoming aware of the rhetorical nature of discourse.'[44] In other words: pondering upon rhetorics by rhetorical means does not help.

However, mathematics and formal logic which cannot be dissolved in rhetorical tropes play an important part in virtually all types of theoretical discourse, including linguistics and aesthetics. (It is not by chance that, so far, Derrida has not attempted to deconstruct a mathematical text.) One could add that a semiotician like Greimas demonstrates on several occasions that it is possible to explain figures such as metaphors or metonymies by relating them to the concepts of *seme* or *sememe*.[45] Seen in this light, Derrida's and de Man's deconstructive arguments appear as Nietzschean and Romantic exaggerations of the importance of tropes; exaggerations which do not take into account *the immanence of formal logic in all kinds of theoretical argument.*

These exaggerations have a long history beginning with the Young Hegelian critique of Hegel's system (cf. chap. 1.2). Like the Young Hegelians, de Man tries to expose the flaws of Hegel's system by emphasising the irreducible ambivalence, the unity of opposites without synthesis. In *The Resistance to Theory* he remarks: 'Binaries, to the extent that they allow and invite synthesis, are therefore the most misleading of differential structures.'[46] In de Man's work, as in the theories of the Young Hegelians, this radical critique of Hegel's dialectical synthesis leads to an emphasis on the particular (i.e. the rhetorical figure and the *expression plane*) and to a rejection of the universal concept, of the notion of *totality*.

De Man's anti-Hegelian, Nietzschean penchant for particularisation explains his critique of the *symbol* and of symbolic aesthetics: of *aesthetic ideology*. A concise and quite useful definition of the latter concept is to be found in Lindsay Water's introduction to de Man's *Critical Writings* (1953-1978): 'It is an ideology that requires that literature be dominated by the knowing subject who ascribes meaning and moral to the text. It is an ideology that monumentalizes literature by setting it up as a symbol of civilization.'[47]

One could add that it is an ideology born within the context of Hegelian *logocentrism*, where art and literature are identified with historical meanings defined by the subject of philosophical discourse. In an article on the function of the symbol and of symbolic thought in Hegel's aesthetics, de Man tries to define the whole of Hegel's aesthetics as an aesthetics of the *symbol*: 'Hegel, then, is a theoretician of the symbol.'[48]

Ignoring completely Hegel's aesthetic critique of the *symbol* and of symbolic art (which the German philosopher identifies with the 'incomplete' conception of art in Persian and especially Egyptian antiquity), de Man asserts that the symbolic principle is the unifying principle *par excellence* which makes it possible for Hegel and the Hegelians (e.g. Hegelian Marxists like Goldmann) to consider works of art as meaningful totalities which appeal to the senses by expressing (univocally) political or moral ideas. According to de Man, Friedrich Schiller was the first to adapt Kantian ethics to the Hegelian demands of a unifying aesthetics, thus laying the foundations of an *aesthetic ideology*. Much later, this aesthetic ideology of meaningful totalities was simplified and vulgarised by the Nazis who used it in order to add an aesthetic dimension to their politics.

As an alternative to the *symbol* and the totalising, *symbol*-oriented *aesthetic ideology* de Man introduces the rhetorical figure of *allegory*. As might have been expected, this figure is interpreted by de Man as expressing disharmony, decomposition, and fragmentation. Commenting on de Man's aesthetics and the contrast between symbol and allegory, Romano Luperini points out that 'the symbol is presented as a unity of appearance and essence, whereas allegory asserts their discrepancy (. . .).'[49]

Pondering on this dissociation of appearance and essence, de Man also discovers a break between subject and object, between thought and reality. Unlike the aesthetics of the *symbol* – i.e. the *aesthetic ideology* – which presuppose the unity of subject and object, the negative aesthetics of allegory presuppose their irreparable break-up.

There is a Kantian and an anti-Hegelian element underlying this argument: the subject constructs all objects in space and time and hence can no longer presume with Hegel that the concept is inherent in reality or that thought and reality can be identified. There is at the same time, however, a genuinely deconstructionist moment: the subject's constructions no longer correspond to reality and contradict each other. For this reason, says de Man, all literary texts turn into allegories of their own unreadability. This unreadability appears simultaneously as an unbridgeable gap between subject and reality, between theoretical and literary discourse.

One of the most important aspects of this allegorical negativity is the *aporia* of meaning which de Man invariably encounters in literature. Like Derrida, he holds that logic, grammar, and rhetorics are not simply different aspects of language, but elements which may come into conflict, and engender *undecidabilities* or *aporias*, i.e. the unreadability of a text. What he calls 'undecidability' ought not to be confused with *polysemy* in the semiotic sense: the coexistence of different *isotopies* (cf. chap. 6.1) which can trigger off diverging reading processes. For it is an *aporia* inherent in the text and hence independent of the attitude or the *horizon of expectations* characteristic of a particular readership.

In this respect, de Man's arguments coincide with those of certain American architects who consider themselves as deconstructionists: 'A deconstructivist architect is therefore not one who dismantles buildings, but one who locates the inherent dilemmas within buildings.'[50] In this text the words 'locates' and 'inherent' are particularly important: for they show that deconstructive thinkers tend to attribute certain qualities to objects, neglecting the idea of the Czech Structuralists and of reader–response criticism that all objects are contingent constructions of particular readers.

In an attempt to understand Yeats's poem *Among Schoolchildren* as an aporetic structure and as an *allegory* of its own unreadability, de Man insists on the undecidable character of the last verses:

> O chestnut-tree, great-rooted blossomer,
> Are you the leaf, the blossom or the bole?
> O body swayed to music, O brightening glance,
> How can we know the dancer from the dance?

Asserting that the question at the end of the poem can be read both as a rhetorical question (it is impossible to distinguish) and as a literal question (it is necessary to distinguish), de Man believes that he has revealed the undecidable or *aporetic* structure of the text. For the latter can be read simultaneously as a representation of organic unity (between the tree and the leaf, between the erotic body and the music) *and* as an attempt at differentiation:

> For it turns out that the entire scheme set up by the first reading can be undermined, or deconstructed, in the terms of the second, in which the final line is read literally as meaning that, since the dancer and the dance are not the same, it might be useful, perhaps even desperately necessary – for the question can be given a ring of urgency, 'Please tell me, how *can* I know the dancer from the dance' – to tell them apart.[51]

However, the necessity invoked by de Man does not impose itself, especially because he isolates the last lines of the poem from the rest, thus renouncing a semantic, syntactic, and phonetic analysis of the text as a whole, as a linguistic structure. In conjunction with de Man's 'aporetic' reading oriented towards undecidability, one could repeat Greimas' critical remark about Barthes' '*ouverture infinie*' of the text: namely that 'it is frequently the result of partial readings'[52], that is to say of incomplete analyses which fail to take into account the global interaction of structures.

The deconstructive contradiction which de Man *projects* into the text appears as arbitrary insofar as it is not accompanied by the self-critical question about the role of the deconstructive metalanguage in the construction of the literary object. Can de Man seriously believe that the aporias detected by him in virtually all texts of world literature (in Proust's novel, Rilke's poem, Rousseau's work) are *inherent* in the analysed objects? Is it not more likely that they are products of his own deconstructive discourse (in the same way as Goldmann's meaningful totalities were products of genetic structuralism)? Would a semiotic reading of Yeats's poem (in the sense of Greimas) not reveal semantic coherence and a hierarchy of isotopies where de Man finds undecidabilities and aporias? What exactly is the role of theoretical metalanguages in the construction of literary objects? This is an important question neither Greimas nor de Man have tried to answer.

5 J. Hillis Miller: Aporia, Repetition, Iterability
Unlike Paul de Man whose thought is rooted in German philosophy (Nietzsche, Heidegger), J. Hillis Miller begins his career as

a critic with the Franco-Swiss phenomenologist Georges Poulet (who taught in the USA) and as a follower of Jean-Pierre Richard's *thematic criticism* (cf. sec. 2). Like Paul de Man he undergoes the influence of New Criticism and defends the method of *close reading* along with an aesthetics of autonomy inspired by Kant and Croce (cf. chap. 2.1). His first works, for example *The Disappearance of God: Five Nineteenth Century Writers* (1963), are marked by Poulet's influence and by Richard's *thematic criticism* with its emphasis on the unification of the universe by the individual author's consciousness. 'Nevertheless, I can say that the work of the Geneva critics took possession of my imagination'[53], remarks Miller in *Victorian Subjects* (1990).

His work constitutes an important aesthetic and methodological link between New Criticism and deconstruction, inasmuch as Miller gradually transforms the method of *close reading* into a refined instrument of deconstruction. For it turns out that the hyper-precision of *close reading* finally subverts the cohesion postulated by the New Critics. Howard Felperin shows that this systematic subversion of New Criticism (of its coherence postulate) forms the common denominator that unites all the Yale deconstructionists: 'What the Yale deconstructionsts, institutional heirs apparent to new criticism, did, was to reveal the formal project of their predecessors as having barely scratched the surface of the rhetorical multiplicity it had set out to explore (. . .).'[54]

In this situation, critics like de Man and Miller can only deconstruct the theoretical foundations of New Criticism by demonstrating, for example, that the meaningful structures described by the New Critics were mere figments of the imagination: 'Unlike the New Critics, deconstructionists argue that you can't take it for granted that a good work of literature is going to be organically unified.'[55] Here the main thrust of American deconstruction is clearly visible. The search for coherence and meaning which was dominant in the 1950s and 1960s, uniting such heterogeneous approaches to literature as New Criticism and Marxism, is replaced in the 80s and 90s by a sustained search for contradictions, aporias, and differences. This search is anti-Hegelian and Nietzschean at the same time.

Like Derrida and Paul de Man, Miller writes in a Young Hegelian and Nietzschean context whenever he criticises the

Hegelian concept of *Aufhebung* or *synthesis* and along with it the entire dialectical tradition. Analysing the relationship between *logocentrism* and nihilism in Shelley's poem *The Triumph of Life*, he points out that the two contradictory terms 'are related to one another in a way which is not antithesis and which may not be synthesized in any dialectical *Aufhebung*'.[56] It is therefore essential to perceive the deconstructive contradiction as an extreme ambivalence in the Nietzschean sense: an ambivalence that excludes all kinds of Hegelian syntheses, thus impairing the dialectical unification process.

The deconstructive antinomies of *Aufhebung* and *synthesis* are *undecidability* and *aporia*. Miller adopts a radically anti–Hegelian and Nietzschean point of view when he rejects all attempts at unification which could yield a meaningful world. After the Nietzschean 'death of God', meaning is irretrievably lost: 'After the disappearance of the gods the poet finds himself in a place where opposites are simultaneously true.'[57]

Put forward in an essay on Wallace Stevens, this thesis is applied by Miller to all the writers and texts he comments on. Be it Shelley's *The Triumph of Life*, George Eliot's *Adam Bede*, Emily Brontë's *Wuthering Heights* or Goethe's *Die Wahlverwandtschaften*, Miller invariably discovers at least two *incompatible* modes of reading which lead to *undecidability* and *aporia*. In *Fiction and Repetition* he summarises his crucial argument in an analysis of *Wuthering Heights*: 'My argument is that the best readings will be the ones which best account for the heterogeneity of the text, its presentation of a definite group of possible meanings which are systematically interconnected, determined by the text, but logically incompatible.'[58]

Commenting on George Eliot's realism in her novel *Adam Bede*, Miller tries to demonstrate how the doctrine of realism expounded in the famous 17th chapter is systematically contradicted and subverted by the author's own writing. On the one hand, Eliot links the aesthetics of realism to a truthful and honest style which renounces fantastic elements and rhetorical ornaments; on the other hand, her text reveals on all levels its dependence *vis-à-vis* the trope, the metaphor, the catachresis, and rhetorics in general. The seventeenth chapter itself owes its persuasive force to the rhetoric of tropes: 'Realistic narration must depend, as this chapter of *Adam*

Bede conspicuously does, on figurative language'[59], explains Hillis Miller in *The Ethics of Reading*.

However, a careful reading of the seventeenth chapter shows that George Eliot simply defines realism as an approach that avoids embellishment and an ornamental style contradicting our everyday experience of individuals as they are. Nowhere does she postulate an incompatibility between realism and the use of tropes. Here, as in the case of Paul de Man, the critical reader wonders to what extent the contradictions and aporias revealed by deconstructive reading are actually to be found in the texts.

Similar problems crop up in Miller's interpretations of William Wordsworth's *Lucy*-poems. In his methodologically very heterogeneous analysis of one of these poems – *A Slumber did my Spirit Seal* – he tries to convince the reader that the word *thing* takes on two incompatible meanings, thus engendering an aporia:

> A slumber did my spirit seal;
> I had no human fears:
> She seemed a thing that could not feel
> The touch of earthly years.
>
> No motion has she now, no force;
> She neither hears nor sees;
> Rolled round in earth's diurnal course,
> With rocks, and stones, and trees.

According to Miller's reading, the heroine of the poem appears as a *thing* in two incompatible ways: as a young 'thing' (Miller refers to the German expression '*junges Ding*') in an anthropomorphous sense and (after her death) as a lifeless body in a physical and natural sense, i.e. as a 'thing' taken literally. Miller believes that no semantic connection can be made between the two meanings of the word *thing*. He diagnoses an 'unbridgeable gap between one meaning of the word "thing" and the other'.[60]

Although it is impossible to consider Miller's interpretation as a whole, it makes sense to focus on the *sememe* (Greimas) 'thing' and on the thing-like character of the heroine, which in the first stanza is associated with the *seme* (Greimas) 'life', in the second stanza with the *seme* 'death'. So far, Miller's way of looking at things seems quite plausible – even from a semiotic point of view. However, a closer look at the poem reveals that there is no unbridgeable gap between the stanzas, because the heroine's thinglike character is defined *negatively* or *privatively* in both stanzas: as *absence of consciousness* ('could not feel'; 'neither hears nor sees') and as a *non-human state* ('no human fears'; 'with rocks, and stones, and trees'). Could it be that these privative elements bridge the gap between 'life' and 'death' detected by Miller, giving birth to the fascinating paradox of the poem that Lucy remains the same in spite of the transition from life to death? This question which is obviously not presented here as an alternative to Miller's global interpretation, suggests that deconstructive analyses might be as one-sided and arbitrary as those of the Marxists or the semioticians.

Along with undecidability and *aporia*, Miller introduces another figure of Nietzschean origin: *repetition* in the sense of Derrida's *iterability*. Following Gilles Deleuze and Jacques Derrida, he distinguishes two kinds of repetition: the Platonic and the Nietzschean, and defines Platonic repetition as a process 'grounded in a solid archetypal model which is untouched by the effects of repetition'.[61] In other words, Plato and his followers (like Greimas and Austin) believe that the repeated unit does not lose its identity: the copy is a copy of the original model (e.g. of Plato's idea or pure form). The Nietzschean repetition is quite a different matter: 'The other, Nietzschean mode of repetition posits a world based on difference. Each thing (. . .) is unique, intrinsically different from every other thing. Similarity arises against the background of this "disparité du fond".'[62] It ought to be clear from what has been said so far that this Nietzschean *repetition* is closely related to Derrida's *itérabilité*.

In an analysis of Thomas Hardy's novel *Tess of the d'Urbervilles*, Miller initially describes the textual function of the *red colour* in such a way that the recurrence of 'red' evokes a *theme* in the sense of Richard or an *isotopy* in the sense of Greimas. The concatenation of 'red things' constructed by Miller is accompanied by sexual connotations: 'the red ribbon in Tess's hair; her mouth (. . .); the strawberry that Alec forces her to eat; the roses that Alec gives her, with which she pricks her chin; the red scratches on her wrists in the raping scene (. . .) the red stains made on her arms (. . .).'[63]

This enumeration of items containing the *seme* 'red' will remind semioticians of Greimas' concepts of *iterativity* and *isotopy*. However, Miller constructs semantic structures only to subvert, to deconstruct them. The 'red things' do not form an *isotopy*, for, says Miller: 'The relation among the links in a chain of meanings in *Tess of the d'Urbervilles* is always repetition with a difference, and the difference is as important as the repetition.'[64] In other words: the process of meaning is not – as with Greimas – a process of integration, but a process of disintegration in the sense of Derrida's *iterability*.

At this point several critical questions arise: 1. How are we to understand Miller's dictum that 'the difference is as important as the repetition'? 2. How can Miller associate (i.e. group together as belonging to one class) the 'red things' without hierarchically subsuming them under the *seme* 'red', thus recognising one of Greimas' fundamental principles of classification? 3. Why is it that most readers tend to ignore the deconstructive mechanisms of semantic disintegration in Hardy's novel?

In a novel such as *Tess of the d'Urbervilles*, difference (which Miller doesn't really define) may be as important as repetition, but this does not mean that chaos reigns supreme and that no coherence whatsoever can be found. For Miller himself describes semantic structures, for example the 'red things' and their sexual connotations. His own descriptions would be impossible without the tacit application of logic and semantics which linguists and semioticians adhere to explicitly. If the novel really deconstructed itself in a process of differentiation or *iterability*, as Miller claims, then most readers would fail to recognise a coherent plot and discard the book in despair. We know, however, that this is not the reaction of the majority of Hardy's readers.

Hence it is legitimate to ask whether Miller means what he says, when he asserts that the ethics of reading consist in respecting the alterity of the text: 'The ethics of reading is the power of the words of the text over the mind and the words of the reader.'[65] If this is the case, then one wonders why there are such discrepancies between deconstructive interpretations of one and the same text. In the last section of this chapter it will appear that Hartman's reading of Wordsworth's poem differs sharply from Miller's.

6 Geoffrey H. Hartman: Negativity, Delay, Indeterminacy
Like the other deconstructionists, Geoffrey H. Hartman has been influenced by Romanticism and Nietzschean philosophy. What makes him particularly interesting within the framework of this chapter is his explicit critique of Hegelian classicism to which he opposes a Romantic and Nietzschean idea of the text.

Following Derrida, Hartman considers the main issues of deconstruction in view of the antagonism between Hegel and Nietzsche. Commenting on the style of Derrida's experimental text *Glas*, he seeks to define its two perspectives: 'One is the past, starting with Hegel who is still with us; the other is the future, starting with Nietzsche who is once again with us (. . .).'⁶⁶ This sentence, already quoted at the end of the first chapter, is a concise presentation of the deconstructive programme in a social and philosophical situation in which a general aversion towards rationalism, Hegelianism, and Marxism makes authors like Hartman turn to Nietzsche for inspiration. 'Composed of explicit or inner quotations, of verbal debris', Hartman explains, '*Glas* (. . .) labors in Hegel's shadow to remove his absoluteness and create a negative or deeply critical work of *philosophic* art.'⁶⁷

The idea is to overcome Hegel's (and Marx's) classicism by Romantic and Nietzschean means. G. Douglas Atkins is quite right in reminding us of Hartman's Romantic roots: his reputation was established as a scholar of Romanticism.⁶⁸ Time and again Hartman himself quotes Friedrich Schlegel and other German Romantics in order to justify his own project of a 'synthesising' criticism 'that would combine art and philosophy'.⁶⁹ Like Schlegel, he praises the fragment and the open character of the text, whose incongruities, ambiguities, and ironies thwart all attempts of totalising reason to construct a coherent whole.

However, Hartman's Romanticism is not simply Romantic in the historical sense: it is mediated by the philosophy of Nietzsche whom Hartman considers quite correctly as Hegel's antipode. Thanks to Nietzsche and his rhetorical, figurative conception of language, the American critic can try to bridge the institutionalised gap between literature and criticism. Adopting a Nietzschean point of view, he can present the new critic not so much as the servant of the original author, but as a creator in his own right. 'For Hartman,' Christopher Norris writes, 'the only way out is for the critic to

throw off his "inferiority complex" and enter wholeheartedly –
with a Nietzschean swagger – into the dance of meaning.'[70]

In his interpretation of Wordsworth's *Lucy*-Poem *A Slumber
did my Spirit Seal* (also interpreted by Miller: cf. sec. 5) Hartman
illustrates what is meant by 'the dance of meaning' in his brand
of deconstruction. Like Roland Barthes who opposes Saussure's
theory of *anagrams* to Saussure's systematic theory of language (cf.
chap. 6.3), Hartman projects textual analysis onto the *expression
plane*, where anagrammatic associations or puns appear to him as the
most salient features. Let us have a second look at Wordsworth's
poem in the light of Hartman's Nietzschean playfulness.

> A slumber did my spirit seal;
> I had no human fears;
> She seemed a thing that could not feel
> The touch of earthly years.
>
> No motion has she now, no force;
> She neither hears nor sees;
> Rolled round in earth's diurnal course,
> With rocks, and stones, and trees.

In his analysis, which starts from Freud's theory of the dream,
Hartman foregrounds certain semantic and phonetic associations
or *anagrams*. He would like to show that Wordsworth uses certain
euphemisms in order to evoke words such as *die* or *grave* and that
Freud's ideas about oneiric associations of words and names are
particularly relevant in this case.

Which associations and *anagrams* has Hartman found in Wordsworth's poem? He concentrates on certain *puns* that can be related
to the theme of death: 'So "diurnal" (line 7) divides into "die"
and "urn", and "course" may recall the older pronunciation of
"corpse".'[71] Commenting on the second stanza, he points out
that its expressive force 'resides predominantly in the euphemistic
displacement of the word *grave* by an image of *gravitation* ("Rolled
round in earth's diurnal course").'[72] He then continues his argu- ·
ment on a phonetic level, considering *trees* (wrongly, according to
Eco)[73] as an *anagram* of *tears*:

> And though there is no agreement on the tone of this stanza, it is
> clear that a subvocal word is uttered without being written out.

It is a word that rhymes with 'fears' and 'years' and 'hears', but which is closed off by the very last syllable of the poem: 'trees'. Read 'tears', and the animating, cosmic metaphor comes alive, the poet's lament echoes through nature as in a pastoral elegy. 'Tears', however, must give way to what is written, to a dull yet definitive sound, the anagram 'trees'.[74]

However, the semantic affinity of *rocks*, *stones*, and *trees* is guaranteed by their belonging to non-human 'earthly nature'. The same cannot be said of *tears* which are quite arbitrarily associated with *trees* thanks to a complete disregard for semantic classification. Hartman's attempt to split the adjective *diurnal* into *die* and *urn* is equally arbitrary, since it cannot be justified in an etymological or semantic context: *diurnal* is of Latin origin, *die* and *urn* are of Germanic and Latin origin respectively, but *urn* (*urna*) has nothing to do with *diurnal* (*diurnus* from *dies* = *day*). All of Hartman's arguments are thus situated on the *expression plane* of language, the associations of which are arbitrarily exploited.

Considered as a whole, Hartman's interpretation is more closely related to Barthes' idea of a *texte scriptible* marked by *signifiance* than to Miller's figure of repetition or to Paul de Man's and Miller's *aporia*. It is quite surprising to find that the central word *thing*, so extensively commented on by Miller, is not even mentioned by Hartman, who, after all, also pretends to be a deconstructionist.

How is this discrepancy between two types of deconstruction to be reconciled with Miller's 'ethics of reading', i.e. with the idea that 'deconstruction is nothing more or less than good reading as such'?[75] But who decides what good reading actually means? Does it mean discovering *aporias* or tracing *anagrams* in the most unlikely shapes and forms? One thing is certain: it is hardly worth trying to relate different deconstructive readings to one another, because they are not complementary. More than any other form of deconstruction, Hartman's criticism is literature about literature in the Romantic sense, in the sense of Friedrich Schlegel who was among the first to imagine the critic as an *alter ego* of the author. His idea of the contemporary critical text which bridges the gap between literature and criticism is Derrida's *Glas*: a collage of philosophy and fiction that resists generic classification.

Globally speaking, Hartman's brand of deconstruction belongs to the pragmatic and essayistic type and differs substantially from Miller's somewhat rigid search for *aporias* and *differences*. It is based on three complementary notions which are worth looking at in a concluding assessment: *negativity*, *delay*, and *indeterminacy*. All three can be related to the common denominator of 'suspended meaning' in the sense of Derrida's *différance*.

G. Douglas Atkins summarises Hartman's idea of negativity and reveals its anti-conceptual (anti-rationalist, anti-Hegelian) bias: 'Deconstruction illustrates this particular "labor of the negative", saving the text through its repeated demonstration that "there is no transparence of the thing to thought. The meaning cannot displace the medium".'[76] This may be a useful idea, but it certainly is not new. For it was one of the favourite assumptions of the New Critics who tirelessly insisted on the impossibility of reducing the 'how' of the text to the 'what' of the message (cf. chap. 2.1).

Unlike the New Critics, Hartman is convinced that an objective or generally acceptable interpretation of a text does not or cannot exist. His analysis of Wordsworth's poem – if it is one – shows to what extent he considers the literary text and the critic's discourse to be inseparable. Hence one aspect of *negativity* is the impossibility to fix meaning objectively by separating it from the subjectivity of the reader.

Other aspects of Hartman's *negativity* are *ambiguity* and *indeterminacy*, both of which make a reduction of literary texts to conceptual structures (ideologies, philosophies) impossible. 'Whatever is being constructed is based on competing principles: the equivocal and equi-vocal character of words.'[77] At this point an affinity between Hartman and the other deconstructionists comes to the fore. Like the others, he develops a criticism geared towards Nietzsche's figure of *ambivalence* which makes the literary and even the philosophical text appear as irreducibly polysemic and plurivocal.

Indeterminacy is less concrete than *ambiguity* and refers to the impossibility to fix textual meanings or images. Commenting on Yeats's *Leda and the Swan*, Hartman identifies indeterminacy with the impossibility to imagine Leda's face: 'The ultimate indeterminacy, then, centers on this face that cannot be imagined.'[78] Again, one could ask whether this idea is as revolutionary as the deconstructionist would like it to be. Isn't it quite similar to Ingarden's and Iser's *Unbestimmtheit* (*indeterminacy*)? Many of

Hartman's statements suggest that he uses quite conventional concepts of criticism wrapped in deconstructionist rhetoric.

His practical advice that in the face of *ambiguity* and *indeterminacy* we ought to read literature with *delay* sounds plausible: 'Delay does not lead to eventual determination; meaning does not cease its wanderings, nor criticism its wonderings.'[79] This final pun closes the deconstructive circle, linking Hartman to Derrida: availing themselves of different rhetorical figures, both thinkers insist on the impossibility of de-fining, de-limiting or closing the text by conceptual means.

Although their theories are a useful and necessary antidote to Hegelian and Marxist *logocentrism*, they completely disregard the fact that most texts have semantic, syntactic, narrative, and phonetic structures recognised and reproduced (although in different ways) by the majority of readers. If there were no presence of meaning, if his texts were not structured, Derrida could not *identify* them in English or German translations. The Swedish linguist Bertil Malmberg seems to confirm this argument when he points out that 'in reality it is therefore the principle of general structures (i.e. of deep structures) and of linguistic universals which explains both the possibility of translation and the transformations within individual languages'.[80] The deconstructionists may be right when insisting on the irreducible particularity of the signifier brought to the fore by *iterability* and *différance* but they tend to overlook the universals of language which make a rational discussion (e.g. about deconstruction) possible.[81]

CHAPTER 8
Lyotard's Postmodern Aesthetics and Kant's Notion of the Sublime

The chapter on deconstruction has shown that aesthetics and literary criticism in contemporary society are marked by an unambiguous rejection of Hegelianism and of Hegelian categories. The harmonious totality which Goldmann declared to be one of the main features of great works, the symbol as a totalising concept, and the identity of meaning in the sense of Greimas' *iterativity* (cf. chap. 6.1) are replaced in deconstruction and postmodernism alike by *contradiction*, *allegory*, and *iterability*. These concepts (or anti-concepts) have a common denominator: negativity. For they negate the possibility of establishing a univocal meaning in the sense of Hegelian dialectics or Greimasian semiotics.

This deconstructionist and postmodern negativity which was in some respects announced by Adorno's negative aesthetics and his rejection of Hegelian conceptualisation is a sign of the times. The modernist search for meaning, so prominent in the works of Kafka, Proust, D. H. Lawrence, Sartre, and other existentialist authors, yields to a postmodern rejection of meaning and the metaphysical search of Marxists, existentialists, and surrealists.

A postmodernist such as Jean-François Lyotard believes that the only acceptable aesthetic response to the social, political, and cultural situation of late capitalism is a radical negation of meaning. In contrast to Barthes, de Man, and Hillis Miller whose negativity is mainly inspired by Nietzsche's critique of metaphysics and language, Lyotard resorts to Kant's theory of the *Sublime* (*das Erhabene*) in order to work out a negative aesthetic, an aesthetic of contradiction and aporia adequate to the late capitalist condition.

Unlike Kant's theory of the *Beautiful* which is based on the notion of *delight* (*Gefallen*), his theory of the *Sublime* is geared towards a contradictory mixture of *attraction* (*Lust*) and *repulsion* (*Unlust*) which results in *awe* (*Achtung*). As a negation of the

Beautiful which harmonises and reconciles, the *Sublime* destroys all notions of unity, harmony, and coherence. 'Sublime is what, by its resistance to the interest of the senses, we like directly'[1], explains Kant, defining this aesthetic phenomenon as a fundamental contradiction between emotions. We are attracted to the Sublime, says Kant, in spite of its awe-inspiring and frightening character. He illustrates this notion by referring to 'threatening rocks', 'thunderclouds piling up in the sky', and 'vulcanoes with all their destructive power'.[2] In the first section of this chapter it will become clear that Kant associates the *Beautiful* with *Understanding* (*Verstand*) and the *Sublime* with *Reason* (*Vernunft*).

Within the present context, it is not Kant's aesthetic as such that is important, but the fact that his concept of the *Beautiful* has influenced New Criticism, Russian Formalism, and Czech Structuralism, whereas his concept of the *Sublime* is being claimed for postmodern aesthetics by Lyotard. For Lyotard's claim is not an isolated case: it confirms other postmodern and deconstructive trends towards contradiction, aporia, and fragmentation. Globally speaking, Kant's *Critique of Judgement* fulfils a somewhat ambiguous and contradictory function in contemporary aesthetics and literary theory. With its concept of the *Beautiful* it has inspired theories of literary autonomy and reader response criticism; through its concept of the *Sublime* it is linked to the postmodern ideas of *contradiction* and *aporia*. The reception of Kant's work shows to what extent philosophical texts can undergo semantic and functional changes, thereby serving very different purposes.

1 From Kant to Lyotard: Postmodern Aesthetics of Disharmony

In his interpretation of Kant's theory of the *Sublime*, Lyotard returns to his theory of the *disagreement* or the *différend*, which he developed in *The Postmodern Condition* (1979) and *The Différend* (1983), in order to demonstrate that a fundamental, irreducible *différend* between the faculties has inspired Kant's notion of the *Sublime*. What exactly does Lyotard mean by *différend* and how does he apply this concept to aesthetics?

Although the theory of the *différend* is complex and some-what heterogeneous, its basic tenets can be summarised here in view of the function which it fulfils in Lyotard's aesthetics. Starting from the postmodern idea *par excellence* that the great *meta-narratives* (*métarécits*) or metaphysical tales of Christianity, Rationalism, Hegelianism, and Marxism are exhausted, because they have lost their credibility[3], Lyotard postulates a linguistic fragmentation and pluralisation of society which none of the exhausted *meta-narratives* can re-integrate. Each social, ethnic or religious group, he argues, has its own particular political, cognitive, ethical, and aesthetic criteria and will not accept a subordination of these criteria to a *meta-narrative* aspiring to universal validity.

The disappearance of universal validity and universally recognised criteria, he says, leads to a radical pluralisation of our linguistic world, marked by the coexistence of incompatible or incommensurate group languages among which communication is well-nigh impossible. In this situation, only two solutions are conceivable according to Lyotard: either the incompatibility of the diverging collective languages is negated in an authoritarian way by their subordination to an encompassing meta-language or *meta-narrative* or their incommensurability and particularity are recognised and respected. In the first case an *injustice* (*tort*) is committed, in the second case we practise what Lyotard calls a *paralogy* (*paralogie*) by accepting a kind of self-determination or autonomy of incommensurate languages.

It is important to note that for Lyotard a conflict between heterogeneous *language games* in the sense of Wittgenstein is a *disagreement* or *différend* that cannot be settled by superimposing a meta-language, thus transforming the conflict into a dispute or lawsuit. Any attempt to adopt this strategy invariably yields an *injustice* or *tort*. A case in point is the attempt to apply the precepts and rules of a nationally valid European or American law to the actions of an ethnic minority whose values and norms are incompatible or incommensurate with those the law is based on.

In the present context it is not possible to discuss the details of Lyotard's theory of the *différend* or to comment on the criticism it has incurred. It seems more relevant to discover its roots in Lyotard's early aesthetic theory, mapped out in his thesis *Discours, figure*, which was published in 1971. It is interesting to observe to what extent the theory of the *différend*, which is usually associated with the idea of social or political injustice, has aesthetic origins. For in his early work Lyotard deals with the aporetic task of the art critic to *speak* about painting and visual art in general without committing an injustice or a *tort* by *verbalising* it, by reducing it to a linguistic object. Starting from the postmodern assumption *avant la lettre* that 'western ratio (. . .) kills art along with the dream'[4], an assumption contained *in nuce* in the aesthetics of F. Th. Vischer and Nietzsche, Lyotard explains: 'A painting should not be read, as the semiologists say nowadays; Klee thought it ought to be *grazed* on (qu'il est à *brouter*) (. . .).'[5]

Following Emmanuel Lévinas' philosophy of alterity which holds that we should not attempt to reduce the Other or otherness to our own concepts and thoughts, he sets out to demonstrate the alterity of colour, of that which invariably eludes concepts and conceptualisation. Words, he argues, will always be an inadequate means for the representation of painting, of its non-verbal figures. Hence there will always be an unbridgeable gap between *discourse* and *figure*: a gap which cannot be accounted for verbally, because we can, after all, only *talk* about the importance of colour and the '*prééminence de la figure*'[6], as Lyotard puts it.

For the first time the *différend* appears here as an irreducible tension between two spheres of experience: between the verbal discourse of philosophy and the figures of painting. 'He has poised the visible figure against discourse itself'[7], remarks John McGowan about the author of *Discours, figure*. Those who follow Hegel in trying to explain painting by conceptual means, one might say, considering *Discours, figure* retrospectively within the context of *Le Différend*, commit an *injustice* or a *tort* by ignoring the alterity of the figure. It follows from this that the discourse about painting can only be imagined as a self-deconstructing discourse which also questions the unity or identity of the speaking subject.

As if he intended to return to the problematic mapped out in his early aesthetic writings, Lyotard turns to Kant's theory of the *Sublime* in order to show in the course of the 1980s that this concept could help us to found an aesthetics of heterogeneity and discrepancy: an aesthetics which in some respects continues the projects of modernism and the avant-garde movements, adapting them to the critical requirements of a postmodern (i.e. late capitalist) situation. For Lyotard would like to understand postmodernism not as a new era, but as a permanent rebirth of modernity. Freud, Duchamp, Bohr, Gertrude Stein, and even

Rabelais, Sterne, and other writers appear to him as representatives of postmodernism, because in their works the paradoxical and the incommensurate come to the fore.

This kind of projection of a contemporary debate into the past is not specific for Lyotard and other postmodernists, but characterises quite a few philosophies and literary theories. Russian Formalists such as Šklovskij considered Laurence Sterne as a precursor of the Futurist avant-garde and its de-familiarising experiments. Derrida and de Man adopt a similar stance when they claim that Rousseau was a deconstructionist *avant la lettre* and that his texts deconstruct themselves. None of these 'retrospective readings' are meant to define Sterne as a postmodern or Futurist novelist or Rousseau as a deconstructionist; rather they are attempts to justify avant-garde, deconstructionist or postmodern perspectives by postulating precedents and creating traditions.

Lyotard's actualisation of Kant's notion of the *Sublime* ought to be understood in this context. The French philosopher does not argue that Kant should be read as a postmodernist, but reads the theory of the *Sublime* as a contribution to the contemporary debate on postmodernism. *In Kant's Sublime he recognises an aesthetic expression of the disagreement (différend).* 'This differend cannot be resolved', he explains and adds: 'But it can be felt as such, as differend. This is the sublime feeling.'[8]

How is the *Sublime* to be understood as *différend*? In the introduction to this chapter it was already pointed out that Kant defines the *Sublime* as a kind of *aporia*: as a feeling of admiration and awe which combines attraction and repulsion. This combination comes about, says Kant, because our reason is able to comprehend phenomena which our senses cannot grasp. The millions of light years which separate us from far-off galaxies can be calculated rationally, but cannot be imagined or felt by the senses. Lyotard takes up this idea when he describes the *Sublime as a fundamental disagreement between that which Reason can think and that which can be imagined or felt by the senses.*

The conflict between *Reason* which is able to think the *Sublime* as an absolute and endless idea and *Understanding* (*Verstand*, in the sense of Kant) as a faculty tied to the senses is represented allegorically by Lyotard: 'Reason thus enters "the scene" in the place of understanding. It challenges the thought that imagines:

"make the absolute that I conceive present with your forms". Yet form is limitation. (. . .) It cannot present the absolute.'[9] The alliance between *Understanding* and the senses may be adequate for the comprehension of the *Beautiful* in the Kantian sense; it fails completely when confronted by the *Sublime*. This is why Kant – long before Lyotard – associated the *Beautiful* with *Understanding* and the *Sublime* with *Reason*, considering that the *Sublime* was beyond the grasp of *Understanding* and the senses.

In this context Lyotard refers to 'the differend of the finite and the infinite'[10] which cannot be settled, because *Understanding* and *Reason* are two different faculties that cannot be reduced to a common denominator or related to one set of criteria. For the norms and rules of the one are not the norms and rules of the other. Thus the postmodern character of the *Sublime* resides in its contradictory and aporetic structure which does not allow for any synthesis in the sense of the Hegelian *Aufhebung*.

As a negation of Hegelian totality and unity it also negates the identity of the *Subject* as a unifying instance. Unlike the *Beautiful* which by its harmony and its aesthetic pleasure contributes decisively to the constitution of subjectivity without a concept, the *Sublime* appears as a mortal challenge to the very existence of the *Subject*. Putting the *Subject* in quotation marks, Lyotard says: 'Taste promised him a beautiful life; the sublime threatens to make him disappear.'[11] For the *Sublime* does not merely combine two heterogeneous modes of knowledge, but also two incompatible sensations: pleasure and awe, admiration and anxiety. The *Subject* is torn between these incompatible drives.

Commenting on the *Sublime*, Lyotard adds: 'The sublime feeling is an emotion, a violent emotion, close to unreason, which forces thought to the extremes of pleasure and displeasure, from joyous exaltation to terror (. . .).'[12] In *L'Enthousiasme* where, following Kant, he associates enthusiasm with the *Sublime*, the enthusiasm inherent in historical revolutions appears on the one hand as 'an extreme mode of the Sublime'[13], on the other hand as an attitude 'close to madness'.[14] This oscillation between pleasure and pain, joy and awe, enthusiasm and madness finally leads to the dissolution of subjectivity which accompanies revolutions and other social crises.

Lyotard's reinterpretation of the Kantian *Sublime* reveals, among other things, the proximity and interrelatedness of Reason and the Irrational, of Reason and Madness. Reason's demand that imagination should represent the *Sublime*, making it accessible to our senses, comes close to Madness, tips over into Madness. This postmodern attempt to relate Reason and Madness to one another, instead of separating them in the traditional rationalist manner, is guided by the critical idea (also to be found in Horkheimer's and Adorno's Critical Theory) that the apparently rational social whole might very well be ruled by Madness and that only a thought inspired by the contradictory and aporetic theory of the *Sublime* can be considered adequate to the contradictions of late capitalism. Within this perspective, Lyotard speaks of a connivance between contemporary capitalism and the avant-garde in the realm of innovation and concludes: 'There is something of the sublime in capitalist economy'.[15]

In this situation, postmodern art and literature are expected to fulfil the well-nigh impossible task of representing the '*imprésentable*' (Lyotard). Time and again Lyotard emphasises that the aesthetics of capitalism are not oriented towards the *Beautiful*, but towards the *Sublime*. If this global assessment is correct, then art and literature of late capitalism (which according to Jameson forms the economic basis of postmodernity)[16] can only obey the laws of sublime *aporia*. Considered from this point of view, postmodern art does not appear as a consumer-friendly revision of avant-garde radicalism in the sense of Eco, but as a further radicalisation and a new revolt in the avant-garde sense.

Peter Bürger, a German theoretician of the avant-garde, does not seem to be aware of this, when he argues that Lyotard continues the modernist tradition and repudiates postmodernism.[17] Although Lyotard rejects the consumer-oriented aesthetics of Eco, Jencks, and Bonito Oliva, his approach is postmodernist insofar as it radicalises the revolt of the historical avant-garde movements without acknowledging their social utopias. In fact, Lyotard's early break with Marxism makes it quite impossible to consider him an heir of Breton's 'surrealist revolution' which was sporadically marked by a Marxist rhetoric.[18]

The postmodern core of Lyotard's aesthetics of the Sublime is his concept of *différend*, announced by *La Condition postmoderne* (1979), where related concepts such as *paralogie, agonistique langagière,* and *hétéromorphie des jeux de langages* are at the centre of the scene, and systematically developed in *Le Différend* (1983). (If one assumes that *différend* is the key concept of Lyotard's postmodern aesthetics because it is inherent in his theory of the *Sublime*, then it is impossible to consider this aesthetics as modernist, as some theoreticians do. For in this case the main representative of postmodernism would not be postmodern.)

In the literary realm, Lyotard's aesthetics of the *Sublime* seems to be close to an experimental and rebellious literature that rejects the communicative structures of a globally commercialised society without espousing the revolutionary discourse and the utopias of modernism, Surrealism, and Futurism. Thomas Pynchon and Kurt Vonnegut in the USA, Felix de Azúa in Spain, Christoph Ransmayr and Werner Schwab in Austria speak a language that bears the marks of conflict and destruction. On the one hand, the texts of these authors react to the destruction of political, aesthetic, moral, and linguistic values in late capitalist society; on the other hand, they develop a style which is a permanent revolt against this devaluation and destruction.

Like Werner Schwab who sums up his aesthetic programme with the word *Sprachzerstörung* (*destruction of language*), Thomas Pynchon writes a text of revolt and defiance, when dealing with the physical, mental, and cultural destructions of World War II:

> KRUPPALOOMA comes this giant *explosion*: water leaps in a surprised blue-green tongue (ever seen a toilet hollering, 'Yikes!'?) out of every single black-lidded bowl, pipes wrench and scream, walls and floor shudder, plaster begins to fall in crescents and powder-sheets as all the chattering transvestites fall silent, reach out to touch anyone nearby as a gesture of preparation for the Voice of the Loudspeaker, saying: 'That was a sodium bomb. Sodium explodes when it touches water'.[19]

Reading this passage, one is reminded of Lyotard's remark that there is something sublime about capitalism: for Pynchon's text also combines fascination and awe, attraction and repulsion, reminding us of the awesome and possibly sublime character of the two World Wars.

2 Lyotard and de Man: The Sublime, Allegory, and Aporia

Lyotard's theory of the *Sublime* not only has a counterpart in postmodern literature, but also in literary criticism. In the preceding chapter, Paul de Man's notions of *allegory* and *aporia* have been presented as figures of disharmony and discord, as critical instruments serving to subvert the *aesthetic ideology* based on the notion of the *symbol*. In what follows it will be argued that a postmodern affinitiy exists between de Man's terminology (which de Man himself never considered to be postmodern) and Lyotard's theory of the *Sublime*.

Introducing the complementary notions of *allegory* and *aporia*, de Man has a problematic in mind which corresponds to that of Lyotard's *Sublime*: an unbridgeable gap between aesthetic phenomena which shatters the foundations of subjectivity. When Lyotard writes that 'the elements are heterogeneous, but their union is necessary: one cannot think one without the other'[20], he also presents, albeit in a very concise manner, Paul de Man's aporetic way of reading (e.g. of W. B. Yeats' poem *Among Schoolchildren*) and the contradictory character of his notion of *allegory*.

Lyotard's Kantian contrast between the unifying *Beautiful* and the disruptive *Sublime* is comparable to de Man's antagonism between *symbol* and *allegory*. Like the *Beautiful*, the *Symbol* is a phenomenon of harmony which tends to present the material and the ideal, thought and world, subject and object as a coherent totality in the Hegelian sense. As was pointed out in chapter 7, de Man criticises this unifying function of the *symbol*, arguing that it contributes decisively to the formation of an *aesthetic ideology* which was later on systematically developed and popularised by National Socialists and Fascists. As a critical alternative to the symbol-oriented *aesthetic ideology*, de Man introduces the figure of *allegory* which he considers to be a radical subversion of symbolic thought.

Some of Lyotard's remarks in *L'Inhumain* show to what extent his critique of ideological thought as a thought of symbolic harmony is akin to de Man's critique of the *symbol*. Commenting on Hildegard Brenner's study of cultural politics under National Socialism and of Hans Jürgen Syberberg's films, he reminds us of the fact that neo-romantic and symbolic forms expressing harmony and unity were used by collaborating artists in order to block the 'negative dialectic' and to replace the negativity of utopian expectation in the sense of Adorno[21] by a positive utopia of the 'nation', the 'Führer' or 'Siegfried'.[22] The aesthetics of the *Sublime*, Lyotard concludes, were thus neutralised and replaced by the politics of myth. Instead of using the expression 'politics of myth'[23] he could have also used de Man's notion of aesthetic ideology.

It becomes clear at this stage that both Lyotard and de Man are not merely interested in an inversion of rationalist and Hegelian theses about the constitution of meaning and totality, but also continue the critical tradition in the sense of Adorno's and Horkheimer's *Ideologiekritik*. In some crucial points, however, the postmodern notion of critique differs from that of Critical Theory. Unlike this theory, which established a close link between negativity, truth ('*Wahrheitsgehalt*', Adorno: cf. chap. 5.2), and the hope for a more humane future, postmodern negativity tends to be purely destructive and to sacrifice the last bourgeois-liberal values Adorno and Horkheimer so obstinately held on to.

The postmodern propensity for the heterogeneous and the particular radicalises Adorno's plea in favour of particularisation by renouncing the critical *concept*, by sacrificing it to rhetoric (Paul de Man) or to the *paralogie* (Lyotard). But in a situation where the concept as an analytic and critical instrument is no longer at the disposal of the Subject of theory, the Subject itself is threatened by disintegration. In postmodernism this disintegration is greeted with a mixture of relief and resignation: it seems not worth saving whatever could not be saved anyway.

The situation of Critical Theory was rather different, and Albrecht Wellmer quite rightly reminds us of the fact that 'the disintegration of the subject in late industrial society' appeared to Adorno and Horkheimer as 'a process of *regression*'.[24] From the point of view of these two thinkers, the negativity of *allegory* and the *Sublime* would only make sense if it could be used critically by an autonomous Subject oriented towards a meaningful historical future. But this historical perspective has been abandoned by postmodernists like Lyotard along with the discredited *meta-narratives* (*métarécits*) of Christianity, Rationalism, and Marxism. Within the postmodern constellation all that is left is a destructive negation of meaning and subjectivity.

It is hardly surprising therefore that Paul de Man does not consider modernity in an historical perspective as a promise of a better future, but as an 'eternal return' in the sense of Nietzsche:

> Paul de Man's discussion of 'Modernism' shows it to be a concept by no means unique to a single period but a recurrent ever-repeated self-subverting move in each period's sense of itself in relation to previous periods. If de Man is right the term 'post-Modern' ist a tautology or an oxymoron, since no writer or critic ever reaches the modern in the sense of the authentically self-born, much less goes beyond it.[25]

The key words in this passage are 'recurrent' and 'ever-repeated': because history is not regarded by de Man and Miller in a Hegelian perspective as a cumulative process or as a progress towards ever higher stages of development and consciousness, but as a cyclic movement in the Nietzschean sense.

All of postmodernism could be considered as a rejuvenation of the Young Hegelian critique and as a Nietzschean revolt against Hegel and Hegelianism. On the one hand, postmodernists such as Lyotard reject the Hegelian idea of totalisation and synthesisation, emphasising the contradictory character of reality, art, and literature, on the other hand, they take issue with Hegel on the notion of history as a dialectic progression.

Both aspects of postmodernism come to the fore in Paul de Man's remarks on Hegelianism which are considered here as characteristic of postmodern thought: 'We are Hegelian when we try to systematize the relationships between the various art forms or genres according to different modes of representation or when we try to conceive of historical periodization as a development, progressive or regressive, of a collective or individual consciousness.'[26] De Man is not a Hegelian of course (as was made clear in the preceding chapter), but would like to show, in very much the same way as Lyotard, that there is no progression in the historical-dialectical sense, that there are no systematic relations between genres and that a work of art does not constitute a coherent totality.

It was one of the aims of this chapter to show that in deconstructionist and postmodernist debates not only Nietzsche's critique of metaphysics and of language has been turned against

Hegel and Hegelianism but also Kant's *Critique of Judgement*. However, it is important to bear in mind that this work – like most philosophical works – can be read in many different ways and that the New Critics, the Russian Formalists, and the Czech Structuralists used it in order to give additional plausibility to their idea that a work of art is a coherent whole, that art is autonomous (self-referential), and that the only correct attitude to adopt towards aesthetic phenomena is a disinterested one. Critics such as Brooks, Wimsatt, Jakobson, and Mukařovský not only believed in the autonomy and the integrity of art but also in the autonomy and integrity of the individual subject: of the spectator or reader whose identity and autonomy was to be confirmed and reinforced by the disinterested character of aesthetic contemplation.

Postmodernists like Lyotard use Kant very differently and for different purposes. For them the *Critique of Judgement* is not primarily a theory of the *Beautiful*, of harmony and autonomy, but an aesthetic of the *Sublime* which negates the individual's autonomy and identity. Along with the actualisation of Nietzsche, this reinterpretation of Kant's aesthetic is a symptom of the times: in the postmodern context the idea of an autonomous and self-identical Subject has lost its credibility which had previously been undermined by modernist doubts and critiques. Modernist writers such as Joyce, Virginia Woolf, Svevo, Pirandello, Proust, and Musil represented and analysed the crisis of the individual Subject long before the postmodern problematic emerged. Lyotard and other postmodernists merely seem to confirm and evaluate the results of a long evolution which the modernists announced at the beginning of the twentieth century.

3 From Lyotard to Vattimo: Two Postmodernisms
Any attempt to identify postmodern aesthetics and literary theory with Lyotard's brand of postmodernism would lead to an inadmissible simplification. For in his book *L'Inhumain* the French philosopher asks the reader not to confuse his 'postmodern condition' with an aesthetics of the 'trans-avant-garde' propagated by the Italian architect Achille Bonito Oliva and the American artist and architect Charles Jencks. According to Lyotard, Oliva and Jencks do not continue or renew the critical project of the historical avant-garde movements, but betray it. They betray it,

Lyotard explains, because they continue to adhere to the aesthetic ideal of harmony and reconciliation (between Subject and Object) which is being systematically exploited by the 'culture industry' (Adorno). As an alternative Lyotard proposes an aesthetics which continues the revolt of the European avant-garde in a different context and by adopting new techniques inspired by Kant's *Sublime* and the 'unrepresentable' in general.[27]

However, Lyotard's alternative is not universally accepted in the postmodern world, and the perspective adopted by Oliva and Jencks is not an isolated phenomenon. In philosophy an aesthetic theory similar to that of Jencks and Oliva has been developed by Gianni Vattimo who agrees on certain points with Lyotard, but disagrees on others. On the whole, his approach appears not so much as a revolt against present day capitalist society, but rather as a confirmation of its dominant trends.

To begin with, he seems to agree with the French author when it comes to acknowledging the irreversible tendency towards pluralisation and particularisation in contemporary European and American society. Like Lyotard, he explains this tendency in conjunction with the disintegration of the great Fascist and Marxist meta-narratives in post-war society. Once the dominant ideology which identified its *ratio* with Reason as a whole collapses, fragmentation sets in and, at the end of the day, the global system of values falls apart into rival reasons, ethics, aesthetics, and cultures. Vattimo speaks of a 'liberation of differences'.[28]

Like Lyotard, he welcomes the result of this process, calling it *heterotopy* (*eterotopia*): a coexistence of many different cultures, reasons, ethics, and aesthetics and an ever-increasing pluralisation of society which can no longer be unified by a single utopian project in the Christian, Rationalist, Marxist-Leninist or Fascist sense. At the same time, the utopian aspirations of the Futurist, Surrealist, and Vorticist avant-garde movements are recognised as futile and replaced by the political and aesthetic pluralism of *heterotopy*. In Vattimo's discourse, the latter appears as a politically and aesthetically valid alternative to the *utopias* of modernity.

Vattimo's perspective also overlaps with Lyotard's when he claims that, along with the meta-narratives, the *Subject* undergoes a process of fragmentation and pluralisation and that subjectivity can only be conceived of as a plurality of competing forces. He speaks of an *'individuality as multiplicity'* (*'individualità come molteplicità'*)[29] and of a *'split subject'* (*'sogetto scisso'*)[30] which corresponds to the postmodern state of fragmentation.

Although Vattimo's outlook overlaps with Lyotard's as far as the pluralist diagnosis and the deconstruction of the individual *Subject* is concerned, it would be an error to postulate a contiguity between 'the postmodern condition' and the Italian philosopher's conception of postmodernism. For Vattimo not only approves the tendency towards particularisation and pluralisation but also welcomes the emergence of a commercialised mass culture which tends to combine high-brow and popular forms of art, bringing about a 'de-differentiation' of the aesthetic sphere analysed by Scott Lash: 'If modernization means the differentiation of fields, postmodernization means at least the partial collapse of some fields into other fields. For example (. . .) the implosion of the aesthetic field into the social field. Or, with "commodification", the collapse of the aesthetic field into the economic field.'[31] However, this kind of 'de-differentiation' or commercialisation of culture which is also announced by Baudrillard's *transesthétique*[32], is fiercely opposed by Lyotard who, as was shown above, is trying to mobilise the contemporary avant-garde against the commercialised culture of late capitalism.

With his aesthetic theory of pluralisation and popularisation Vattimo stands much closer to authors such as Jencks, Oliva, and Eco who adopt a conciliatory attitutde towards commercialised culture, arguing, among other things, that it meets the needs of democratic society. Democracy or capitalism? Like Adorno – but unlike Vattimo, Jencks, Oliva, and Eco – Lyotard, the former Marxist, the avant-garde thinker, tends to believe that the notion of democracy is ideological eyewash designed to camouflage the power structure of late capitalism. Having abandoned all hopes linked to the idea of a proletarian revolution or to the idea of the 1968 student revolt, he projects his aversion towards the capitalist system into the aesthetic sphere: into a theory of the *Sublime* considered as adequate to the negativity and the destructive drives of contemporary capitalist society.

The question is of course what this kind of theory can achieve in an increasingly one-dimensional society that tends to marginalise artistic revolts or to integrate them as exotic (but commercialised) happenings which consumers of revolutionary nostalgia can enjoy without running too many revolutionary risks. The complementary question concerns Lyotard's theory of the *Subject*: if it is true that the postmodern *Subject* is pluralised (Vattimo and Lyotard seem to agree on this) and that the aesthetic *Sublime* threatens it with death, then a critical attitude in the sense of Adorno's and Horkheimer's Critical Theory becomes inconceivable. For *Subjects* are so weakened that they are no longer capable of formulating a coherent critique of the system within which they are functioning. This is precisely what Adorno and Horkheimer were afraid of when they insisted on strengthening the autonomy of the individual *Subject*. The common denominator of postmodern theories seems to be the fact that they have resigned themselves to the loss of individual autonomy.

However, the confrontation of postmodern theories with Critical Theory was merely a side-effect of the present argument; its basic aim was to reveal the relative heterogeneity of postmodern aesthetics and (more important) to show to what extent Kantian aesthetics, which were interpreted by New Critics, Formalists, and Structuralists in terms of individual and artistic autonomy, can be re-interpreted in such a way that they turn into a negation of autonomy and the *Subject*. In both cases, however, Kant's *Critique of Judgement* serves as a basis for anti-Hegelian criticism.

CHAPTER 9
Towards a Critical Theory of Literature

So far the chapters of this book had a predominantly descriptive, explicative, and critical function. The underlying idea was that some of the most important literary theories could be understood as Kantian, Hegelian or Nietzschean aesthetics and that the differences and antagonisms between these theories were ultimately due to the fundamental incompatibility between these three philosophical positions. The complementary idea was that for different reasons literary theories inspired by Kant and Nietzsche emphasise the *expression plane* in the sense of Hjelmslev, whereas theories inspired by Hegel foreground the *content plane* or the conceptual aspects of art and literature.

Although it is neither possible nor desirable to solve all of the problems which have been dealt with in this book, the present chapter can be read as an attempt to map out a critical theory of literature which oscillates between the Kantian and the Hegelian position inasmuch as it postulates a limited polysemy of the literary text which can be read in many different ways but not arbitrarily. Different readers will read a text in many different and even incompatible manners, but they will usually agree on the identity of the text (i.e. the object of their discussion) and some of its salient features. In the course of history many diverging interpretations of a literary work are conceivable, but they are bound to overlap in crucial points as long as the identity of the object – its title, its phonetic, semantic, and narrative structures – is not in doubt.

In other words, this chapter postulates the existence of *constant* or *universally recognisable* textual features such as titles, phonetic elements, syntactic and narrative units (stanzas, chapters, parts of a novel) or semantic structures. Now, anybody who has read the sixth chapter attentively or is familiar with semantics and semiotics is bound to object at this point that each semiotic, each semantic theory will identify different structures and that even authors of narrative theories will disagree when asked to define narrative sequences in a novel such as Jane Austen's *Pride and Prejudice* or George Eliot's *Middlemarch*. This is undoubtedly true, and it would be somewhat foolish to argue that semantic and narrative structures in these novels can be defined once and for all. However, it is also true that in a novel such as Albert Camus' *L'Etranger* (*The Outsider*) the division of the text into two parts (both in the French original and in the English translation of 1946) has been recognised by all critics without exception.

Hence it seems to be one of the tasks of literary theory to describe the dialectic between openness and closure, between polysemy and monosemy, between that which can be univocally defined on a conceptual level and the ambiguous: that which escapes conceptual definition, thus keeping in motion the open-ended process of interpretation. As in the sixth chapter, the idea is that literary theory ought to become aware of the dialectics between *iterativity* in the sense of Greimas and *iterability* in the sense of Derrida.

In other words, neither Kant's notion 'without concept', nor Nietzsche's rhetorical approach, nor Hegel's conceptually definable *totality* is the whole truth. The truth – if it exists – should be looked for in the nexus between that which is definable and that which is not. Unfortunately, this crucial point cannot be located geometrically. It can only be approached dialogically by comparing different constructions of one and the same object within heterogeneous theories.

The essential concepts here are: *construction* and *heterogeneity*. For if we are to avoid the mimetic misunderstanding according to which the discourse of theory (or of literature) reflects reality, we have to assume with semioticians and constructivists[1] that each theoretical discourse constructs its objects in a particular way, i.e. according to certain criteria and linguistic mechanisms which will be discussed in detail further on. This theoretical and ideological particularity of theories explains (at least partly) their heterogeneity. For each theory constructs its objects in accordance with a particular social, political point of view that is partly incompatible with the perspectives of other theories.

However, it will be argued in the course of this chapter that this inevitable heterogeneity which is due to the ideological diversity of society is not only a disadvantage and an obstacle to mutual understanding, but also an asset to scientific communication. For (it will be argued) an agreement between ideologically heterogeneous theories on a particular point is more relevant and more interesting than an agreement within a theoretical group or school. At the same time it will be shown that Stanley Fish's notion of an *interpretive community* (cf. chap. 4.3) is not sophisticated enough, because it is based on the simple assumption that an interpretation adopted by a collective or a community should be preferred to an individual attribution of meaning. It will be shown that it is not enough to found interpretation on collective norms and values but that it is necessary to take into account the incompatibilities and conflicts between collectively supported attributions of meaning, turning such controversies dialectically into a theoretically productive element.

1 Literary Theory between Kant, Hegel, and Nietzsche
The literary theory which will be presented in this chapter can be viewed as an attempt to rethink the problematic of Adorno's *Aesthetic Theory* (cf. chap. 5.2) and of Critical Theory in general in the light of recent philosophical, sociological, and literary debates. Adorno's position is quite exceptional inasmuch as he avoids both Kant's sceptical stance, which excludes the search for truth (*Wahrheitsgehalt*, Adorno) in the aesthetic realm, and Hegel's conceptual absolutism which eventually dissolves art in philosophy or science (*Wissenschaft*), as Hegel himself says. At the same time, Adorno introduces essayistic, aphoristic, and paratactic elements into the discourse of philosophy, thus following a Nietzschean impulse which later on becomes dominant in French and American deconstruction.[2]

Although the theoretical approach mapped out here will take into account some of the more convincing Nietzschean and deconstructive critiques of Hegelianism and *logocentrism*, it will not follow the Nietzschean drive towards rhetorics and a literarisation of theory (in the sense of de Man and Hartman). Instead of sacrificing theory to literature, it will systematically oscillate between Kant's refusal to conceptualise art and Hegel's claim that a conceptual definition is possible. It will thus follow the movement of philosophical aesthetics as described by Mikel Dufrenne: 'A subjectivist aesthetic under the aegis of Kant, an objectivist aesthetic under the aegis of Hegel: this contrast will dominate the entire history of aesthetics (. . .).'[3] This is undoubtedly a simplification, because it does not take into account Nietzsche's rhetorical or linguistic turn which – as has been shown throughout this book – had a lasting impact on aesthetics and literary criticism.

However, it is a useful simplification, because it marks the two philosophical poles between which most literary theories develop and interact. A critical theory of literature will refuse to let itself be absorbed by Kantian, Hegelian or Nietzschean discourse and instead try to move dialectically between Hegelian conceptualisation and the Kantian or Nietzschean negation of it. It will take into account Adorno's famous dictum that works of art are riddles or enigmas and that the theoretical approach to art does not imply a solution of the enigma but rather an explanation why it cannot be solved.[4] Adopting a semiotic terminology, one could say that we expect literary theory to describe and explain as accurately as possible the relationship between *expression plane* and *content plane*, *polysemy* and *monosemy* or *openness* and *closure*.

Those who are inclined to believe that reader-response criticism and deconstruction have once and for all demonstrated the openness of literary texts in what Barthes calls '*l'infini du langage*', should be reminded not only of Hegelian Marxism which they may consider as obsolete for political reasons, but also of Jean-Pierre Richard's *thematic analysis* and the semiotics of Greimas who claims that undecidability, openness, and the plurality of meanings are mainly due to incomplete, superficial, and unsystematic readings.

In a very different context, Tzvetan Todorov, a former Formalist, holds that literature would be worthless 'if it did not make a better understanding of life possible'. He adds: 'It is not only a quest for truth, but it is also this.'[5] This is certainly not an example of literary Hegelianism, but Todorov's renewal of the existential components of literature indicates that the trend towards Nietzschean deconstruction may not be irreversible and that the concepts of meaning and truth might return to the centre of the critical scene.

However, this kind of prognosis should not be read as an unqualified rejection of Kant's principle 'without concept'. For

Kant's *Critique of Judgement* contains a number of very plausible arguments, some of which were discussed here in conjunction with Anglo-American New Criticism, Russian Formalism, Czech Structuralism, and reader-response criticism. The *expression plane* cannot be reduced to the *content plane* and has to be considered as a permanent source of *polysemy* (polysemic signifiers resist conceptual definitions); the different semantic structures of a literary text cannot always be hierarchically ordered within the framework of a closed totality (in the Hegelian-Marxist or Greimasian sense); the meanings which are projected into the text in the course of its reception by metalanguages such as phenomenology, psycho-analysis, Marxism or deconstruction are subject to historical change which also affects the metalanguages. Hence the meaning of the heterogeneous and polysemic literary text cannot be fixed.

It should be added – and it is Derrida's merit to have insisted on this aspect of the hermeneutic process – that even conceptual (legal, political, scientific) texts do not guarantee a univocal reception. The original meaning of the American *Declaration of Independence* as intended by its authors may not be accessible to us any more and the text is anything but a univocal message, as Derrida already pointed out in the Mid-Eighties. The works of Kant, Hegel, and Marx have given birth to as many heresies as the Bible, and it can therefore be assumed that their polysemies and contradictions are as pronounced as those of the holy text.

The protracted controversies triggered off by Thomas S. Kuhn's *The Structure of Scientific Revolutions* (1962) reveal, among other things, that even scientific texts are not immune to the virus of polysemy. Margaret Masterman, for example, found at least 21 different meanings of *paradigm*, the key concept of Kuhn's book: 'possibly more, not less'[6], she added laconically.

Considering this – possibly inevitable – polysemy of scientific texts, theoreticians of literature might be tempted to forget about the question what a literary text *means*. Even after a thousand interpretations of Milton's *Paradise Lost* or Kafka's *The Trial* it may not be possible to fix the meaning of these texts. As a reader of Kafka, the theoretician may find consolation in the idea that even the '*man from the country*' ('*der Mann vom Lande*') does not succeed in gaining access to the *Law* and to the *Truth* he seeks. However, this consoling idea itself reveals a certain degree of univocity in Kafka's text: the man from the country does not succeed in gaining access to the *Law*. From a Greimasian point of view, this univocity could be summed up in the phrase 'the failure of the actant-Subject to obtain the desired Object'. This failure seems to be a univocal fact which the numerous polysemies of the text cannot put in doubt.

As a matter of fact, Kafka's polysemic parable *Before the Law* which has given rise to so many interpretations and controversies is structured by a relatively simple *actantial model* (in the sense of Greimas). A Subject, the man from the country, is confronted by an Anti-Subject, the guard, who succeeds in preventing him from acquiring the desired Object, i.e. access to the Law. The story ends univocally with the victory of the Anti-Subject over the dying Subject. It can therefore be said to represent the failure of the Subject.

Many a competent reader will obviously object that this is a somewhat trivial assessment of the parable which fails to take into account its semantic complexity and especially the fact that at the end it opens onto a paradox: the man for whom the entrance to the Law had been reserved and kept open was prevented from entering. However, this very statement presupposes another univocal element: namely the fact that the text ends in a paradox. Moreover, a careful reading reveals that this paradox is doubled by a second paradox: the man from the country, it is said, might not even be able to bear the sight of the Law, i.e. of the object he desires. Right at the beginning of the parable, the guard draws our attention to this difficulty:

> But take note: I am powerful. And I am only the lowest door-keeper. But from room to room stand door-keepers each more powerful than the last. The mere aspect of the third is more than even I can endure. (*Merke aber: Ich bin mächtig. Und ich bin nur der unterste Türhüter. Von Saal zu Saal stehen aber Türhüter, einer mächtiger als der andere. Schon den Anblick des dritten kann nicht einmal ich mehr vertragen.*)[7]

Paradoxically, the Law seems to attract the man by its light: although his sight deteriorates rapidly, he recognises 'a radiance which breaks out imperishably from the door to the law' ('*im Dunkel einen Glanz, der unverlöschlich aus der Türe des Gesetzes bricht*'.)[8]

In other words, the Law is defined in the parable as a space (*'von Saal zu Saal'*) and as a source of light, and the paradox emerges because the hero desires something the sight of which he might not be able to bear and because he is prevented from using the entrance which was reserved for him. Adopting a Greimasian perspective, one could argue that an unknown Addresser entrusts a Subject with a task the Subject is unable to accomplish.

Although it is not possible here to envisage a detailed analysis of the parable, it can be shown that the text can be defined both on the semantic and on the narrative level as a structured (although polysemic) unit. Contrary to deconstructionist opinion, *iterativity* (chap. 6.1) as repetition of textual units does not lead, in this particular case, to the disintegration of meaning, but to its consolidation: e.g. by making the guard appear in the eighth sentence of the parable as the Anti-Subject and towards the end as a victorious Anti-Subject.

Naturally, it would also be possible to apply Derrida's notion of *iterability* to Kafka's text in order to show how it is deconstructed by its paradoxes: 'In a certain way', writes Derrida, *'Vor dem Gesetz* is the story of this inaccessibility, of this inaccessibility to the story, the history of this impossible history, the map of this forbidden path: no itinerary, no method, no path to accede to the law, to what would happen there, to the *topos* of its occurrence.'[9] However, the mere fact that the topic of a text is 'inaccessibility' does not mean that its structures are beyond description and comprehension.

All depends on our aesthetic point of view. Do we believe in a rationalist or Hegelian aesthetic, which emphasises univocal textual elements on the semantic and narrative level, or in a Kantian or Nietzschean aesthetic which draws our attention to the paradoxes and polysemies of the text? A Nietzschean theory in the deconstructive sense would underline the fact that the victory of the Anti-Subject blatantly contradicts the last sentences of the parable: 'This entrance was meant only for you. I shall now go and close it.' (*'Dieser Eingang war nur für dich bestimmt. Ich gehe jetzt und schließe ihn.'*)[10]

However, it would be somewhat unsatisfactory to conclude that relativism is inevitable and that the meaning of a text simply depends on the point of view or the aesthetics of its reader. It seems more rewarding to establish a dialectical relationship between the apparently incompatible aesthetics in order to show that they are complementary. For even the sketchy analysis of Kafka's parable may have shown that coherence and contradiction, monosemy and polysemy coexist in a literary text. Any attempt to read the text *either* as a coherent and univocal whole *or* as a self-deconstructing paradox is doomed to failure.

On a semantic level, the arguments put forward so far are even better illustrated by Albert Camus' novel *L'Etranger* (*The Outsider*) which has elicited almost as many critical comments as Kafka's *The Trial*. The question is not so much whether these comments are confirmed by 'the text' (which only exists as a read and interpreted text), but whether the consensus of these comments reveals some of the basic semantic and narrative structures. In the last part of this chapter this consensus will be analysed in detail and related to the concepts of *dialogical theory* and *interdiscursive dialogue*.

In numerous interpretations of Albert Camus' novel *L'Etranger*, a consensus has come to the fore concerning the semantic oppositions between the elements of *fire* and *water*, between the *sun* and the *sea*. The text of the novel seems to justify this consensus, insofar as the narrator's discourse associates systematically (in very much the same way as later on in *La Peste*, 1947) the *sea* with *life* and the *sun* with *death*. A few moments before Meursault shoots the Arab on the beach, he seeks to escape from the sun which seems to determine his actions: '(. . .) I was thinking of the cold, clear stream behind it, and longing to hear again the tinkle of running water. Anything to be rid of the glare (. . .).' ('*J'avais envie de retrouver le murmure de son eau, envie de fuir le soleil . . .*').[11] The text states univocally that it is the same sun which tormented the narrator during his mother's funeral, influencing all of his actions: 'It was just the same sort of heat as at my mother's funeral (. . .).' ('*C'était le même soleil que le jour ou j'avais enterré maman . . .*')[12] (The English translation is hopelessly inaccurate: in the first quotation it renders 'soleil' with 'glare', in the second it substitutes 'heat'/'chaleur' for 'sun'/'soleil', thus producing an unnecessary semantic shift which weakens the semantic structure of the original.)

This fundamental semantic opposition between *fire* and *water* (*sun* and *sea*) is confirmed by several psychoanalytic interpretations which relate the *sun* to the masculine, the *water* to the feminine principle. J. Fletcher, for example, interprets the antagonism between Meursault and the *sun* as a conflict between father and son who fight for the possession of the female objects (*Object-Actants*, Greimas would say) 'water' and 'earth'. Henning Krauss, who in his psychoanalytic interpretation of *L'Etranger* also believes that the sun symbolises the masculine, the water the feminine principle, defines Camus' mythical Nature as a bisexual being which violates Meursault.[13]

What matters here, is not so much the validity or originality of these interpretations, but the fact that they recognise the funda- mental semantic opposition between *fire* and *water* which structures Camus' novel. This is what Jean-Claude Coquet means (cf. chap. 6) when he points out that all phenomenological, psychoanalytical or sociological interpretations ought to set out from the '*primary or linguistic meaning*' ('*sens primaire ou linguistique*')[14] of a text. However, there are many competing linguistic, semiotic, and semantic theories, and we should therefore resist the temptation to fix this primary meaning monologically within the framework of a particular theoretical metalanguage (e.g. Greimas' semiotics). The text structure as 'primary meaning' cannot be fixed in a monologue, but only in the course of a theoretical dialogue involving heterogeneous theories and points of view.

It is crucial to realise, however, that the identity and identifiability of a text depends on the existence of recognisable features (e.g. the title)[15] and structures: the division of Camus' *L'Etranger* into two parts or narrative sequences (reproduced in all translations) is a case in point. Without such basic phonetic, semantic, syntactic, and narrative structures a text could not be *identified* by competing interpretations, and this would give rise to the ontological question whether they are actually dealing with the same object. This question arises whenever a critic focuses on a translation, while other critics concentrate on the original, for original and translation are different objects.

In the following sections, the aesthetic problems of interpreta- tion and object constitution will be projected into two closely related contexts: the context of *ideology* and the context of *theory*. It will be shown that all theories are also ideologies in the general sense (i.e. value systems) and that a theoretical dialogue about liter- ary or other objects is only possible if the ideological factor is taken into account. In other words: each theory interprets or constructs a literary object in accordance with particular ideological criteria and value judgements. It seems important to find out how theoretical constructions of literary objects come about in an ideological and linguistic context and how they can be related to one another dialogically. For only dialogically produced knowledge, that is knowledge yielded by the cooperation of hetergeneous theories can be said to go beyond the prejudice of theoretical monologue: beyond the prejudice cultivated by the members of ideologically and theoretically homogeneous groups. It will be argued that the dialogue between ideologically heterogeneous theories is the only remedy against monological blindness and dogmatism.

2 Towards a Critique of Ideology: Ideology as Sociolect and Discourse
What exactly is the role of ideology in literary theory? The role of ideology in the social and cultural sciences can hardly be overestimated. It is a well-known fact that conservative, liberal, Marxist, and feminist interpretations of Romanticism or modernism differ quite substantially and that Marxists tend to associate postmodernism with late capitalism (Jameson, Eagleton), while some feminists consider it to be a predominantly masculine phenomenon. Unlike Terry Eagleton who recognises in postmodernism 'a grisly parody of socialist utopia'[16], Linda Hutcheon criticises it in a feminist perspective: 'Feminisms are not really either compatible with or even an example of postmodern thought, as a few critics have tried to argue; if anything, together they form the single most powerful force in changing the direction in which (male) postmodernism was heading but, I think, no longer is.'[17]

Is postmodernism 'late capitalist', is it 'male', is it 'feminist' or simply radically 'pluralist' and democratic as Wolfgang Welsch in Germany is trying to argue?[18] In spite of their obvious divergencies, these definitions of postmodernism have one feature in common: they are ideological, because they are the products of different kinds of socio-political *engagement*. Bonnie Kime Scott's book *Refiguring Modernism. The Women of 1928* (1995) is another case in point: it is an ideological attempt to re-interpret modernism and the role of female writers within this period from a feminist point of view. The idea is to *reconstruct* this period (usually associated with male writers such as T. S. Eliot, W. B. Yeats, E. Pound)[19] in a feminist perspective, thus presenting a different modernism: a dissenting historical construction.

Similarly, conservative, Marxist, feminist, and deconstructionist interpretations of individual authors can be considered as ideologically motivated constructions, none of which can be identified with the interpreted (or reconstructed) works. Thus Terry Eagleton's Marxist construction of George Eliot's work has very little in common with J. Hillis Miller's deconstructionist approach[20], and Georg Lukács' Marxist-Hegelian critique which defines Kafka as a decadent modernist, loading the concept of modernism with negative connotations[21], is incompatible with Adorno's reconstruction of Kafka's work which makes the latter appear as a negative aesthetic and a critique of rationalist capitalism.[22] In none of these cases can we assume that the interpretation is a truthful representation of the object as such. For the polysemic literary text resists all attempts to identify it with a particular theoretical and ideological discourse, reminding us of the fact that it pleases 'without concept', as the Kantians would say.

However, in the present situation this Kantian maxim can no longer be considered as the ultimate wisdom; for we do assume (even if we are not Hegelians) that literary texts tend to have a meaning and that not all attributions of meaning or interpretations are equivalent. Bertolt Brecht intended his Epic Theatre to bring about a radical critique of capitalist society, and Federico Tomaso Marinetti, the founder of Italian Futurism, saw in the Futurist avant-garde an aesthetic corollary of the Fascist movement. It would be ludicrous to assume that the texts of these authors are intended to please 'without concept'.

It seems necessary therefore to take the constructions of aesthetic or literary meaning very seriously and to ask *how they come about in particular ideologies and how (if at all) they can be compared on a theoretical level.* The first question will be dealt with in this section, the second question in the last section of this chapter. Both questions are based on the semiotic and constructivist assumption that theoretical objects are not given but constructed and that we are only aware of objects inasmuch as they are our constructions.[23] However, constructions of social, economic, political or literary objects are not merely theoretical, they are also ideological, as the above examples have shown and as the semiotician Luis J. Prieto has repeatedly pointed out.[24]

We should therefore return to the first question and ask how objects are constructed within ideologies. In order to answer this question it seems necessary to go one step further and inquire into the semiotic (i.e. discursive) nature of ideologies. How can ideologies be defined as linguistic structures? How do they function on a lexical, semantic, and macrosyntactic (narrative) level?

To begin with, ideologies can be considered as collective languages or *sociolects* which are – at least partly – made up of specific vocabularies or lexical repertoires, specific modes of classification (taxonomies), and specific narrative structures or discourses. It could be argued that *sociolects* do not exist as such but only as discourses spoken in every day life by individuals, groups or organisations. In other words, *sociolect* and *discourse* are two different things: the *sociolect* is a theoretical abstraction comparable to Saussure's *langue*. It does not exist as such in social reality and should be defined as *the hypothetical totality of discourses conceivable within the semantic system of a certain social group.*

Each sociolect and all of its discourses are marked by specific lexical units which acquire a symptomatic character insofar as a group language (liberal, feminist, Marxist-Leninist or psychoanalytic) is identified as a discourse in relation to these characteristic units which frequently have the effect of signals. The discourses of the psychoanalytic sociolect, for example, are immediately identified in conjunction with lexical units, such as 'unconscious', 'repression', 'lapsus', 'transference', etc. The reactions these words elicit may range from immediate rejection (e.g. by supporters of empirical psychology) to uncritical approval (by speakers of the psychoanalytic language). Naturally, such approval does not exclude factions and schisms within the sociolect as the numerous conflicts between 'Freudians' and 'Jungians' have shown. Similarly, Marxist-Leninist discourses can be easily identified thanks to symptomatic lexical units such as 'state monopoly capitalism', 'imperialism', 'class struggle', etc. They may provoke violent reactions not only on behalf of liberal or conservative discourses but also by Marxists who reject Leninism.

More important than lexical units which have a symptomatic or 'recognition' value are the semantic mechanisms which make it possible for the speaking Subject to model reality according to certain individual positions and interests. Thus the word 'unconscious' only acquires a psychoanalytic meaning if it is integrated by the Subject of discourse into a particular *class* of lexical units along with concepts like 'repression', 'lapsus', 'libido', etc. In other words, the definition of concepts is closely linked to the process of selection and classification, one of the most important activities of the speaking Subject.

One of the results of this activity – both in ideological and in theoretical discourses – is the construction of an object. The object of psychoanalysis, 'the unconscious', for example, is the product of certain definitions and classifications (taxonomies) which distinguish the discourses of psychoanalysis from other specialised languages. Political discourses show to what extent selections, definitions, and classifications determine the construction of geo-political objects. How is Catalonia to be classified? As a Spanish province, along with Andalusia, Aragon, and Valencia – or as a nation and a potential nation state, along with Portugal, Sweden, and France? Anyone familiar with the Yugoslavian crisis is bound to realise that definitions and classifications form an important link between semantics and politics. Are Serbian and Croatian to be considered as one language ('Serbo-Croatian'), or are they to be treated as two separate languages? Is Macedonian a language in its own right, or are we to adopt the Bulgarian classification (definition) according to which it is a Bulgarian dialect?

Similar links between semantics and politics can be observed in the construction of literary objects. George Eliot's *Adam Bede* could be defined as a 'Victorian novel' within a conservative ideology; it appears as the representation of a semantic contrast between individualist and corporate values in Terry Eagleton's Marxist perspective: '(. . .) A potentially tragic collision between "corporate" and "individualist" ideologies is consistently defused and repressed by the forms of Eliot's fiction.'[25] The object '*Adam Bede*' could also be constructed from a feminist point of view and interpreted as a plea for emancipation: Dinah, the Methodist preacher, would then appear not so much as a fervent interpreter of the Gospel, but as one of the first liberated women in Victorian literature. In this context the inner monologue of one of the characters would appear as based on sexist prejudice: '"A sweet woman", the stranger said to himself, "but surely nature never meant her for a preacher".'[26] None of these interpretations can be said to be wrong; they are based on very different semantic selections and classifications. The question (to be dealt with in the next section) is how they can be related to the text and to one another.

The lexical and semantic levels, although very important, are only part of the discourse; the third level is the syntactic-narrative structure which also determines the object constitutions of ideological and theoretical discourses. Politicians, philosophers, and scientists do not simply select, define, and classify (classification presupposes relevance criteria and selection), but also *tell a story*: the history of Spain and Catalonia, the history of modern Yugoslavia, the history of the novel or of modernism. In almost every political, economic or literary commentary a 'story' or narrative structure can be detected which – according to the classification and the *actantial models* involved (cf. chap 6.1) – we consider as realistic, unrealistic or absurd.

The actantial models of psychoanalysis (*Ego, Superego, Id*), which are regularly used to constitute an object called 'neurosis', have time and again been questioned and even ridiculed; at the same time the very existence of psychoanalytic objects such as 'neurosis', 'unconscious' or 'lapsus' has been denied. However, psychoanalysis is not the only science which has been in trouble because the credibility of its semantic and narrative object constructions has been questioned. Sociological narratives, such as Max Weber's theory of rationalisation, Durkheim's theory of differentiation (division of labour), and Marx's theory of the class struggle have been exposed to radical criticism in which the referential value of the constructs involved is invariably at stake. In literary criticism the situation is not very different. Marxist and existentialist narratives may have been partly superseded by feminist or postmodernist ones, but the latter have certainly not met with universal approval. It is the fate of ideologies and theories as ideologies to be recognised only within restricted socio-linguistic contexts or *sociolects*. Outside these contexts their validity is in doubt.

At this stage a socio-semiotic definition of ideology seems possible: *Ideology is a discourse based on the lexical repertoire, the semantic oppositions and classifications as well as on the narrative models of a sociolect*. Its structure and function can only be understood dialogically in the sense that each ideological discourse (indirectly: *sociolect*) articulates the interests of a particular social group or organisation and hence opposes the interests, classifications, definitions, and narratives of other groups in an historical *socio-linguistic situation*. The latter is to be considered as the global historical interaction of all sociolects and discourses in a particular society.

Gunter Kress und Robert Hodge describe this interaction of languages in *Language as Ideology*: 'In this way classification becomes the site of tension and struggle – on one level between individuals, as each tries to impose his or her system on others or gives way to superior power. On another level, the struggle goes on between social, ethnic, national, or racial groupings.'[27] This can be read as a fair description of the contemporary *socio-linguistic situation*. One might wish to add that at any point alliances and symbioses between ideological *sociolects* are conceivable and that the vocabularies and semantic classifications of Marxism, feminism, psychoanlysis, and anarchism can mix, yielding new combinations such as feminist psychoanalysis, anarchist Marxism, etc.

Seen in this light, ideology scarcely differs from the theoretical discourses of the social sciences in which definitions, distinctions, and classifications are among the most important activities of the speaking Subject (*sujet d'énonciation*, Greimas). Hence the assumption seems legitimate that all discourses, including those of the social sciences, are ideological in the sense defined here. They too, because of their definitions, classifications, and narrative schemes, can be attributed to sociolects and hence to collective points of view and interests. In this respect one could speak of a *general definition of ideology* which comes close to that proposed by Karl Mannheim in *Ideology and Utopia*:

> Whereas the particular conception of ideology designates only part of the opponent's assertions as ideologies – and this only with reference to their content, the total conception calls into question the opponent's total *Weltanschauung* (including his conceptual apparatus), and attempts to understand these concepts as an outgrowth of the collective life of which he partakes.[28]

In the present context, Mannheim's 'total conception' of ideology comes close to ideology as *sociolect*: in both cases the entire *perspective* of an individual or group is at stake. Unlike Mannheim's notion of ideology which is mainly sociological and philosophical (a product of the Sociology of Knowledge), the concept proposed here is a semiotic construction which projects the problem of ideology onto a lexical, semantic, and narrative level.

In the case of Mannheim it remains a problem, because the founder of the Sociology of Knowledge fails to introduce a viable distinction between ideology and science or ideology and theory. He believes that *detached intellectuals (freischwebende Intelligenz)* might be in a position situated above all ideologies or particular perspectives and allowing for a critical distance vis-à-vis all collective value systems. Mannheim's approach was criticised by Max Horkheimer from the point of view of Critical Theory and by Lucien Goldmann in a Marxist context. Both thinkers find it hard to believe in the 'detachment' of intellectuals and quite rightly point out that in most cases intellectuals are in the forefront of ideological battles.[29] (Good examples are the writers of the Auden generation in Britain, Barrès and Maurras in France, Marinetti in Italy, and Lenin, Bakunin or Trotsky in Russia.) Therefore the neutrality of critical intellectuals can no longer be considered as a solution to the problems of ideology.

The solution proposed here *in view of a new approach towards theory* aims at the discourse structure as such. Going beyond ideology is not the privilege of a particular social group, but the capacity of the Subject of discourse (the speaking or writing Subject) to avoid certain semantic and narrative mechanisms of dogmatisation which preclude us from understanding social objects and from seeking an open dialogue with others. Taking into account what has been said so far, ideological discourse can be defined as follows: *Originating in a particular group language or sociolect, ideology is a discourse governed by the semantic dichtomy and the corresponding narrative techniques (hero/antagonist). Its Subject is either not prepared or not able to reflect on its semantic and syntactic procedures and present them as an object of open discussions. Instead it considers its discourse as the only possible (true, natural) one and identifies it monologically with its actual and potential referents.*

This means that we have to work with *two complementary concepts* of ideology (as a linguistic structure): ideology as a group language or sociolect and ideology as a dualistic, dogmatic discourse which identifies itself with its objects, thus precluding dialogue. Although it is impossible to avoid or go beyond ideology in the first sense (as theoreticians and private individuals we can hardly avoid adopting a liberal, feminist, Marxist, conservative or ecological point of view), it seems perfectly possible to avoid the dualistic and dogmatic mechanisms of ideology in the second, the negative sense. Avoiding these mechanisms is indispensable for the emergence of theory.

The presence of ideology in literary criticism has long prevented the latter from becoming theoretical and from engaging in theoretical discussions within the realm of the social sciences. Not only Hegelians and Marxists, but also New Critics and Structuralists have claimed, time and again, to have discovered the 'true meaning' of the text. Even deconstructionists tend to argue that the aporias or contradictions which they construct and subsequently project into their literary objects are *inherent* in these objects: 'The "unreadability" is not located in the reader but in the text itself'[30], explains J. Hillis Miller. Elsewhere he adds: 'I would say that I think my reading of Yeats' poem is right, that all right-thinking people will come, given enough time, to my reading.'[31]

Both statements are ideological in the sense defined above: in the first sentence, Miller identifies his discourse (the discourse of 'unreadability') with the object as such; in the second sentence, he imposes his discourse as a dualistic monologue (right/wrong) upon all right-thinking people. There is no room for dissent: for who wouldn't want to be among 'all the right-thinking people'? It may be Miller's democratic right to choose deconstruction (feminism, Marxism, anarchism) as his ideology in the general sense, in the sense of *sociolect*; but he should be criticised for being ideological in the negative sense: in the sense of *dualism* (dichotomy), *identification*, and *monologue*.

3 Towards a Critical Theory of Literature

Within the context of literary criticism, a theory is needed which does not renounce conceptualisation and interpretation of texts, but at the same time refuses to identify the literary text with one of its contingent interpretations or theoretical metatexts. It will oscillate between the Kantian dictum 'without concept' and the

Hegelian insistence on univocal definition or conceptualisation. It will try to approach literary meaning on a dialogical level, relating heterogeneous theories to one another in order to confront their dissenting voices with their points of consensus. The idea underlying this project is a systematic dialectic between dissent and agreement which in the end might reveal some of the constant structures of literary texts – without which there would be no identifiable objects. But what exactly is theory as discourse?

Symmetrically to the negative definition of ideology, theoretical discourse could be defined as follows: *Theoretical discourse originates – just like ideological discourse – in one or several sociolects and as a particular system of norms and values articulates viewpoints and interests. In contrast to the ideological Subject, the Subject of theoretical discourse reflects upon its social and linguistic situation (its origin or genesis) as well as upon its semantic and syntactic mechanisms in an attempt to avoid dualism (dichotomy). It reveals its own contingency and particularity, thus opening its discourse to a dialogue with heterogeneous theories (languages). Simultaneously, it presents its objects as contingent constructs which do not exclude alternative constructions within competing discourses and sociolects.*[32]

This notion of theory does not imply any kind of relativism. For I may be convinced – at least for the time being – that my construction of Yeats's poem *Among Schoolchildren* or of Kafka's parable *Before the Law* is the best one without asserting that it is the only possible one and without excluding alternatives. In the course of time, I may discover, 1. that other interpreters have revealed textual elements which I had overlooked, but which confirm my construction; 2. that others have put forward arguments which I had not thought of and which make me modify my construction; 3. that others have revealed new elements and put forward new and convincing arguments which invalidate my construction in part or as a whole.

The crucial question is who 'the others' are. Are they people who belong to my scientific or theoretical group and speak *my sociolect* (e.g. Critical Theory, Critical Rationalism or the Sociology of Knowledge) or do they belong to another group whose *sociolect* is partly incompatible with mine? This question, which is crucial for the understanding of the type of theoretical dialogue proposed here, is not radically new, for it was raised – in two very different contexts and forms – by Karl Mannheim in *Ideology and Utopia* (1929) and about a decade later by Maurice Halbwachs (a sociologist of the Durkheim-School) in his article 'La Psychologie collective du raisonnement' (1938).

Mannheim draws a clear – and very useful – distinction between a theoretical dialogue involving individuals from one and the same group or 'perspective' and a dialogue between two or more heterogenous groups or 'perspectives'. It seems worthwhile to reproduce Mannheim's argument integrally in order to avoid misunderstandings and in order to make a concrete comparison with Halbwachs possible:

> In the case of situationally conditioned thought, objectivity comes to mean something quite new and different: a) there is first of all the fact that in so far as different observers are immersed in the same system, they will, on the basis of the identity of their conceptual and categorical apparatus and through the common universe of discourse thereby created, arrive at similar results, and be in a position to eradicate as an error everything that deviates from this unanimity; b) and recently there is a recognition of the fact that when observers have different perspectives, 'objectivity' is attainable only in a more roundabout fashion. In such a case, what has been correctly but differently perceived by the two perspectives must be understood in the light of the differences in structure of these varied modes of perception. An effort must be made to find a formula for translating the results of one into those of the other and to discover a common denominator for these varying perspectivistic insights.[33]

Maurice Halbwachs seems to tackle similar problems when he points out towards the end of his article: 'A number of different logics have thus emerged, each of which is exclusively valid within the group which draws its inspiration from it and which has laid down its rules.'[34] (The word 'logic' is used here in a very broad sense, meaning 'way of reasoning'.)

For the argument developed here the following points made by Mannheim and Halbwachs are of particular importance: 1. Communication between scientific groups differs qualitatively from communication within a group. 2. Communication between groups is possible only if certain translation rules are agreed on.

3. Mannheim's expression 'correctly but differently perceived' seems to indicate that the discourses of different scientific groupings may converge in crucial points.

Within the context of this chapter, it seems possible and desirable to go one step further and to transform factors considered by Mannheim and Halbwachs as obstacles to communication – namely the heterogeneous 'perspectives' of groups – into an asset of theoretical dialogue. The obstacle turns into an advantage when we argue that *intersubjectivity* or the intersubjective testing of hypotheses *within* a group or *sociolect* is less suitable for challenging collective (ideological) prejudice than *interdiscursivity* or the interdiscursive testing of hypotheses *between* groups or sociolects. The very heterogeneity of ideological groupings and languages thus appears as a guarantee against collective dogmatisation and prejudice.

It goes without saying, however, that *interdiscursivity* or the theoretical dialogue between groups is far more intricate and cumbersome than *intersubjectivity* within a homogeneous group, not merely because ideological interests and doxa constantly hamper the flow of information, but also because translation rules are not readily available in a situation where the semantics of sociolects may seem to be incommensurate.

However, all contemporary *sociolects* are embedded in a particular *socio-linguistic situation* (cf. above) and hence connected by the natural, everyday language of a certain society at a particular moment in history. Incommensurability which Jean-François Lyotard would like to turn into a rule[35] therefore seems to be the exception. Nevertheless, Lyotard is perfectly right to remind us of the dangers looming in any confrontation of heterogeneous discourses and in any attempt to apply the criteria of one type of discourse to another type. A fruitful dialogue between discourses seems only possible when the alterity and autonomy of each participating language is respected.[36]

This is the reason why the differentiation of ideology and theory is so important here. For only a discourse which is prepared to shed the shackles of ideological *identification, dualism,* and *monologue* and present its objects as possible and contingent constructions can enter into a dialogical relationship with heterogeneous discourses in order to construct a common political, economic or literary object. In other words: the *interdiscursive dialogue* proposed here presupposes a systematic critique of ideological discourse (in the negative sense) and a dialogical theory able to move between sociolects.

The German constructivist Paul Lorenzen[37] describes this dialogical movement between heterogeneous languages in three steps: 1. Comparing such languages, the interlocutors may discover that some of their concepts can be used as synonyms. This fortunate coincidence is not simply due to chance, but to the fact that all sociolects are *secondary modelling systems* in the sense of Lotman[38], which are solidly rooted in the *primary system* of natural language. The latter can always be used as a means of informal communication between group languages. 2. The second case described by Lorenzen is one of partial discrepancy: the language of our interlocutor contains concepts and distinctions which we have not thought of, but which we can integrate into our language by modifying it. 3. In the third case, says Lorenzen, the introduction of our interlocutor's concepts and distinctions (classifications) into our own language can lead to contradictions. In this case, he says, our discourse and that of our partner have to be re-examined. He should have added that in the course of this re-examination we may come to realise that the two discourses (sociolects) are partly or globally incompatible or incommensurate in the sense of Lyotard.

However, incompatibility or incommensurability are usually relative, and the debates about the *concept of ideology* in social philosophy and the social sciences reveal to what extent a *partial* consensus can be reached between heterogeneous languages. The partial character of theoretical consensus is due to a permanent dialectic between agreement and dissent, between confirmation and negation.

Considering the phenomenon of ideology from the point of view of Critical Theory (in the sense of Adorno and Horkheimer) and from the point of view of Critical Rationalism (in the sense of Popper and Hans Albert), it is relatively easy to trace the turns of this dialectic and to discern a partial consensus which yields an interdiscursive definition of *ideology*. Although Critical Theory and Critical Rationalism start from very different premises – the authors of Critical Theory standing close to Hegel and Marx, the authors of Critical Rationalism standing closer to Kant and Max Weber –

they tend to agree on the following aspects of ideology: 1. ideology is a dualist or manichean discourse which 2. has a monological structure, 3. identifies itself with 'reality', and 4. develops rhetorical mechanisms which make it immune against critique (e.g. 'it is a well-known fact that', 'the average person needs/does not need', 'God, humanity, the nation wants', etc.).[39] However, this partial consensus turns into dissent as soon as the interlocutors realise that in Critical Theory the alternative to this kind of ideological discourse is dialectical thought aiming at the unity of opposites as an alternative to dualism, at essayism and parataxis as alternatives to identity and monologue, etc. Critical Rationalists, whose alternatives to ideology are empirical orientation, refutability (criticability), and testing of hypotheses, could never agree with the alternatives proposed by Critical Theory.

However, this fundamental dissent is a guarantee that the partial consensus reached is a *consensus in heterogeneity* and therefore not brought about by ideological prejudice of a collective. For the ideologies involved are incompatible in most respects: whereas Critical Rationalists embrace almost unconditionally the values of liberalism and individualism, the representatives of Critical Theory adopt a very sceptical and critical attitude towards these values. *Within* the sociolects of Critical Theory and Critical Rationalism, consensus may very well be based on epistemological and ideological prejudice: on what everybody considers as 'evident' in a particular situation. But what is evident *within* a group may cease to be evident *between* groups.

This dimension of theory and theoretical dialogue is completely obliterated in Stanley Fish's approach which was dealt with in the last part of the fourth chapter. Having rejected the idea that meaning is to be found in the text itself or that it is attributed to the text by the individual reader[40], Fish thinks that he has found the solution by introducing the notion of *interpretive community* (cf. chap. 4.3):

> This, then, is the explanation for the stability of interpretation among different readers (they belong to the same community). It also explains why there are disagreements and why they can be debated in a principled way: not because of a stability in texts, but because of a stability in the makeup of interpretive

communities and therefore in the opposing positions they make possible.[41]

Fish's solution is theoretically weak, because, instead of trying to imagine a theoretical dialogue between *interpretive communities*, he sets out to persuade his contemporaries to adhere to his *interpretive community*:

> In the end I both gave up generality and reclaimed it: I gave it up because I gave up the project of trying to identify the one true way of reading, but I reclaimed it because I claimed the right, along with everyone else, to argue for a way of reading, which, if it became accepted, would be, for a time at least, the true one. In short, I preserved generality by rhetoricizing it.[42]

This is obviously confusing theory with rhetorics and fashion. One might just as well resort to political propaganda or to the techniques of advertising.

The problem is that Fish, who does not seem to be familiar with Mannheim's and Halbwachs' theories, does not envisage going beyond the problem of *interpretive community* in order to relate the languages or sociolects of different *interpretive communities* to one another, thus bringing about a theoretical, an interdiscursive dialogue. In the case of *ideology*, this kind of dialogue shows that the construction or definition of an object can be situated between different group languages and thus preserved from total historical contingency or arbitrariness.

This argument also applies to the interpretation of literary texts. Like the works of George Eliot, Kafka, and Camus, Marcel Proust's novel *A la recherche du temps perdu* has been interpreted in many different theoretical and ideological contexts. Every year new interpretations of this text appear and demonstrate that it cannot be identified with its Marxist, psychoanalytic, feminist or deconstructionist meanings – or *aesthetic objects*, as Mukařovský would say (cf. chap. 3). Nevertheless, it is not simply 'without concept', because time and again heterogeneous interpretations of it converge in crucial points.

One such point is the *weakening of the narrative structure* or syntax in this novel. This process is observed and described by Adorno within the context of Critical Theory, by Michel Grimaud in a psychoanalytic context, by Gilles Deleuze within a philosophy which has come to be considered as postmodern, and by Georges Poulet from a phenomenological point of view. While Adorno and Michel Zéraffa analyse the weakening of the narrative structure in Proust's novel on a sociological level, relating it to the crisis of the individual subject[43], Michel Grimaud minutely describes how Proust replaces narrative and syntactic techniques by oneiric associations: 'An onomastic study of Mme Cambremer's name shows to what extent all of Proust's work functions like a dream.'[44] Should anyone argue that the discourses of Critical Theory and those of psychoanalysis are not really heterogeneous, since both Adorno and Habermas attempted to integrate psychoanalysis into their theories, one could point to Gilles Deleuze's reconstruction of the *Recherche* in *Proust et les signes*, where Proust's novel appears as an associative structure and (as in Adorno's case) a radical critique of the hierarchically organised traditional novel: of linear narration.[45] Finally, Georges Poulet draws our attention to this structural aspect of Proust's novel by demonstrating how this text imperceptibly transforms narrative chronology and causality into a *spatial* vision: how it transforms time into space.[46]

It is neither possible nor meaningful in this context to give a detailed account of these interpretations. The idea behind this inevitably sketchy comparison is that interpretations do not simply change as *interpretive communities* or *sociolects* succeed one another in time but that they confirm – on an interdiscursive or intercollective level – the existence of certain structures. These structures (e.g. the semantic opposition between fire and water in Camus' *The Outsider*) may be interpreted in many different ways by Christians, Marxists, feminists, psychoanalysts or phenomenologists, but they keep recurring in virtually all interpretations which consider the text as a whole (and not just one specific stylistic or grammatical aspect).

Although this can be taken to mean that constant elements or structures do exist in literary texts, it does not imply that these structures can be immediately perceived within a particular theoretical perspective. Only a theoretical dialogue in the interdiscursive sense can confirm their existence. Moreover, it can lead to the discovery of aspects and elements we might never become aware of if we limited ourselves monologically to one perspective. At the same time, it sheds new light on the conceptuality of literature: although Camus' or Proust's text cannot be identified with its phenomenological, Marxist, feminist or psychoanalytic interpretation (i.e. with a particular ideological meaning), it is made up of structures none of these interpretations can afford to disregard.

Naturally, a comparison of theories and their interpretations is not an acceptable substitute for a living dialogue, i.e. a real confrontation between theoretical positions which are invariably based on ideologies. However, such a dialogue seems to be the most attractive alternative to the traditional hermeneutic practice which consists in identifying texts monologically with their psychoanalytic, Marxist, feminist or deconstructionist meanings. It certainly appears as an alternative to Stanley Fish's attempt to make one particular critic's interpretation or 'way of reading' seem acceptable for a certain period of time. Although theory is no longer a search for eternal truths or for objectivity, it does aim at a certain degree of universality – a universality not imposed in an abstract, rationalist manner, but obtained by a permanent dialogue between particular and heterogeneous positions.

Notes

CHAPTER 1

1 A. Martinet, *La Linguistique synchronique. Etudes et recherches* (Paris, PUF, 1968), p. 27.

2 J. Lyons, *Semantics I* (Cambridge-London-New York, Cambridge University Press, 1977), p. 71.

3 L. Hjelmslev, *Prolegomena to a Theory of Language* (Madison-London, University of Wisconsin Press, 1969), p. 59.

4 I. Kant, *Critique of Judgement* (Indianapolis-Cambridge, Hackett Publishing Company, 1987), p. 162.

5 I. Kant, *Critique of Judgement*, op. cit., p. 156.

6 I. Kant, *Critique of Judgement*, op. cit., p. 128.

7 E. M. Forster, *Two Cheers for Democracy* (London, Edward Arnold, 1951), p. 99.

8 I. A. Richards, *Principles of Literary Criticism* (London-Henley, Routledge & Kegan Paul [1924] 1976), p. 59.

9 G. Bras, *Hegel et l'art* (Paris, PUF, 1989), p. 60.

10 Winckelmann, J. J., *Geschichte der Kunst des Altertums* (reprint of the 1934 Vienna ed.) (Darmstadt, Wiss. Buchgesellschaft, 1993).

11 G. W. F. Hegel, *Aesthetics. Lectures on fine Art*, vol. 1 (Oxford, The Clarendon Press, 1975), p. 309.

12 G. W. F. Hegel, *Aesthetics*, vol. 2, op. cit., p. 964.

13 G. W. F. Hegel, *Science of Logic*, vol. 2 (London, Allen and Unwin, 1929), p. 466.

14 L. Goldmann, in: L. Goldmann and Th. W. Adorno, 'Deuxième colloque international sur la Sociologie de la Littérature, Royaumont.' (Discussion extraite des actes du colloque), in: *Revue de l'institut de sociologie*, no. 3-4, 1973, p. 540.

15 M. Frank, *Der unendliche Mangel an Sein. Schellings Hegelkritik und die Anfänge der Marxschen Dialektik* (Munich, Fink, 1992) (2nd ed.), p. 112.

16 F. W. J. Schelling, *Texte zur Philosophie der Kunst* (Stuttgart, Reclam, 1982), p. 165.

17 F. Schlegel, 'Über die Unverständlichkeit', in: F. Schlegel, *Kritische Ausgabe III* (Paderborn, Schöningh, 1967), p. 366.

18 Ibid., p. 370.

19 Ibid.
20 G. H. Hartmann, *The Unremarkable Wordsworth* (Minneapolis, University of Minnesota Press, 1987), p. 141.
21 Cf. M. Eßbach, *Die Junghegelianer. Soziologie einer Intellektuellengruppe* (Munich, Fink, 1988), p. 124–31.
22 S. Hook, *From Hegel to Marx. Studies in the Intellectual Development of Karl Marx* (Ann Arbor, The University of Michigan Press, 1966) (2nd ed.), p. 152.
23 Cf. K. Löwith, *Von Hegel zu Nietzsche. Der revolutionäre Bruch im Denken des neunzehnten Jahrhunderts* (Hamburg, Meiner, 1986) (9th ed.), p. 63. Also: M. Eßbach, *Die Junghegelianer*, op. cit., p. 165-9.
24 F. Th. Vischer, 'Kritik meiner Ästhetik', in: F. Th. Vischer, *Kritische Gänge* IV (ed. R. Vischer) (Munich, Meyer & Jessen, 1922), p. 287.
25 F. Th. Vischer, *Das Schöne und die Kunst. Zur Einführung in die Ästhetik* (Stuttgart, Verlag der J. C. Cottaschen Buchhandlung, 1898) (2nd ed.), p. 43.
26 M. M. Bakhtin, *Rabelais and his World* (Cambridge (Mass.)-London, M.I.T. Press, 1968), p. 44.
27 Ibid.
28 Ibid.
29 Cf. K. Löwith, *Von Hegel zu Nietzsche*, op. cit., p. 392-8.
30 F. Nietzsche, *Beyond Good and Evil. Prelude to a Philosophy of the Future* (London, Penguin, 1990), p. 34.
31 F. Nietzsche, 'Über Wahrheit und Lüge im außermoralischen Sinn', in: F. Nietzsche, *Werke* V, (ed. K. Schlechta) (Munich, Hanser, 1980), p. 319.
32 Ibid., p. 314.
33 Cf. S. Stelzer, *Der Zug der Zeit. Nietzsches Versuch der Philosophie* (Meisenheim am Glan, A. Hain, 1979), p. 5.
34 F. Nietzsche, *Die fröhliche Wissenschaft*, in: F. Nietzsche, *Werke* III, op. cit., p. 113.
35 R. Barthes, *S/Z* (London, Jonathan Cape, 1975), p. 5.
36 P. de Man, *The Resistance to Theory* (Minneapolis, Univeristy of Minnesota Press, 1986), p. 14.
37 G. H. Hartman, *Saving the Text. Literature/Derrida/Philosophy* (Baltimore-London, The Johns Hopkins University Press, 1981), p. 28.

CHAPTER 2

1 E. M. Thompson, *Russian Formalism and Anglo-American New Criticism. A Comparative Study* (The Hague, Mouton, 1971).
2 B. Croce, *What is Living and What is Dead in the Philosophy of Hegel*

(London, Macmillan, 1915), p. 27.

3   B. Croce, *Aesthetic As Science of Expression and General Linguistic* (London, Macmillan, 1909), p. 59.

4   Ibid., p. 58.

5   Ibid., p. 111.

6   Ibid.

7   Ibid., p. 120.

8   Cf. B. Croce, *Aesthetica in nuce* (Bari, Laterza, 1985) (10th ed.), p. 18.

9   T. S. Eliot, *The Sacred Wood. Essays on Poetry and Criticism* (London, Methuen [1920] 1960), p. viii.

10 W. K. Wimsatt (in collaboration with M. C. Beardsley), *The Verbal Icon. Studies in the Meaning of Poetry* (New York, Noonday Press, 1958), p. 222.

11 Ibid., p. 244.

12 W. K. Wimsatt, 'Battering the Object: The Ontological Approach', in: *Contemporary Criticism* (London, Edward Arnold, 1970), p. 81.

13 I. A. Richards, *Principles of Literary Criticism* (London-Henley, Routledge & Kegan Paul [1924] 1976), p. 58.

14 Ibid.

15 Cf. W. Kayser, *Das sprachliche Kunstwerk* (Bern, Francke, 1948).

16 C. Brooks, *The Well Wrought Urn. Studies in the Structure of Poetry* (San Diego-New York-London, Harcourt Brace Jovanovitch, 1949), p. 266.

17 C. Brooks and R. Penn Warren, *Understanding Poetry* (New York, Holt-Rinehart-Wilson [1938] 1976), p. 1.

18 Ibid., p. 6.

19 J. C. Ransom, *The New Criticism* (Norfolk (Conn.), New Directions, 1941), p. 287.

20 C. Brooks, *The Well Wrought Urn*, op. cit., p. 74.

21 Ibid., p. 236.

22 W. K. Wimsatt (M. C. Beardsley), *The Verbal Icon*, op. cit., p. 21.

23 Ibid.

24 W. K. Wimsatt and C. Brooks, *Literary Criticism. A Short History*, vol. 2: *Romantic Criticism* (London, Routledge & Kegan Paul [1957] 1970), p. 508.

25 Ibid., p. 512.

26 P. Bourdieu, *Les Règles de l'art. Genèse et structure du champ littéraire* (Paris, Seuil, 1992), p. 394.

27 In this context P. Bourdieu also criticises T. E. Hulme 'pour qui la contemplation artistique est un "intérêt détaché" (*detached interest*)'. Cf. P. Bourdieu, *Les Règles de l'art*, op. cit., p. 393.

28 E. M. Thompson, *Russian Formalism and Anglo-American New Criticism*, op. cit., pp. 66-7.

29 Ibid., p. 57.

30 A. A. Hansen-Löve, *Der russische Formalismus* (Vienna, Verlag der Österreichischen Akademie der Wissenschaften, 1978), p. 78.

31 P. Steiner, *Russian Formalism. A Metapoetics* (Ithaca-New York, Cornell University Press, 1984), p. 48.

32 V. Šklovskij, 'Der Zusammenhang zwischen dem Verfahren der Sujetfügung und den allgemeinen Stilverfahren', in: J. Striedter (ed.), *Russischer Formalismus* (Munich, Fink, 1969), p. 51.

33 J. Barth, *Lost in the Funhouse* (New York-London, Doubleday [1968] 1988), p. 72.

34 N. Gorlov, 'Qu'est-ce que le futurisme?', in: G. Conio (ed.), *Le Formalisme et le futurisme russes devant le marxisme* (Lausanne, L'Age d'Homme, 1975), p. 177.

35 Ibid., p. 171.

36 L. Jakubinskij, in: P. Steiner, *Russian Formalism*, op. cit., pp. 149-50.

37 R. Jakobson, 'Futurizm', in: R. Jakobson, *Selected Writings*, vol. 3 (The Hague, Mouton, 1981), pp. 718-19.

38 Th. G. Winner, 'Roman Jakobson and Avantgarde Art', in: Roman Jakobson. *Echoes of his Scholarship* (ed. by D. Armstrong and C. Van Schoonveld) (Lisse, Peter de Ridder, 1977), p. 512.

39 E. M. Thompson, *Russian Formalism and Anglo-American New Criticism*, op. cit., p. 68.

40 A. V. Lunačarskij, 'Der Formalismus in der Kunstwissenschaft', in: H. Günther (ed.), *Marxismus und Formalismus* (Frankfurt-Berlin-Vienna, Ullstein, 1976), p. 89.

41 L. Trockij, *Literature and Revolution* (London, Redwords, 1991), chap. V.

42 Cf. V. Erlich, *Russian Formalism: History – Doctrine* (The Hague, Mouton, 1969) (3rd ed.); A. A. Hansen-Löve, *Russischer Formalismus*, op. cit.; P. Steiner, *Russian Formalism*, op. cit.

43 Cf. Ch. Hibbert, *The Making of Charles Dickens* (London, Book Club Associates, 1967), chap. VI: 'The Chronicle Reporter'.

44 Cf. T. Benett, *Formalism and Marxism* (London, Routledge, 1989), G. Conio (ed.), *Le Formalisme et le futurisme russes devant la marxisme*, op. cit.; H. Günther (ed.), *Marxismus und Formalismus*, op. cit. and W. G. Walton, 'V. N. Vološinov: A Marriage of Formalism and Marxism', in: P. V. Zima (ed.), *Semiotics and Dialectics. Ideology and the Text* (Amsterdam, Benjamins, 1981).

45 T. Benett, *Formalism and Marxism*, op. cit., p. 96.

CHAPTER 3

1 Cf. M. Jůzl, *Otakar Hostinský* (Prague, Melantrich, 1980), p. 109: 'Hostinský intended to found empirically the evidence of aesthetic judgements analysed by Kant and Herbart.'

2 Cf. J. Mukařovský, 'Strukturalismus v estetice a ve vědě o literatuře' ('Structuralism in Aesthetics and the Science of Literature'), in: J. Mukařovský, *Kapitoly z české poetiky*, vol. 1 (Prague, Melantrich, 1941), p. 27.

3 O. Sus, 'On the Genetic Preconditions of Czech Structuralist Semiology and Semantics. An Essay on Czech and German Thought', in: *Poetics* 4 (Mouton), 1972, p. 40.

4 In the sense of Terry Eagleton in: *Criticism and Ideology* (London, Verso, 1978), p. 44.

5 'Les Thèses de 1929', in: *Le Cercle de Prague*, Change 3 (Paris, 1969), p. 36.

6 Ibid., p. 39.

7 R. Jakobson, 'Novejšaja russkaja poezija. Nabrosok pervyij: Podstupak k Chlebnikovu' ('The Most Recent Russian Poetry. First Sketch: Towards Chlebnikov'), in: R. Jakobson, *Selected Writings*, vol. 5 (Den Haag, Mouton, 1979), p. 305.

8 R. Jakobson and K. Pomorska, *Dialogues* (Cambridge Mass., The MIT Press, 1983), p. 9.

9 R. Jakobson, 'What is Poetry?', in: R. Jakobson, *Selected Writings*, vol. 3 (*Poetry of Grammar and Grammar of Poetry*) (The Hague-Paris-New York, Mouton, 1981), p. 750.

10 R. Jakobson, 'Linguistics and Poetics', in: R. Jakobson, *Selected Writings*, vol. 3 (*Poetry of Grammar and Grammar of Poetry*) (The Hague-Paris-New York, Mouton, 1981), p. 27.

11 P. Steiner, 'The conceptual Basis of Prague Structuralism', in: L. Matejka (ed.), *Sound, Sign and Meaning. Quinquagenery of the Prague Linguistic Circle* (Ann Arbor, University of Michigan, 1978), p. 361.

12 R. Jakobson, 'The Dominant', in: R. Jakobson, *Selected Writings*, vol. 3, op. cit., p. 751.

13 J. Užarević, 'Problema poetičeskoj funkcii' ('The Problem of the Poetic Function'), in: *Materialy meždunarodnogo kongressa: '100 let R. O. Jakobson'*, Moscow, 18-23 December 1996, Moscow, Rossijskij Gosudarstvennyj Gumanitarnyj Universitet (Moscow, 1996), p. 119.

14 J. Mukařovský, 'Die Ästhetik der Sprache', in: Jan Mukařovský, *Studien zur strukturalistischen Ästhetik und Poetik* (Munich, Hanser, 1974), p. 136.

15 J. Mukařovský, 'Umění a světový názor' ('Art and World Vision'), in: J. Mukařovský, *Studie z estetiky* (Prague, Odeon, 1966), p. 246.

16 J. Mukařovský, 'Záměrnost a nezáměrnost v umění' ('Determinacy and Indeterminacy in Art'), in: Jan Mukařovský, *Studie z estetiky*, op. cit., p. 100. Mukařovský explains: 'Not the poet and the construction of his work are primarily responsible for the semantic gesture: for an important part belongs to the recipient (vnímatel).'

17 M. Červenka, 'New Perspectives on Czech Structuralism', in: *PTL* 4 (1979), p. 368.

18 K. Chvatík, *Tschechoslowakischer Strukturalismus. Theorie und Geschichte* (Munich, W. Fink, 1981), p. 36.

19 Cf. M. Jankovič, *Nesamozřejmost smyslu* (Prague, Československý Spisovatel, 1991), pp. 28-9.

20 Ibid., p. 35.

21 Ibid., p. 24.

22 J. Mukařovský, 'Problémy estetické hodnoty' ('Problems of Aesthetic Value'), in: Jan Mukařovský, *Cestami poetiky a estetiky* (Prague, Československý Spisovatel, 1971), p. 33.

23 J. Mukařovský, 'Dialektické rozpory v moderním umění' ('Dialectical contradictions in Modern Art'), in: J. Mukařovský, *Studie z estetiky*, op. cit., p. 258.

24 K. Teige, 'Poème, monde, homme', in: *Change* 10 (1972), p. 136.

25 J. Mukařovský, 'Problémy estetické hodnoty' ('Problems of Aesthetic Value'), in: J. Mukařovský, *Cestami poetiky e estetiky*, op. cit., p. 18.

26 Cf. H. Uyttersprot, *Eine neue Ordnung der Werke Kafkas* (Antwerpen, Orion, 1957).

27 J. Mukařovský, 'Pojem celku v terorii umění' ('The Notion of Totality in Art Theory'), in: J. Mukařovský, *Cestami poetiky a estetiky*, op. cit., p. 91.

28 Cf. J. Mukařovský, 'Může mít estetická hodnota v umění platnost všeobecnou?' ('Can Aesthetic Value in Art Acquire Universal Validity?'), in: J. Mukařovský, *Studie z estetiky*, op. cit., p. 80.

29 J. Mukařovský, 'Estetická norma' ('Aesthetic Norm'), in: J. Mukařovský, *Studie z estetiky*, op. cit., p. 75.

30 K. Chvatík, *Tschechoslowakischer Strukturalismus*, op. cit., p. 14.

31 J. Mukařovský, *Kapitel aus der Ästhetik* (Frankfurt, Suhrkamp, 1970), p. 108.

32 Cf. R. Wellek and A. Warren, *Theory of Literature* (Harmondsworth, Penguin, 1963) (3rd ed.), pp. 24-5.

33 J. Mukařovský, 'Umění jako semiologický fakt' ('Art as a Semiological Fact'), in: J. Mukařovský, *Studie z estetiky*, op. cit., p. 88.
34 P. Steiner, 'The Conceptual Basis of Prague Structuralism', in: L. Matejka (ed.), *Sound, Sign and Meaning*, op. cit., p. 363.
35 F. Vodička, 'Response to Verbal Art', in: L. Matejka and I. R. Titunik (eds.), *Semiotics of Art. Prague School Contributions* (Cambridge (Mass.), The MIT Press, 1976), p. 205.
36 F. Vodička, *Die Struktur der literarischen Entwicklung* (Munich, W. Fink, 1976), p. 70.
37 Ibid., p. 64.
38 F. Vodička, 'Response to Verbal Art', in: L. Matejka and I.R. Titunik (eds.), *Semiotics of Art*, op. cit., p. 206.

CHAPTER 4

1 W. K. Wimsatt (M. C. Beardsley), *The Verbal Icon. Studies in the Meaning of Poetry* (New York, Noonday Press, 1958), p. 222 and S. Fish, *Self-Consuming Artifacts. The Experience of Seventeenth-Century Literature* (Berkeley-Los Angeles-London, University of California Press, 1972), p. 383.
 2 Cf. W. Kayser, *Das sprachliche Kunstwerk* (Bern, Francke, 1948).
 3 H.-G. Gadamer, *Truth and Method* (New York, The Seabury Press, 1975), p. 88.
 4 H.-G. Gadamer, *Kleine Schriften II. Interpretationen* (Tübingen, Mohr-Siebeck, 1967), p. 6.
 5 H.-G. Gadamer, *Truth and Method*, op. cit., p. 39.
 6 H.-G. Gadamer, *Kleine Schriften II*, op. cit., p. 1.
 7 Cf. K. Mannheim, *Strukturen des Denkens* (eds D. Kettler, V. Meja and N. Stehr) (Frankfurt, Suhrkamp, 1980), p. 230.
 8 H.-G. Gadamer, *Truth and Method*, op. cit., p. 273.
 9 H. R. Jauss, in: R. T. Segers, 'Hans Robert Jauss over receptie-onderzoek, Konstanz en de toekomst van de universiteit', in: R. T. Segers (ed.), *Lezen en laten lezen* (The Hague, Nijhoff, 1981), p. 207.
10 H. R. Jauss, *Ästhetische Erfahrung und literarische Hermeneutik* (Frankfurt, Suhrkamp, 1982), p. 17.
11 M. Foucault, 'What is an Author?', in: P. Rabinow (ed.), *The Foucault Reader* (New York, Pantheon Books, 1984), pp. 102-3: 'As a result, the mark of the writer is reduced to nothing more than the singularity of his absence; he must assume the role of the dead man in the game of writing.'
12 H. R. Jauss, *Toward an Aesthetic of Reception* (Minneapolis, University of Minnesota Press, 1982), p. 20.

13 Cf. note 7.
14 H. R. Jauss, 'Racines und Goethes Iphigenie', in: R. Warning (ed.), *Rezeptionsästhetik* (Munich, Fink, 1975), p. 360.
15 Ibid., p. 374.
16 H. R. Jauss, *Ästhetische Erfahrung und literarische Hermeneutik*, op. cit., p. 246.
17 Ibid., p. 265.
18 H. R. Jauss, *Studien zum Epochenwandel der ästhetischen Moderne* (Frankfurt, Suhrkamp, 1989), pp. 289-90.
19 H. R. Jauss, *Ästhetische Erfahrung und literarische Hermeneutik*, op. cit., p. 823.
20 M. Naumann et al., *Gesellschaft, Literatur, Lesen. Literaturrezeption in theoretischer Sicht* (Berlin-Weimar, Aufbau, 1973), pp. 126-7.
21 J. Stückrath, *Historische Rezeptionsforschung. Ein kritischer Versuch zu ihrer Geschichte und Theorie* (Stuttgart, Metzler, 1979), p. 119.
22 Cf. J. Jurt, 'Für eine Rezeptionssoziologie', in: *Romanistische Zeitschrift für Literaturgeschichte* no. 1-2, 1979.
23 M. Naumann et al., *Gesellschaft, Literatur, Lesen*, op. cit., pp. 73-4.
24 W. Iser, 'Im Lichte der Kritik', in: R. Warning (ed.), *Rezeptionsästhetik*, op. cit., p. 337.
25 Cf. Th. W. Adorno, *Against Epistemology: A Metacritique: Studies in Husserl and the Phenomenological Antinomies* (Oxford, Blackwell, 1982).
26 Ch. Brontë, *Jane Eyre* (Oxford-New York, Oxford University Press ['The World's Classics'] 1980), p. 7.
27 Cf. J.-P. Sartre, *L'Imagination* (Paris, PUF [1936] 1969), p. 147.
28 R. Ingarden, *Vom Erkennen des literarischen Kunstwerks* (Tübingen, Niemeyer, 1968), p. 28.
29 R. Ingarden, *Das literarische Kunstwerk* (Tübingen, Niemeyer, 1972) (4th ed.), p. 325.
30 Ibid.
31 Ibid.
32 Cf. G. H. Hartman, *Criticism in the Wilderness. The Study of Literature Today* (New Haven-London, Yale University Press, 1980), p. 38.
33 K. Rosner, 'Ingarden's Philosophy of Literature and the Analysis of Artistic Communication', in: P. Graff and S. Krzemień-Ojak (eds), *Roman Ingarden and Contemporary Polish Aesthetics* (Warsaw, Polish Scientific Publishers, 1975), p. 215.
34 W. Iser, *The Act of Reading. A Theory of Aesthetic Response* (London-Henley, Routledge & Kegan Paul, 1978), p. 13.
35 Ibid., p. 7.
36 Ibid., p. 7.

37 Ibid., p. 22.
38 Ibid., p. 65.
39 Ibid., p. 86.
40 Ibid., p. 87.
41 T. Hardy, *A Pair of Blue Eyes* (London-New York, Penguin [1872-3] 1994), p. 151.
42 W. Iser, *Das Fiktive und das Imaginäre* (Frankfurt, Suhrkamp, 1991), pp. 47-8.
43 W. Iser, *The Implied Reader. Patterns of Communication in Prose Fiction from Bunyan to Beckett* (Baltimore-London, The Johns Hopkins University Press, 1974), p. 37.
44 Ibid., p. 55.
45 W. Iser, *The Act of Reading*, op. cit., p. 92.
46 More clearly than any other text Italo Calvino's novel *If on a Winter's Night a Traveller* (London, Minerva, 1992) illustrates the role of the fictive reader.
47 Cf. W. Booth, *The Rhetoric of Fiction* (Chicago, University of Chicago Press, 1961).
48 W. Iser, *Laurence Sternes 'Tristram Shandy'. Inszenierte Subjektivität* (Munich, Fink, 1987), p. 151.
49 W. Iser, 'Die Appellstruktur der Texte' (Constance, Universitäts-verlag, 1970), p. 8.
50 W. Iser, *Der Akt des Lesens* (Munich, Fink, 1976), p. 133.
51 W. Iser, *The Implied Reader*, op. cit., p. 261.
52 S. Fish, 'Why No One's Afraid of Wolfgang Iser', in: S. Fish, *Doing What Comes Naturally* (Oxford, Clarendon Press, 1989), p. 75.
53 Ibid., p. 77.
54 Ibid.
55 Ibid., p. 76.
56 Ibid.
57 S. Fish, *Is There a Text in This Class? The Authority of Interpretive Communities* (Cambridge (Mass.)-London, Harvard University Press, 1982) (2nd ed.), p. 7.
58 S. Fish, *Self-Consuming Artifacts. The Experience of Seventeenth-Century Literature* (Berkeley-Los Angeles-London, University of California Press, 1972), p. 418.
59 Cf. A. J. Greimas and J. Courtés, *Semiotics and Language. An Analytical Dictionary* (Bloomington, Indiana University Press, 1982): *reading*.
60 S. Fish, *Is There a Text in this Class?*, op. cit., p. 14.
61 Ibid.
62 Ibid., p. 319.

CHAPTER 5

1 Cf. T. Eagleton, *Marxism and Literary Criticism* (London, Methuen, 1976), chap. 4.

2 Cf. L. Althusser, *For Marx* (London, Allen Lane, 1969).

3 K. Marx and F. Engels, *Über Kunst und Literatur*, vol. 2 (Berlin, Dietz, 1967), p. 322.

4 S. S. Prawer, *Karl Marx and World Literature* (Oxford, Clarendon Press, 1976), p. 97.

5 K. Marx and F. Engels, *Über Kunst und Literatur*, op. cit., p. 82.

6 S. S. Prawer, *Karl Marx and World Literature*, op. cit., p. 96.

7 Cf. M. Rose, *Marx's lost Aesthetic: Karl Marx and the Visual Arts* (Cambridge, Cambridge University Press, 1984), p. 86 – and S. S. Prawer, *Karl Marx and World Literature*, op. cit., p. 22.

8 G. Lukács, *The Theory of the Novel* (London, Merlin Press, 1970), p. 15.

9 G. Lukács, *Ästhetik* (Neuwied-Berlin, Luchterhand, 1972), vol. 2, p. 138.

10 G. Lukács, 'Balzac und der französische Realismus', in: G. Lukács, *Probleme des Realismus*, vol. 3 (Neuwied-Berlin, Luchterhand, 1971), p. 477.

11 G. Lukács, *Ästhetik*, op. cit., vol. 4, p. 169.

12 Cf. G. Lukács, 'Franz Kafka oder Thomas Mann?', in: G. Lukács, *Die Gegenwartsbedeutung des kritischen Realismus*, vol. 4, *Probleme des Realismus* I (Neuwied-Berlin, Luchterhand, 1971), p. 550.

13 Cf. L. Goldmann, 'Introduction aux premiers écrits de Georges Lukács', in: G. Lukács, *La Théorie du roman* (Paris, Gonthier, 1963), pp. 187-90.

14 Cf. S. Naïr and M. Lowy, *Goldmann – ou la dialectique de la totalité* (Paris, Seghers, 1973), pp. 14-24.

15 L. Goldmann, *The Hidden God. A Study of the Tragic vision in the Pensées of Pascal and the Tragedies of Racine* (London, Routledge, 1964), p. 19: 'The essential meaning of the work (. . .) and the meaning which the individual and partial elements take on when the work is looked at as a whole.'

16 Cf. Cl. Lévi-Strauss, *Structural Anthropology* (New York-London, Basic Books), 1963.

17 L. Goldmann, in: L. Goldmann and Th. W. Adorno, 'Deuxième colloque international sur la Sociologie de la Littérature. Discussion extraite des actes du colloque', in: *Revue de l'Institut de Sociologie* (Brussels), no. 3/4 (1973), p. 540.

18 Cf. H. Marcuse, *Counterrevolution and Revolt* (Boston, Beacon Press,

1972).
19 Cf. R. Kager, *Herrschaft und Versöhnung. Einführung in das Denken Theodor W. Adornos* (Frankfurt-New York, Campus, 1988), p. 205. Kager relates Benjamin's concept of mimesis to body language and dance.
20 R. Tiedemann, *Studien zur Philosophie Walter Benjamins* (Frankfurt, Suhrkamp, 1973), p. 38.
21 W. Benjamin, 'Zur Sprachphilosophie und Erkenntniskritik', in: W. Benjamin, *Gesammelte Schriften*, vol. 6 (Frankfurt, Suhrkamp, 1977), p. 26.
22 Ch. Baudelaire, 'Mon cœur mis à nu', in: Ch. Baudelaire, *Œuvres complètes*, vol. 1 (Paris, Gallimard, Bibl. de la Pléiade, 1975), p. 678.
23 W. Benjamin, 'Der Surrealismus', in: W. Benjamin, *Gesammelte Schriften*, vol. 2.1, op. cit., p. 301.
24 S. Lash, *Sociology of Postmodernism* (London-New York, Routledge, 1990), p. 156.
25 Cf. Th. W. Adorno, *Aesthetic Theory* (London, The Athlone Press, 1997), p. 45: 'The "exhibition value" that, according to Benjamin, supplants "cult value" is an *imago* of the exchange process.'
26 M. Zenck, *Kunst als begriffslose Erkenntnis* (Munich, Fink, 1977), pp. 97-8.
27 Th. W. Adorno, *Negative Dialectics* (London, RKP, 1973), pp. 354-60.
28 Ibid., pp. 141-2.
29 Cf. Th. W. Adorno, 'Parataxis. On Hölderlin's Late Poetry', in: *Notes to Literature II* (New York, Columbia University Press, 1992), pp. 131-40. Also: R. Bubner, 'Kann Theorie ästhetisch werden?', in: *Materialien zur ästhetischen Theorie. Th. W. Adornos Konstruktion der Moderne* (eds B. Lindner and W. M. Lüdke) (Frankfurt, Suhrkamp, 1979), pp. 119-20.
30 Th. W. Adorno, *Aesthetic Theory*, op. cit., pp. 115-16: 'This psychological posture is that of an "intolerance to ambiguity", an impatience with what is ambivalent and not strictly definable (. . .).'
31 Ibid., p. 128.
32 Ibid., p. 205.
33 Ibid., p. 229.
34 Cf. B. Karsenti, *Marcel Mauss. Le fait social total* (Paris, PUF, 1994).
35 Cf. Th. W. Adorno, 'Stefan George', in: Th. W. Adorno, *Notes to Literature II*, op. cit., pp. 181-5.
36 Th. W. Adorno, 'The Artist as Deputy', in: Th. W. Adorno, *Notes to Literature I* (New York, Columbia University Press, 1991), p. 107.

37 L. Hutcheon, *A Poetics of Postmodernism. History, Theory, Fiction* (London-New York, Routledge, 1988), pp. 25-6.

38 M. M. Bakhtin, *Rabelais and his World* (Cambridge (Mass.)-London, M.I.T. Press, 1968), p. 44.

39 Cf. for example M. M. Bakhtin, *Literaturno-kritičeskie stat'i* (Moscow, Chudožestvennaja Literatura, 1986), p. 41, where Nietzsche's thought is considered as 'half-scientific' (polunaučnoje).

40 R. Grübel, 'Zur Ästhetik des Wortes bei Michail Bachtin', in: M. M. Bachtin, *Die Ästhetik des Wortes* (Frankfurt, Suhrkamp, 1979), p. 59.

41 Ibid.

42 M. M. Bakhtin, *Rabelais and his World*, op. cit., p. 312.

43 M. M. Bakhtin, *Problems of Dostoevsky's Poetics* (Manchester, Manchester University Press, 1984), p. 90.

44 M. M. Bakhtin, *The Dialogic Imagination: Four Essays* (ed. M. Holquist) (Austin, University of Texas Press, 1981), p. 7.

45 R. Lachmann, 'Intertextualität als Sinnkonstitution. Andrej Belyijs Petersburg und die "fremden" Texte', in: *Poetica* no. 15 (1983), p. 70.

46 H. Günther, *Die Verstaatlichung der Literatur. Entstehung und Funktionsweise des sozialistisch-realistischen Kanons in der sowjetischen Literatur der 30er Jahre* (Stuttgart, Metzler, 1984), p. 135.

47 Cf. P. V. Zima, 'Bakhtin's Young Hegelian Aesthetics', in: *Critical Studies*, vol. 1, no. 2 (1989).

48 A. Callinicos, *Against Postmodernism. A Marxist Critique* (Cambridge, Polity Press, 1989), p. 9.

49 T. Eagleton, *Against the Grain. Essays 1975-1985* (London-New York, Verso, 1986), p. 132.

50 T. Eagleton, *The Illusions of Postmodernism* (Oxford-Cambridge (Mass.), Basil Blackwell, 1996), p. 65.

51 F. Jameson, *Postmodernism, or, The Cultural Logic of Late Capitalism* (Durham-North Carolina, Duke University Press, 1991), p. 62.

52 Ibid., p. 298.

53 Ibid., pp. 298-9.

54 Cf. F. Jameson, 'Postmodernism, or, The Cultural Logic of Late Capitalism', in: *New Left Review*, no. 146 (1984), pp. 53-92.

55 F. Jameson, *Postmodernism, or, The Cultural Logic of Late Capitalism*, op. cit., p. 400.

56 N. Luhmann, *Soziale Systeme* (Frankfurt, Suhrkamp, 1987), pp. 464-5 and pp. 542-3.

57 Th. W. Adorno, *Minima Moralia. Reflections from Damaged Life* (London, NLB, 1974), p. 50.

CHAPTER 6

1   A. J. Greimas, *Maupassant. The Semiotics of Text. Practical Exercises* (Amsterdam-Philadelphia, John Benjamins, 1988), p. 37.

2   A. J. Greimas, 'Pour une théorie du discours poétique', in: *Essais de sémiotique poétique* (Paris, Larousse, 1972), p. 16.

3   Ibid., p. 13.

4   A. J. Greimas and J. Courtés, *Semiotics and Language. An Analytical Dictionary* (Bloomington, Indiana University Press, 1982): isotopy.

5   For a more thorough definition of pluri-isotopy cf. A. J. Greimas and J. Courtés, *Semiotics and Language*, op. cit.: pluri-isotopy.

6   F. Rastier, 'Systématique des isotopies', in: *Essais de sémiotique poétique*, op. cit., p. 96.

7   J.-Cl. Coquet, *Sémiotique littéraire. Contribution à l'analyse sémantique du discours* (Tours, Mâme, 1973), p. 69.

8   A. J. Greimas, *Structural Semantics. An Attempt at a Method* (Lincoln-London, University of Nebraska Press, 1983), p. 264.

9   A. J. Greimas, *Maupassant*, op. cit., p. 45.

10 Ibid., p. 246.

11 Cf. Cl. Bremond, *Logique du récit* (Paris, Seuil, 1973), p. 89.

12 A. Jefferson, 'Semiotics of a Literary Text', in: *PTL* 3 (1977), p. 584.

13 Cf. F. K. Stanzel, *A Theory of Narrative* (Cambridge, Cambridge University Press, 1984) and G. Genette, *Narrative Discourse: An Essay on Method* (Ithaca, Cornell University Press, 1980).

14 Cf. J.-Cl. Coquet (ed.), *Sémiotique. L'Ecole de Paris* (Paris, Hachette, 1982), in particular: M. Arrivé, 'La Sémiotique littéraire', pp. 139-43.

15 U. Eco, *La struttura assente* (Milan, Bompiani, 1968), p. 162.

16 U. Eco, *Einführung in die Semiotik* (Munich, Fink, 1972), p. 154. (The German version diverges from the Italian original – *La struttura assente* – and the English translation.)

17 U. Eco, *A Theory of Semiotics* (Bloomington-London, Indiana University Press, 1976), p. 272.

18 U. Eco, *Einführung in die Semiotik*, op. cit., p. 155.

19 U. Eco, *I limiti dell'interpretazione* (Milan, Bompiani, 1990), p. 111.

20 U. Eco, *The Limits of Interpretation* (Bloomington, Indiana University Press, 1990), p. 21. (The English and the Italian editions are not identical.)

21 U. Eco, *The Role of the Reader. Explorations in the Semiotics of Texts* (London, Hutchinson, 1981), pp. 247-56.

22 U. Eco, *Semiotica e filosofia del linguaggio* (Torino, Einaudi, 1984), p. 71.

23 U. Eco, *Interpretation and Overinterpretation* (ed. S. Collini) (Cambridge, Cambridge University Press, 1992), p. 65.

24 Ibid., p. 64.

25 W. Hüllen 'Erzählte Semiotik. Betrachtungen zu Umberto Ecos "Der Name der Rose"', in: *Literatur im Kontext. Festschrift für Helmut Schrey* (ed. R. Haas and Ch. Klein-Braley) (Sankt Augustin, Hans Richarz, 1985), p. 129.

26 U. Eco, *Reflections on the Name of the Rose* (London, Secker and Warburg, 1985), p. 67.

27 R. Barthes, *The Semiotic Challenge* (Oxford, Blackwell, 1988), p. 5.

28 Ibid.

29 Ibid., p. 6.

30 Ibid., p. 7.

31 R. Barthes, *S/Z* (London, Jonathan Cape, 1975), p. 5. (Paris, Seuil, 1970, p. 12.)

32 R. Barthes, *L'Obvie et l'obtus. Essais critiques III* (Paris, Seuil, 1982), p. 252.

33 R. Barthes, 'Rasch', in: *Langue, discours, société. Pour Emile Benveniste* (Paris, Seuil, 1975), p. 228.

34 R. Barthes, *The Rustle of Language* (Oxford, Basil Blackwell, 1986), p. 203.

35 Ibid., p. 233.

36 R. Barthes, *The Semiotic Challenge*, op. cit., p. 154.

37 Ibid., p. 156.

38 J.-J. Goux, *Freud, Marx. Economie et symbolique* (Paris, Seuil, 1973), p. 125.

39 R. Barthes, *Le Bruissement de la langue. Essais critiques IV* (Paris, Seuil, 1984), p. 207.

40 R. Barthes, *S/Z*, op. cit., p. 173.

41 R. Barthes, *Essais critiques* (Paris, Seuil, 1964), p. 69.

42 R. Barthes, *The Grain of the Voice. Interviews 1962-1980* (London, Jonathan Cape, 1985), p. 191.

43 Cf. R. Barthes, *Sade, Fourier, Loyola* (Baltimore, The Johns Hopkins University Press, 1997).

44 R. Barthes, *Le grain de la voix. Interviews* (Paris, Seuil, 1981), p. 243.

45 R. Barthes, *S/Z*, op. cit., p. 9.

46 Ibid., p. 8.

47 V. Jouve, *La Littérature selon Roland Barthes* (Paris, Minuit, 1986), p. 53.

48 R. Barthes, in: G. de Mallac and M. Eberbach, *Roland Barthes* (Paris, Editions Universitaires, 1971), p. 108.

49 R. Barthes, *The Semiotic Challenge*, op. cit., p. 175.
50 L.-J. Calvet, *Roland Barthes. Un regard politique sur le signe* (Paris, Payot, 1973), p. 143.
51 R. Barthes, *S/Z*, op. cit., p. 24.
52 Ibid., p. 41.
53 A. J. Greimas, 'Roland Barthes: una biografia da costruire', in: *Mitologie di Roland Barthes. I Testi e gli Atti* (eds P. Fabbri and I. Pezzini) (Parma, Società Produzioni Editoriali, 1986), p. 308.

CHAPTER 7

1 J. Derrida, *Of Grammatology* (Baltimore-London, The Johns Hopkins University Press, 1976), p. 272.
2 J. Derrida, *L'Archéologie du frivole. Lire Condillac* (Paris, Denoël-Gonthier, 1973), pp. 112-13.
3 J. Derrida, *Of Grammatology*, op. cit., p. 24.
4 Ibid., p. 26.
5 J. Derrida, *Glas* (Lincoln-London, University of Nebraska Press, 1986), p. 26.
6 Ibid., p. 8.
7 J. Derrida, *Memoires for Paul de Man* (New York, Columbia University Press, 1986), p. 137.
8 J. Derrida, *La Voix et le phénomène* (Paris, PUF, 1967), p. 15.
9 Ibid., p. 83.
10 J. Derrida, *Margins of Philosophy* (Chicago, University of Chicago Press, 1982), p. 132.
11 M. Heidegger, *Identität und Differenz* (Pfullingen, Neske, 1957), p. 64.
12 Ch. Norris, *The Deconstructive Turn. Essays in the Rhetoric of Philosophy* (London-New York, Routledge, 1983), p. 24.
13 A. J. Greimas, *Structural Semantics. An Attempt at a Method* (Lincoln-London, University of Nebraska Press, 1983), p. 65.
14 F. Schlegel, 'Über die Unverständlichkeit', in: F. Schlegel, *Kritische Ausgabe*, vol. 3 (Paderborn, Schöningh, 1967), p. 370.
15 F. Nietzsche, 'Menschliches Allzumenschliches' in: F. Nietzsche, *Werke*, vol. 2 (Munich, Hanser, 1980), p. 440.
16 J. Derrida, *The Postcard. From Socrates to Freud and Beyond* (Chicago-London, The University of Chicago Press, 1987), p. 165.
17 F. Nietzsche, 'Über Wahrheit und Lüge im außermoralischen Sinne', in: F. Nietzsche, *Werke*, vol. 5, op. cit., p. 314.
18 J. Derrida, *Writing and Difference* (London-Henley, RKP, 1978), p. 280.
19 J. Derrida, *Margins*, op. cit., p. 318.

20 Ibid., p. 327.

21 F. de Saussure, *Course in General Linguistics* (Glasgow-New York, Fontana-Collins, 1974), p. 116.

22 J. Derrida, 'La Différance', in: *Théorie d'ensemble* (Paris, Seuil, 1968), p. 53.

23 J. Derrida, *Writing and Difference*, op. cit., p. 25.

24 Ibid.

25 D. Fricke, 'Jean-Pierre Richard', in: *Französische Literaturkritik in Einzeldarstellungen* (ed. W.-D. Lange) (Stuttgart, Kröner, 1975), p. 187.

26 S. Mallarmé, 'Préface à Vathek', in: *Œuvres complètes* (Paris, Gallimard, Bibl. de la Pléiade, 1945), p. 568.

27 J.-P. Richard, *L'Univers imaginaire de Mallarmé* (Paris, Seuil, 1961), p. 380.

28 Ibid.

29 Ibid., p. 422.

30 Ibid., p. 424.

31 Ibid., p. 432.

32 Ibid., p. 22.

33 Ibid., p. 417.

34 J. Derrida, *La Dissémination* (Paris, Seuil, 1972), p. 236. (J. Derrida, *Dissemination* (London, The Athlone Press, 1981), p. 207: 'this signifier having in the last instance no signified'.)

35 Ibid., p. 271.

36 Ibid.

37 Ibid., p. 258.

38 D. Lehmann, *Signs of the Times. Deconstruction and the Fall of Paul de Man* (New York, Poseidon Press, 1991), p. 79 and p. 24.

39 P. de Man, *Blindness and Insight* (New York-Oxford, Oxford University Press, 1971), p. 109.

40 P. de Man, *The Resistance to Theory* (Minneapolis, University of Minnesota Press, 1986), p. 14.

41 Ibid.

42 Ibid., p. 19.

43 G. W. F. Hegel, *Vorlesungen über die Ästhetik*, vol. 1 (Frankfurt, Suhrkamp, 1970), p. 518. (G. W. F. Hegel, *Aesthetics. Lectures on Fine Art*, vol. 1 (Oxford, Clarendon Press, 1975), p. 404: '[. . .] image and meaning are no longer distinguished and the image directly affords only the abstract meaning itself instead of a concrete picture. If, for example, we are to take begreifen in a spiritual sense, then it does not occur to us at all to think of a perceptible grasping by the hand'.)

44　J. Culler, *Framing the Sign. Criticism and Institutions* (Oxford, Blackwell, 1988), p. 122.
45　Cf. A. J. Greimas and J. Courtés, *Semiotics and Language. An Analytical Dictionary* (Bloomington, Indiana University Press, 1982): *seme* and *sememe*.
46　P. de Man, *Resistance to Theory*, op. cit., p. 109.
47　L. Waters, in: P. de Man, *Critical Writings. 1953-1978* (Minneapolis, University of Minnesota Press, 1989), p. LVII.
48　P. de Man, 'Sign and Symbol in Hegel's Aesthetics', in: *Critical Inquiry* 8 (1982), p. 765.
49　R. Luperini, 'Per una rivalutazione dell'allegoria da Benjamin a de Man', in: M. D'Ambrosio (ed.), *Il testo, l'analisi, l'interpretazione* (Naples, Liguori, 1995), p. 70.
50　M. Wigley, in: P. Johnson and M. Wigley, *Deconstructivist Architecture* (New York, The Museum of Modern Art, 1988), p. 13.
51　P. de Man, *Allegories of Reading. Figural Language in Rousseau, Nietzsche, Rilke, and Proust* (New Haven-London, Yale University Press, 1979), pp. 11-12.
52　A. J. Greimas and J. Courtés, *Semiotics and Language*, op. cit.: *lexeme*.
53　J. Hillis Miller, *Victorian Subjects* (London-New York, Harvester-Wheatsheaf, 1990), p. 215.
54　H. Felperin, *Beyond Deconstruction* (Oxford, Clarendon Press, 1985), pp. 107-8.
55　J. Hillis Miller, *Theory now and then* (London-New York, Harvester-Wheatsheaf, 1991), p. 86.
56　Ibid., p. 151.
57　J. Hillis Miller, *Tropes, Parables, Performatives. Essays on Twentieth-Century Literature* (London-New York, Harvester-Wheatsheaf, 1990), p. 36.
58　Ibid., p. 36.
59　J. Hillis Miller, *The Ethics of Reading. Kant, de Man, Eliot, Trollope, and Benjamin* (New York, Columbia Univ. Press, 1987), p. 73.
60　J. Hillis Miller, *Theory now and then*, op. cit., p. 181.
61　J. Hillis Miller, *Fiction and Repetition. Seven English Novels* (Cambridge (Mass.), Harvard University Press, 1982), p. 6.
62　Ibid.
63　Ibid., p. 123.
64　Ibid., p. 128.
65　J. Hillis Miller, *Victorian Subjects*, op. cit., p. 255.
66　G. H. Hartman, *Saving the Text* (Baltimore-London, The Johns Hopkins University Press, 1980), p. 28.

67 G. H. Hartman, *Criticism in the Wilderness. The Study of Literature Today* (New Haven-London, Yale University Press, 1980), p. 38.
68 Cf., G. Douglas Atkins, *Geoffrey Hartman. Criticism as Answerable Style* (London-New York, Routledge, 1990), p. 27.
69 G. H. Hartman, *Criticism in the Wilderness*, op. cit., p. 38.
70 Ch. Norris, *Deconstruction. Theory and Practice* (London-New York, Routledge, 1991) (revised ed.), p. 92.
71 G. H. Hartman, *Easy Pieces* (New York, Columbia University Press, 1985), p. 149.
72 Ibid.
73 Cf., U. Eco, *Interpretation and Overinterpretation* (Cambridge, Cambridge University Press, 1992) (ed. S. Collini), p. 61. Commenting on Hartman's interpretation of Wordsworth's poem, Eco points out that '"tears" is not an anagram of "trees".' He explains: 'If we want to prove that a visible text A is the anagram of a hidden text B, we must show that all the letters A, duly reorganized, produce B. If we start to discard some letters, the game is no longer valid.'
74 G. H. Hartman, *Easy Pieces*, op. cit., p. 149.
75 J. Hillis Miller, *The Ethics of Reading*, op. cit., p. 10.
76 G. Douglas Atkins, *Geoffrey Hartman*, op. cit., p. 131.
77 G. H. Hartman, *Saving the Text*, op. cit., p. 14.
78 G. H. Hartman, *Criticism in the Wilderness*, op. cit., p. 35.
79 I. Salusinszky, Interview with G. H. Hartman, in: I. Salusinszky, *Criticism in Society* (London-New York, Methuen, 1987), p. 77.
80 B. Malmberg, 'Derrida et la sémiologie: quelques notes marginales', in: *Semiotica* 11, 2 (1974), p. 196.
81 Cf. P. V. Zima, 'Semiótica, estética y desconstrucción: ¿Iteratividad o iterabilidad?', in: *Actas del V Simposio Internacional de la Asociación Andaluza de Semiótica* (eds J. Valles, J. Heras and M. I. Navas) (Almería, University of Almería, 1995), p. 33.

CHAPTER 8

1 I. Kant, *Critique of Judgement* (Indianapolis-Cambridge, Hackett Publishing Company, 1987), p. 127.
2 Ibid., p. 120.
3 Cf. J.-F. Lyotard, *The Postmodern Condition. A Report on Knowledge* (Minneapolis, University of Minnesota Press, 1984).
4 J.-F. Lyotard, *Discours, figure* (Paris, Klincksieck, 1971), p. 14.
5 Ibid.
6 Ibid., p. 18.
7 J. McGowan, *Postmodernism and its Critics* (Ithaca-London, Cornell University Press, 1991), p. 182.

8   J.-F. Lyotard, *Lessons on the Analytic of the Sublime* (Stanford, Stanford University Press, 1994), p. 234.

9   Ibid., p. 123.

10 Ibid., p. 151.

11 Ibid., p. 144.

12 Ibid., p. 228.

13 J.-F. Lyotard, *L'Enthousiasme* (Paris, Galilée, 1986), p. 61.

14 Ibid., p. 63.

15 J.-F. Lyotard, *The Inhuman. Reflections on Time* (Cambridge, Polity, 1991), p. 105.

16 Cf. F. Jameson, *Postmodernism, or, The Cultural Logic of Late Capitalism* (Durham, Duke University Press, 1991), p. 400.

17 Cf. P. Bürger, 'Eine Ästhetik des Erhabenen', in: Ch. Bürger, 'Moderne als Postmoderne: Jean-François Lyotard', in: Ch. Bürger and P. Bürger (eds), *Postmoderne: Alltag, Allegorie und Avantgarde* (Frankfurt, Suhrkamp, 1987), p. 138.

18 Cf. A. Breton, *Manifestes du surréalisme* (Paris, Gallimard, 1969), p. 113.

19 Th. Pynchon, *Gravity's Rainbow* (London, Picador, 1975), p. 690.

20 J.-F. Lyotard, *Lessons on the Analytic of the Sublime*, op. cit., p. 95.

21 Cf. Th. W. Adorno, *Negative Dialectics* (London, Routledge & Kegan Paul, 1973), pp. 158-61.

22 Cf. J.-F. Lyotard, *The Inhuman* (Cambridge-Oxford, Polity-Blackwell, 1991), p. 104.

23 Ibid.

24 A. Wellmer, *Zur Dialektik von Moderne und Postmoderne* (Frankfurt, Suhrkamp, 1993) (5th ed.), pp. 74-5.

25 J. Hillis Miller, *Theory now and then* (New York-London, Harvester-Wheatsheaf, 1991), p. 210.

26 P. de Man, 'Sign and Symbol in Hegel's Aesthetics', in: *Critical Inquiry* no. 3 (1982), p. 763.

27 Cf. J.-F. Lyotard, *The Inhuman* (Cambridge-Oxford, Polity-Blackwell, 1988), pp. 119-24.

28 G. Vattimo, *The Transparent Society* (Baltimore, The Johns Hopkins University Press, 1992), chap. 1.

29 G. Vattimo, *Al di là del soggetto. Nietzsche, Heidegger e l'ermeneutica* (Milan, Feltrinelli, 1991) (4th ed.), p. 49.

30 Ibid.

31 S. Lash, *Sociology of Postmodernism* (London-New York, Routledge, 1990), p. 252.

32 Cf. J. Baudrillard, *La Transparence du mal* (Paris, Galilée, 1990), pp. 22-7: 'Transesthétique'.

CHAPTER 9

1 The important authors in this context are: L. J. Prieto, *Pertinence et pratique. Essai de sémiologie* (Paris, Minuit, 1975) and Radical Constructivists such as H. Maturana, 'Neurophysiology of Cognition', in: P. Garvin (ed.), *Cognition: Principles of Biological Autonomy* (New York, Elsevier-North Holland, 1979).

2 For a comparison of Adorno's approach with deconstruction cf. P. V. Zima, *Die Dekonstruktion. Einführung und Kritik* (Tübingen, Francke, 1994) (*La Déconstruction. Une critique* [Paris, PUF, 1994]).

3 M. Dufrenne, *Esthétique et philosophie*, vol. 2 (Paris, Klincksieck, 1976), p. 26.

4 Cf. Th. W. Adorno, *Aesthetic Theory* (London, The Athlone Press, 1997), pp. 118-36.

5 T. Todorov, *Critique de la critique. Un roman d'apprentissage* (Paris, Seuil, 1984), pp. 188-9.

6 M. Mastermann, 'The Nature of a Paradigm', in: I. Lakatos and A. Musgrave (eds), *Criticism and the Growth of Knowledge* (Cambridge, Cambridge University Press, 1970), p. 61.

7 F. Kafka, *The Trial* (London, Penguin, 1994), p. 166. (*Der Prozeß* [Frankfurt, Fischer, 1960], pp. 155-6.)

8 Ibid., p. 167. (Ibid., p. 156.)

9 J. Derrida, 'Before the Law', in: J. Derrida, *Acts of Literature* (ed. D. Attridge) (New York-London, Routledge, 1992), p. 196.

10 F. Kafka, *The Trial*, op. cit., p. 167. (*Der Prozeß*, op. cit., p. 156.)

11 A. Camus, *The Outsider* (Harmondsworth, Penguin, 1961), p. 62. (*L'Etranger* [Paris, Gallimard, (1942) 1957], p. 87).

12 A. Camus, *The Outsider*, op. cit., p. 63. (*L'Etranger*, op. cit., p. 89.)

13 Cf. J. Fletcher, 'Interpreting L'Etranger', in: *The French Review* no. 1 (Winter, 1970) and H. Krauss, 'Zur Struktur des Etranger', in: *Zeitschrift für französische Sprache und Literatur* LXXX, no. 3, p. 218.

14 J.-Cl. Coquet, *Sémiotique littéraire. Contribution à l'analyse sémantique du discours* (Tours, Mâme, 1972), p. 27.

15 Cf. L. H. Hoek, *La Marque du titre. Dispositifs sémiotiques d'une pratique textuelle* (The Hague-Paris-New York, Mouton, 1980), p. 292: '*invariants* du titre'.

16 T. Eagleton, *Against the Grain. Selected Essays* (London-New York, Verso, 1986), p. 132.

17 L. Hutcheon, *The Politics of Postmodernism* (London-New York, Routledge, 1989), p. 142.

18 Cf. W. Welsch, *Unsere postmoderne Moderne* (Weinheim, VCH, 1991) (3rd ed.), p. 36.

19 Cf. B. K. Scott, *Refiguring Modernism. The Women of 1928* (Bloomington-Indianapolis, Indiana University Press, 1995).

20 Cf. J. H. Miller, 'Reading Writing: Eliot', in: J. H. Miller, *The Ethics of Reading* (New York, Columbia University Press, 1987), chap. IV.

21 Cf. G. Lukács, 'Franz Kafka oder Thomas Mann?', in: G. Lukács, *Die Gegenwartsbedeutung des kritischen Realismus, Werke, vol. 4, Probleme des Realismus I* (Neuwied-Berlin, Luchterhand, 1971), p. 550.

22 Cf. Th. W. Adorno, 'Notes on Kafka', in: *Th. W. Adorno, Prisms* (Cambridge (Mass.), The M.I.T. Press, 1981), pp. 247-9.

23 Cf. E. von Glasersfeld's introduction to Radical Constructivism: E. von Glasersfeld, 'Einführung in den radikalen Konstruktivismus', in: P. Watzlawick (ed.), *Die Erfundene Wirklichkeit* (Munich, Piper, 1985) (3rd. ed.), pp. 24-5.

24 Cf. L. J. Prieto, *Pertinence et pratique*, op. cit., chap. V: 'Pertinence et idéologie'.

25 T. Eagleton, *Criticism and Ideology. A Study in Marxist Literary Theory* (London, Verso, 1978), p. 112.

26 G. Eliot, *Adam Bede* (London, Penguin [1859] 1985), p. 67.

27 G. Kress and R. Hodge, *Language as Ideology* (London, Routledge, 1979), p. 63-64.

28 K. Mannheim, *Ideology and Utopia. An Introduction to the Sociology of Knowledge* (London-Henley, Routledge & Kegan Paul [1936] 1976), p. 50.

29 Cf. M. Horkheimer, 'Ein neuer Ideologiebegriff?', in: V. Meja and N. Stehr (eds), *Der Streit um die Wissenssoziologie*, vol. 2, *Rezeption und Kritik der Wissenssoziologie* (Frankfurt, Suhrkamp, 1982), pp. 488-9 and: L. Goldmann, *Sciences humaines et philosophie* (Paris, Gonthier, 1966), p. 52.

30 J. Hillis Miller, *Theory now and then* (London-New York, Harvester, Wheatsheaf, 1991), p. 345.

31 Ibid., p. 196.

32 These definitions of the ideological and the theoretical discourse were proposed for the first time in: P. V. Zima, *Ideologie und Theorie. Eine Diskurskritik* (Tübingen, Francke, 1989), pp. 55-6 and in: P. V. Zima, 'Ideology and Theory. The Relationship between Ideological and Theoretical Discourses', in: *Recherches sémiotiques/Semiotic Inquiry*, no. 2-3 (1991), pp. 148-9.

33 K. Mannheim, *Ideology and Utopia*, op. cit., p. 270.

34 M. Halbwachs, *Classes sociales et morphologie* (Paris, Minuit, 1972), p. 150.

35 Cf. J.-F. Lyotard, *The Differend: Phrases in Dispute* (Minneapolis, University of Minnesota Press, 1988), nos. 178-81.

36 Ibid.
37 P. Lorenzen, *Konstruktive Wissenschaftstheorie* (Frankfurt, Suhrkamp, 1974), p. 114.
38 Cf. J. M. Lotman, *Structure of Aesthetic Texts* (Ann Arbor, Michigan Slavic Contributions, 1977), chap. II.
39 Cf. P. V. Zima, *Ideologie und Theorie*, op. cit., chap. VIII, where the ideological attribution of discourses to mythical instances such as 'history', 'the people' or 'destiny' is analysed.
40 S. Fish, *Is There a Text in This Class? The Authority of Interpretive Communities* (Cambridge (Mass.)-London, Harvard University Press, 1980), p. 14.
41 Ibid., p. 15.
42 Ibid., p. 16.
43 Cf. Th. W. Adorno, 'Kleine Proust-Kommentare', in: Th. W. Adorno, *Noten zur Literatur II* (Frankfurt, Suhrkamp, 1961), p. 95 and: M. Zéraffa, *La Révolution romanesque* (Paris, UGE [10/18] 1969), p. 262.
44 M. Grimaud, 'La Rhétorique du rêve. Swann et la psychanalyse', in: *Poétique* no. 33 (1978), p. 98.
45 G. Deleuze, *Proust et les signes* (Paris, PUF, 1970), pp. 141-2.
46 G. Poulet, *L'Espace proustien* (Paris, Gallimard, 1963), pp. 134-5.

Bibliography

Note:This bibliography mainly contains titles regarding the *theories of literature* dealt with in the individual chapters.

Adorno, Th. W., *Negative Dialectics* (London, Routledge & Kegan Paul, 1973).

Adorno, Th. W., *Minima Moralia. Reflections from Damaged Life* (London, NLB, 1974).

Adorno, Th. W., 'Notes on Kafka', in: Th. W. Adorno, *Prisms* (Cambridge (Mass.), The M.I.T. Press, 1981).

Adorno, Th. W., *Against Epistemology: A Metacritique: Studies in Husserl and the Phenomenological Antinomies* (Oxford, Blackwell, 1982).

Adorno, Th. W., *Aesthetic Theory* (London, Athlone, 1997).

Adorno, Th. W., 'The Artist as Deputy', in: Th. W. Adorno, *Notes to Literature I* (New York, Columbia University Press, 1991).

Adorno, Th. W., 'Parataxis. On Hölderlin's Late Poetry', in: *Notes to Literature II* (New York, Columbia University Press, 1992).

Althusser, L,. *For Marx* (London, Allen Lane, 1969).

Arvon, H., *Marxist Aesthetics* (Ithaca, Cornell University Press, 1970).

Bakhtin, M. M., *Rabelais and his World* (Cambridge (Mass.)-London, M.I.T. Press, 1968).

Bakhtin, M. M., *The Dialogic Imagination: Four Essays* (ed. M. Holquist) (Austin, University of Texas Press, 1981).

Bakhtin, M. M., *Problems of Dostoevsky's Poetics* (Manchester, Manchester University Press, 1984).

Bakhtin, M. M., *Literaturno-kritičeskie stat'i* (Moscow, Chudožestvennaja Literatura, 1986).

Barthes, R., *Essais critiques* (Paris, Seuil, 1964).

Barthes, R., 'Rasch', in: *Langue, discours, société. Pour Emile Benveniste* (Paris, Seuil, 1975).

Barthes, R., *S/Z* (London, Jonathan Cape, 1975).

Barthes, R., *L'Obvie et l'obtus. Essais critiques III* (Paris, Seuil, 1982).

Barthes, R., *The Grain of the Voice. Interviews 1962-1980* (London, Jonathan Cape, 1985).

Barthes, R., *The Rustle of Language* (Oxford, Basil Blackwell, 1986).

Barthes, R., *The Semiotic Challenge* (Oxford, Blackwell, 1988).

Baudrillard, J., *La Transparence du mal* (Paris, Galilée, 1990).

Benett, T., *Formalism and Marxism* (London, Routledge, 1989).

Benjamin, W., *Understanding Brecht* (London, NLB, 1973).

Benjamin, W., 'The Work of Art in the Age of Mechanical Reproduction', in: W. Benjamin, *Illuminations* (London, Fontana, 1973).

Benjamin, W., 'Zur Sprachphilosophie und Erkenntniskritik', in: W. Benjamin, *Gesammelte Schriften*, vol. 6 (Frankfurt, Suhrkamp, 1977).

Best, S. and Kellner, D., *Postmodern Theory. Critical Interrogations* (London, Macmillan, 1991).

Booth, W., *The Rhetoric of Fiction* (Chicago, University of Chicago Press, 1961).

Bourdieu, P., *Les Règles de l'art. Genèse et structure du champ littéraire* (Paris, Seuil, 1992).

Bras, G., *Hegel et l'art* (Paris, PUF, 1989).

Bremond, Cl., *Logique du récit* (Paris, Seuil, 1973).

Brooks, C. *The Well Wrought Urn. Studies in the Structure of Poetry* (San Diego-New York-London, Harcourt-Brace-Jovanovitch, 1949).

Brooks, C. and Penn Warren, R., *Understanding Poetry* (New York, Holt-Rinehart-Wilson [1938] 1976).

Bubner, R., 'Kann Theorie ästhetisch werden?', in: *Materialien zur ästhetischen Theorie. Th. W. Adornos Konstruktion der Moderne* (eds B. Lindner and W. M. Lüdke) (Frankfurt, Suhrkamp, 1979).

Bürger, P., 'Eine Ästhetik des Erhabenen', in: Ch. Bürger, 'Moderne als Postmoderne: Jean-François Lyotard', in: Ch. Bürger and P. Bürger (eds), *Postmoderne: Alltag, Allegorie und Avantgarde* (Frankfurt, Suhrkamp, 1987).

Callinicos, A., *Against Postmodernism. A Marxist Critique* (Cambridge, Polity Press, 1989).

Calvet, L.-J., *Roland Barthes. Un regard politique sur le signe* (Paris, Payot, 1973).

Červenka, M., 'New Perspectives on Czech Structuralism', in: *PTL* 4 (1979).

Chvatík, K., *Tschechoslowakischer Strukturalismus. Theorie und Geschichte* (Munich, W. Fink, 1981).

Conio, G. (ed.), *Le Formalisme et le futurisme russes devant le marxisme* (Lausanne, L'Age d'Homme, 1975).

Coquet, J.-Cl., *Sémiotique littéraire. Contribution à l'analyse sémantique du discours* (Tours, Mâme, 1972).

Coquet, J.- Cl. (ed.), *Sémiotique. L'Ecole de Paris* (Paris, Hachette, 1982).

Critchley, S., *The Ethics of Deconstruction. Derrida and Levinas* (Oxford, Blackwell, 1992).

Croce, B., *Aesthetic As Science of Expression and General Linguistic* (London, Macmillan, 1909).

Croce, B., *What is Living and What is Dead in the Philosophy of Hegel* (London, Macmillan, 1915).

Croce, B., *Aesthetica in nuce* (Bari, Laterza, 1985) (10th ed.).

Culler, J., *The Pursuit of Signs. Semiotics, Literature, Deconstruction* (London-Melbourne, Routledge & Kegan Paul, 1981).

Culler, J., *On Deconstruction. Theory and Criticism after Structuralism* (Ithaca-New York, Cornell University Press, 1982).

Culler, J., *Framing the Sign. Criticism and Institutions* (Oxford, Blackwell, 1988).

De Saussure, F., *Course in General Linguistics* (Glasgow-New York, Fontana-Collins, 1974).

De Man, P., *Blindness and Insight* (New York-Oxford, Oxford University Press, 1971).

De Man, P., *Allegories of Reading. Figural Language in Rousseau, Nietzsche, Rilke, and Proust* (New Haven-London, Yale University Press, 1979).

De Man, P., 'Sign and Symbol in Hegel's Aesthetics', in: *Critical Inquiry* no. 3 (1982).

De Man, P., *The Resistance to Theory* (Minneapolis, University of Minnesota Press, 1986).

De Man, P., *Critical Writings. 1953-1978* (Minneapolis, University of Minnesota Press, 1989).

Deleuze, G., *Proust et les signes* (Paris, PUF, 1970).

Derrida, J., *La Voix et le phénomène* (Paris, PUF, 1967).

Derrida, J., 'La Différance', in: *Théorie d'ensemble* (Paris, Seuil, 1968).

Derrida, J., *L'Archéologie du frivole. Lire Condillac* (Paris, Denoël-Gonthier, 1973).

Derrida, J., *Of Grammatology* (Baltimore-London, The Johns Hopkins University Press, 1976).

Derrida, J., *Writing and Difference* (London-Henley, Routledge & Kegan Paul, 1978).

Derrida, J., *Dissemination* (London, The Athlone Press, 1981).

Derrida, J., *Margins of Philosophy* (Chicago, University of Chicago Press, 1982).

Derrida, J., *Glas* (Lincoln-London, University of Nebraska Press, 1986).

Derrida, J., *Memoires for Paul de Man* (New York, Columbia University Press, 1986).

Derrida, J., *The Postcard. From Socrates to Freud and Beyond* (Chicago-London, The University of Chicago Press, 1987).

Derrida, J., 'Before the Law', in: J. Derrida, *Acts of Literature* (ed. D. Attridge) (New York-London, Routledge, 1992).

Douglas Atkins, G., *Geoffrey Hartman. Criticism as Answerable Style* (London-New York, Routledge, 1990).

Dufrenne, M., *Esthétique et philosophie* (2 vols.) (Paris, Klincksieck, 1976).

Eagleton, T., *Marxism and Literary Criticism* (London, Methuen, 1976).

Eagleton, T., *Criticism and Ideology. A Study in Marxist Literary Theory* (London, Verso, 1978).

Eagleton, T., *Literary Theory: An Introduction* (Oxford, Blackwell, 1983).

Eagleton, T., *Against the Grain. Selected Essays* (London-New York, Verso, 1986).

Eagleton, T., *The Illusions of Postmodernism* (Oxford-Cambridge (Mass.), Basil Blackwell, 1996).

Eco, U., *A Theory of Semiotics* (Bloomington-London, Indiana University Press, 1976).

Eco, U., *The Role of the Reader. Explorations in the Semiotics of Texts* (London, Hutchinson, 1981).

Eco, U., *Semiotica e filosofia del linguaggio* (Torino, Einaudi, 1984).

Eco, U., *Reflections on the Name of the Rose* (London, Secker and Warburg, 1985).

Eco, U., *The Limits of Interpretation* (Bloomington, Indiana University Press, 1990).

Eco, U., *Interpretation and Overinterpretation* (ed. S. Collini) (Cambridge, Cambridge University Press, 1992).

Eliot, T. S., *The Sacred Wood. Essays on Poetry and Criticism* (London, Methuen [1920] 1960).

Eßbach, M., *Die Junghegelianer. Soziologie einer Intellektuellengruppe* (Munich, Fink, 1988).

Felperin, H., *Beyond Deconstruction* (Oxford, Clarendon Press, 1985).

Fish, S., *Self-Consuming Artifacts. The Experience of Seventeenth-Century Literature* (Berkeley-Los Angeles-London, University of California Press, 1972).

Fish, S., *Is There a Text in This Class? The Authority of Interpretive Communities* (Cambridge (Mass.)-London, Harvard University Press, 1982) (2nd ed.).

Fish, S., 'Why No One's Afraid of Wolfgang Iser', in: S. Fish, *Doing What Comes Naturally* (Oxford, Clarendon Press, 1989).

Fletcher, J., 'Interpreting *L'Etranger*', in: *The French Review* no. 1 (Winter, 1970).

Frank, M., *Der unendliche Mangel an Sein. Schellings Hegelkritik und die Anfänge der Marxschen Dialektik* (Munich, Fink, 1992) (2nd ed.)

Fricke, D., 'Jean-Pierre Richard', in: *Französische Literaturkritik in Einzeldarstellungen* (ed. W.-D. Lange) (Stuttgart, Kröner, 1975).

Gadamer, H.-G., *Kleine Schriften II. Interpretationen* (Tübingen, Mohr-Siebeck, 1967).

Gadamer, H.-G., *Truth and Method* (New York, The Seabury Press, 1975).

Genette, G., *Narrative Discourse: An Essay on Method* (Ithaca, Cornell University Press, 1980).

Genette, G., *L'Œuvre d'art I. Immanence et transcendance* (Paris, Seuil, 1994).

Genette, G., *L'Œuvre d'art II. La Relation esthétique* (Paris, Seuil, 1997).

Goldmann, L., 'Introduction aux premiers écrits de Georges

Lukács', in: G. Lukács, *La Théorie du roman* (Paris, Gonthier, 1963).

Goldmann, L., *The Hidden God. A Study of the Tragic vision in the Pensées of Pascal and the Tragedies of Racine* (London, Routledge, 1964).

Goldmann, L., *Sciences humaines et philosophie* (Paris, Gonthier, 1966).

Goldmann, L., Adorno, Th. W., 'Deuxième colloque international sur la Sociologie de la Littérature, Royaumont.' (Discussion extraite des actes du colloque), in: *Revue de l'institut de sociologie*, no. 3-4 (1973).

Goux, J.-J., *Freud, Marx. Economie et symbolique* (Paris, Seuil, 1973).

Greimas, A. J., 'Pour une théorie du discours poétique', in: *Essais de sémiotique poétique* (Paris, Larousse, 1972).

Greimas, A. J. and Courtés, J., *Semiotics and Language. An Analytical Dictionary* (Bloomington, Indiana University Press, 1982).

Greimas, A. J., *Structural Semantics. An Attempt at a Method* (Lincoln-London, University of Nebraska Press, 1983).

Greimas, A. J., 'Roland Barthes: una biografia da costruire', in: *Mitologie di Roland Barthes. I Testi e gli Atti*, eds P. Fabbri and I. Pezzini (Parma, Società Produzioni Editoriali, 1986).

Greimas, A. J., *Maupassant. The Semiotics of Text. Practical Exercises* (Amsterdam-Philadelphia, John Benjamins, 1988).

Grimaud, M., 'La Rhétorique du rêve. Swann et la psychanalyse', in: *Poétique* no. 33 (1978).

Grübel, R., 'Zur Ästhetik des Wortes bei Michail Bachtin', in: M. M. Bachtin, *Die Ästhetik des Wortes* (Frankfurt, Suhrkamp, 1979).

Günther, H. (ed.), *Marxismus und Formalismus* (Frankfurt-Berlin-Vienna, Ullstein, 1976).

Günther, H., *Die Verstaatlichung der Literatur. Entstehung und Funktionsweise des sozialistisch-realistischen Kanons in der sowjetischen Literatur der 30er Jahre* (Stuttgart, Metzler, 1984).

Hansen-Löve, A. A., *Der russische Formalismus* (Vienna, Verlag der Österreichischen Akademie der Wissenschaften, 1978).

Harland, R., *Superstructuralism: The Philosophy of Structuralism and Post-Structuralism* (London, Methuen, 1987).

Hartman, G. H., *Criticism in the Wilderness. The Study of Literature Today* (New Haven-London, Yale University Press, 1980).

Hartman, G. H., *Easy Pieces* (New York, Columbia Univ. Press, 1985).

Hartmann, G. H., *The Unremarkable Wordsworth* (Minneapolis, University of Minnesota Press, 1987).

Hawthorne, J., *A Glossary of Contemporary Literary Theory* (London-New York, Edward Arnold, 1992).

Hegel, G. W. F., *Aesthetics. Lectures on fine Art*, vol. 1 (Oxford, The Clarendon Press, 1975).

Heidegger, M., *Identität und Differenz* (Pfullingen, Neske, 1957).

Hiersche, A. and Kowalski, E. (eds.), *Literaturtheorie und Literaturkritik in der frühsowjetischen Diskussion. Standorte − Programme − Schulen* (Berlin-Weimar, Aufbau-Verlag, 1990).

Hillis Miller, J., *Fiction and Repetition. Seven English Novels* (Cambridge (Mass.), Harvard University Press, 1982).

Hillis Miller, J., *The Ethics of Reading. Kant, de Man, Eliot, Trollope, and Benjamin* (New York, Columbia University Press, 1987).

Hillis Miller, J., *Victorian Subjects* (London-New York, Harvester-Wheatsheaf, 1990).

Hillis Miller, J., *Tropes, Parables, Performatives. Essays on Twentieth-Century Literature* (London-New York, Harvester-Wheatsheaf, 1990).

Hillis Miller, J., *Theory now and then* (London-New York, Harvester-Wheatsheaf, 1991).

Hjelmslev, L., *Prolegomena to a Theory of Language* (Madison-London, University of Wisconsin Press, 1969).

Hoek, L. H., *La Marque du titre. Dispositifs sémiotiques d'une pratique textuelle* (The Hague-Paris-New York, Mouton, 1980).

Holquist, M., *Dialogism. Bakhtin and his World* (London, Routledge, 1990).

Holub, R. C., *Reception Theory: A Critical Introduction* (London-New York, Routledge, 1984).

Hook, S., *From Hegel to Marx. Studies in the Intellectual Development of Karl Marx* (Ann Arbor, The University of Michigan Press, 1966) (2nd ed.).

Horkheimer, M., 'Ein neuer Ideologiebegriff?', in: V. Meja and N. Stehr (eds), *Der Streit um die Wissenssoziologie*, vol. 2, *Rezeption und Kritik der Wissenssoziologie* (Frankfurt, Suhrkamp, 1982).

Hüllen, W., 'Erzählte Semiotik. Betrachtungen zu Umberto Ecos "Der Name der Rose"', in: *Literatur im Kontext. Festschrift für Helmut Schrey*, eds R. Haas and Ch. Klein-Braley (Sankt Augustin, Hans Richarz, 1985).

Hutcheon, L., *A Poetics of Postmodernism. History, Theory, Fiction* (London-New York, Routledge, 1988).

Hutcheon, L., *The Politics of Postmodernism* (London-New York, Routledge, 1989).

Ingarden, R., *Vom Erkennen des literarischen Kunstwerks* (Tübingen, Niemeyer, 1968).

Ingarden, R., *Das literarische Kunstwerk* (Tübingen, Niemeyer, 1972) (4th ed.).

Iser, W., 'Die Appellstruktur der Texte' (Constance, Universitätsverlag, 1970).

Iser, W., *The Implied Reader. Patterns of Communication in Prose Fiction from Bunyan to Beckett* (Baltimore-London, The Johns Hopkins University Press, 1974).

Iser, W., *The Act of Reading. A Theory of Aesthetic Response* (London-Henley, Routledge & Kegan Paul, 1978).

Iser, W., *Laurence Sternes 'Tristram Shandy'. Inszenierte Subjektivität* (Munich, Fink, 1987).

Iser, W., *Das Fiktive und das Imaginäre* (Frankfurt, Suhrkamp, 1991).

Jakobson, R., 'Novejšaja russkaja poezija. Nabrosok pervyj: Podstupak k Chlebnikovu' ('The Most Recent Russian Poetry. First Sketch: Towards Chlebnikov'), in: R. Jakobson, *Selected Writings*, vol. 5 (Den Haag, Mouton, 1979).

Jakobson, R., 'Futurizm', in: R. Jakobson, *Selected Writings*, vol. 3 (The Hague, Mouton, 1981).

Jakobson, R., 'Linguistics and Poetics', in: R. Jakobson, *Selected Writings*, vol. 3 (The Hague-Paris-New York, Mouton, 1981).

Jakobson, R., 'What is Poetry?', in: R. Jakobson, *Selected Writings*, vol. 3 (The Hague-Paris-New York, Mouton, 1981).

Jakobson, R. and Pomorska, K., *Dialogues* (Cambridge Mass., The MIT Press, 1983).

Jameson, F., 'Postmodernism, or, The Cultural Logic of Late Capitalism', in: *New Left Review*, no. 146 (1984).

Jameson, F., *Postmodernism, or, The Cultural Logic of Late Capitalism* (Durham-North Carolina, Duke University Press, 1991).

Jankovič, M., Nesamozřejmost smyslu (Prague, Československý Spisovatel, 1991).

Jauss, H. R., 'Racines und Goethes Iphigenie', in: R. Warning (ed.), *Rezeptionsästhetik* (Munich, Fink, 1975).

Jauss, H. R., *Toward an Aesthetic of Reception* (Minneapolis, University of Minnesota Press, 1982).

Jauss, H. R., *Ästhetische Erfahrung und literarische Hermeneutik* (Frankfurt, Suhrkamp, 1982).

Jauss, H. R., *Studien zum Epochenwandel der ästhetischen Moderne* (Frankfurt, Suhrkamp, 1989).

Jefferson, A., 'Semiotics of a Literary Text', in: *PTL* 3 (1977).

Johnson, P. and Wigley, M., *Deconstructivist Architecture* (New York, The Museum of Modern Art, 1988).

Jouve, V., *La Littérature selon Roland Barthes* (Paris, Minuit, 1986).

Jurt, J., 'Für eine Rezeptionssoziologie', in: *Romanistische Zeitschrift für Literaturgeschichte* no. 1-2 (1979).

Jůzl, M., *Otakar Hostinský* (Prague, Melantrich, 1980).

Kager, R., *Herrschaft und Versöhnung. Einführung in das Denken Theodor W. Adornos* (Frankfurt-New York, Campus, 1988).

Kant, I., *Critique of Judgement* (Indianapolis-Cambridge, Hackett Publishing Company, 1987).

Kayser, W., *Das sprachliche Kunstwerk* (Bern, Francke, 1948).

Krauss, H., 'Zur Struktur des *Etranger*', in: *Zeitschrift für französische Sprache und Literatur* LXXX, no. 3.

Lachmann, R., 'Intertextualität als Sinnkonstitution. Andrej Belyijs Petersburg und die "fremden" Texte', in: *Poetica* no. 15 (1983).

Lash, S., *Sociology of Postmodernism* (London-New York, Routledge, 1990).

Lehmann, D., *Signs of the Times. Deconstruction and the Fall of Paul de Man* (New York, Poseidon Press, 1991).

Les Thèses de 1929, in: *Le Cercle de Prague*, Change 3 (Paris, 1969).

Lévi-Strauss, Cl., *Structural Anthropology* (New York-London, Basic Books, 1963).

Link, H., *Rezeptionsforschung. Eine Einführung in Methoden und Probleme* (Stuttgart-Berlin, Kohlhammer, 1976).

Lotman, J. M., *Structure of Aesthetic Texts* (Ann Arbor, Michigan Slavic Contributions, 1977).

Lukács, G., *The Theory of the Novel* (London, Merlin Press, 1970).

Lukács, G., 'Franz Kafka oder Thomas Mann?', in: G. Lukács, *Die Gegenwartsbedeutung des kritischen Realismus, Werke*, vol. 4, *Probleme des Realismus I* (Neuwied-Berlin, Luchterhand, 1971).

Lukács, G., 'Balzac und der französische Realismus', in: G. Lukács, *Probleme des Realismus, Werke*, vol. 3 (Neuwied-Berlin, Luchterhand, 1971).

Lukács, G., *Ästhetik* (4 vols.) (Neuwied-Berlin, Luchterhand, 1972).

Lunačarskij, A. V., 'Der Formalismus in der Kunstwissenschaft', in: H. Günther (ed.), *Marxismus und Formalismus* (Frankfurt-Berlin-Vienna, Ullstein, 1976).

Luperini, R., 'Per una rivalutazione dell'allegoria da Benjamin a de Man', in: M. D'Ambrosio (ed.), *Il testo, l'analisi, l'interpretazione* (Naples, Liguori, 1995).

Lyons, J., *Semantics* (2 vols.) (Cambridge-London-New York, Cambridge University Press, 1977).

Lyotard, J.-F., *Discours, figure* (Paris, Klincksieck, 1971).

Lyotard, J.-F., *The Postmodern Condition. A Report on Knowledge* (Minneapolis, University of Minnesota Press, 1984).

Lyotard, J.-F., *L'Enthousiasme* (Paris, Galilée, 1986).

Lyotard, J.-F., *The Differend: Phrases in Dispute* (Minneapolis, University of Minnesota Press, 1988).

Lyotard, J.-F., *The Inhuman. Reflections on Time* (Cambridge, Polity, 1991).

Lyotard, J.-F., *Lessons on the Analytic of the Sublime* (Stanford, University Press, 1994).

Mallac de, G. and Eberbach, M., *Roland Barthes* (Paris, Editions Universitaires, 1971).

Malmberg, B., 'Derrida et la sémiologie: quelques notes marginales', in: *Semiotica* 11, 2 (1974).

Mannheim, K., *Ideology and Utopia. An Introduction to the Sociology of Knowledge* (London-Henley, Routledge & Kegan Paul [1936] 1976).

Mannheim, K., *Strukturen des Denkens*, eds D. Kettler, V. Meja and N. Stehr (Frankfurt, Suhrkamp, 1980).

Marcuse, H., *Counterrevolution and Revolt* (Boston, Beacon Press, 1972).

Martinet, A., *La Linguistique synchronique. Etudes et recherches* (Paris, PUF, 1968).

Marx, K. and Engels, F., *Über Kunst und Literatur* (2 vols.) (Berlin, Dietz, 1967).

Matejka, L. (ed.), *Sound, Sign and Meaning. Quinquagenery of the Prague Linguistic Circle* (Ann Arbor, University of Michigan, 1978).

Matejka, L. and Titunik, I. R. (eds), *Semiotics of Art. Prague School Contributions* (Cambridge Mass., The MIT Press, 1976).

McGowan, J., *Postmodernism and its Critics* (Ithaca-London, Cornell University Press, 1991).

McHale, B., *Constructing Postmodernism* (London-New York, Routledge, 1992).

Mukařovský, J., 'Strukturalismus v estetice a ve vědě o literatuře' ('Structuralism in Aesthetics and the Science of Literature'), in: J. Mukařovský, *Kapitoly z české poetiky* vol. 1 (Prague, Melantrich, 1941).

Mukařovský, M., 'Umění a světový názor' ('Art and World Vision'), in: J. Mukařovský, *Studie z estetiky* (Prague, Odeon, 1966).

Mukařovský, J., *Kapitel aus der Ästhetik* (Frankfurt, Suhrkamp, 1970).

Mukařovský, J., 'Problémy estetické hodnoty' ('Problems of Aesthetic Value'), in: Jan Mukařovský, *Cestami poetiky a estetiky* (Prague, Československý Spisovatel, 1971).

Mukařovský, M., 'Die Ästhetik der Sprache', in: Jan Mukařovský, *Studien zur strukturalistischen Ästhetik und Poetik* (Munich, Hanser, 1974).

Naïr, S. and Lowy, M., *Goldmann ou la dialectique de la totalité* (Paris, Seghers, 1973).

Naumann M. et. al., *Gesellschaft, Literatur, Lesen. Literaturrezeption in theoretischer Sicht* (Berlin-Weimar, Aufbau, 1973).

Nietzsche, F., 'Menschliches Allzumenschliches', in: *Werke*, vol. 2 (Munich, Hanser, 1980).

Nietzsche, F., 'Über Wahrheit und Lüge im außermoralischen Sinn', in: F. Nietzsche, *Werke*, vol. 5 (Munich, Hanser, 1980).

Nietzsche, F., *Beyond Good and Evil. Prelude to a Philosophy of the Future* (London, Penguin, 1990).

Norris, Ch., *The Deconstructive Turn. Essays in the Rhetoric of Philosophy* (London–New York, Routledge, 1983).

Norris, Ch., *Paul de Man. Deconstruction and the Critique of Aesthetic Ideology* (London–New York, Routledge, 1988).

Norris, Ch., *Deconstruction. Theory and Practice* (London–New York, Routledge, 1991) (revised ed.).

Poulet, G., *L'Espace proustien* (Paris, Gallimard, 1963).

Prawer, S. S., *Karl Marx and World Literature* (Oxford, Clarendon Press, 1976).

Prieto, L. J., *Pertincence et pratique. Essai de sémiologie* (Paris, Minuit, 1975).

Ransom, J. C., *The New Criticism* (Norfolk (Conn.), New Directions, 1941).

Richard, J.-P., *L'Univers imaginaire de Mallarmé* (Paris, Seuil, 1961).

Richards, I. A., *Principles of Literary Criticism* (London–Henley, Routledge & Kegan Paul (1924), 1976).

Rose, M., *Marx's lost Aesthetic: Karl Marx and the Visual Arts* (Cambridge, Cambridge University Press, 1984).

Rosner, K., 'Ingarden's Philosophy of Literature and the Analysis of Artistic Communication', in: P. Graff and S. Krzemień-Ojak (eds), *Roman Ingarden and Contemporary Polish Aesthetics* (Warsaw, Polish Scientific Publishers, 1975).

Salusinszky, I., *Criticism in Society* (London–New York, Methuen, 1987).

Sartre, J.-P., *L'Imagination* (Paris, PUF, (1936), 1969).

Schelling, F. W. J., *Texte zur Philosophie der Kunst* (Stuttgart, Reclam, 1982).

Schlegel, F., 'Über die Unverständlichkeit', in: F. Schlegel, *Kritische Ausgabe*, vol. 3 (Paderborn, Schöningh, 1967).

Scott, B. K., *Refiguring Modernism. The Women of 1928* (Bloomington–Indianapolis, Indiana University Press, 1995).

Segers, R. T., 'Hans Robert Jauss over receptie-onderzoek, Konstanz en de toekomst van de universiteit', in: R. T. Segers (ed.), *Lezen en laten lezen* (The Hague, Nijhoff, 1981).

Šklovskij, V., 'Der Zusammenhang zwischen dem Verfahren der

Sujetfügung und den allgemeinen Stilverfahren', in: J. Striedter (ed.), *Russischer Formalismus* (Munich, Fink, 1969).

Stanzel, F. K., *A Theory of Narrative* (Cambridge, Cambridge University Press, 1984).

Steiner, P., 'The conceptual Basis of Prague Structuralism', in: L. Matejka (ed.), *Sound, Sign and Meaning. Quinquagenery of the Prague Linguistic Circle* (Ann Arbor, University of Michigan, 1978).

Steiner, P., *Russian Formalism. A Metapoetics* (Ithaca–New York, Cornell University Press, 1984).

Stelzer, S., *Der Zug der Zeit. Nietzsches Versuch der Philosophie* (Meisenheim am Glan, A. Hain, 1979).

Stückrath, J., *Historische Rezeptionsforschung. Ein kritischer Versuch zu ihrer Geschichte und Theorie* (Stuttgart, Metzler, 1979).

Sus, O., 'On the Genetic Preconditions of Czech Structuralist Semiology and Semantics. An Essay on Czech and German Thought', *Poetics* 4 (Mouton) (1972).

Teige, K., 'Poème, monde, homme', in: *Change* 10 (1972).

Thompson, E. M., *Russian Formalism and Anglo-American New Criticism. A Comparative Study* (The Hague, Mouton, 1971).

Tiedemann, R., *Studien zur Philosophie Walter Benjamins* (Frankfurt, Suhrkamp, 1973).

Todorov, T., *Mikhaïl Bakhtine: le principe dialogique – suivi de Ecrits du Cercle de Bakhtine* (Paris, Seuil, 1981).

Todorov, T., *Critique de la critique. Un roman d'apprentissage* (Paris, Seuil, 1984).

Trockij, L., *Literature and Revolution* (London, Redwords, 1991), chap. V.

Užarević, J., 'Problema poetičeskoj funkcii' ('The Problem of the Poetic Function'), in: *Materialy meždunarodnogo kongressa: '100 let R. O. Jakobson'*, Moscow, 18-23 December 1996, Moscow, Rossijskij Gosudarstvennyj Gumanitarnyj Universitet (Moscow, 1996).

Vattimo, G., *Al di là del soggetto. Nietzsche, Heidegger e l'ermeneutica* (Milan, Feltrinelli, 1991) (4th ed.).

Vattimo, G., *The Transparent Society* (Baltimore, The Johns Hopkins University Press, 1992).

Vischer, F. Th., *Das Schöne und die Kunst. Zur Einführung in die Ästhetik* (Stuttgart, Verlag der J. C. Cottaschen Buchhandlung, 1898) (2nd ed.).

Vischer, F. Th., 'Kritik meiner Ästhetik', in: F. Th. Vischer, *Kritische Gänge* IV (ed. R. Vischer) (Munich, Meyer & Jessen, 1922).

Vodička, F., *Die Struktur der literarischen Entwicklung* (Munich, W. Fink, 1976).

Vodička, F., 'Response to Verbal Art', in: L. Matejka and I.R. Titunik (eds), *Semiotics of Art. Prague School Contributions* (Cambridge Mass., The MIT Press, 1976).

Warning, R., *Rezeptionsästhetik* (Munich, Fink, 1975).

Weimann, R., *Literaturgeschichte und Mythologie. Methodologische und historische Studien* (Frankfurt, Suhrkamp, 1977).

Wellek, R. and Warren, A., *Theory of Literature* (Harmondsworth, Penguin, 1963) (3rd ed.).

Wellmer, A., *Zur Dialektik von Moderne und Postmoderne* (Frankfurt, Suhrkamp, 1993) (5th ed.).

Welsch, W., *Unsere postmoderne Moderne* (Weinheim, VCH, 1991) (3rd ed.).

Williams, R., *Marxism and Literature* (Oxford, Oxford University Press, 1977).

Wimsatt, W. K. and Brooks, C., *Literary Criticism. A Short History* (2 vols.) (Chicago-London, University of Chicago Press, 1957).

Wimsatt, W. K., (in collaboration with M. C. Beardsley), *The Verbal Icon. Studies in the Meaning of Poetry* (New York, Noonday Press, 1958).

Wimsatt, W. K., 'Battering the Object: The Ontological Approach', in: *Contemporary Criticism* (London, Edward Arnold, 1970).

Winckelmann, J. J., *Geschichte der Kunst des Altertums* (reprint of the 1934 Vienna ed.) (Darmstadt, Wiss. Buchgesellschaft, 1993).

Winner, Th. G., 'Roman Jakobson and Avantgarde Art', in: *Roman Jakobson. Echoes of his Scholarship*, ed. by D. Armstrong and C. Van Schoonveld (Lisse, Peter de Ridder, 1977).

Zenck, M., *Kunst als begriffslose Erkenntnis* (Munich, Fink, 1977).

Zéraffa, M., *La Révolution romanesque* (Paris, UGE [10/18] 1969).

Zima, P. V. (ed.), *Semiotics and Dialectics. Ideology and the Text* (Amsterdam, J. Benjamins, 1981).

Zima, P. V., 'Bakhtin's Young Hegelian Aesthetics', in: *Critical Studies*, vol. 1, no. 2 (1989).

Zima, P. V., *Ideologie und Theorie. Eine Diskurskritik* (Tübingen, Francke, 1989).

Zima, P. V., 'Ideology and Theory. The Relationship between Ideological and Theoretical Discourses', in: *Recherches sémiotiques/Semiotic Inquiry*, no. 2-3 (1991).

Zima, P. V., *Die Dekonstruktion. Einführung und Kritik* (Tübingen, Francke, 1994) (*La Déconstruction. Une critique* [Paris, PUF, 1994]).

Zima, P. V., 'Semiótica, estética y desconstrucción: ¿Iteratividad o iterabilidad?', in: *Actas del V Simposio Internacional de la Asociación Andaluza de Semiótica*, eds J. Valles, J. Heras and M. I. Navas (Almería, University of Almería, 1995).

Index